Mean Streets is a field study of young people who have left home and school and are living on the streets of Toronto and Vancouver. This book includes the personal narratives and explanatory accounts, in their own words, of some of the more than four hundred young people who participated in the summer-long study, which featured intensive personal interviews. The study examines why youth take to the streets, their struggles to survive on the street, their victimization and involvement in crime, their associations with other street youth, especially within "street families," their contacts with the police, and their efforts to leave the street and rejoin conventional society. Major theories of youth crime are analyzed and reappraised in the context of a new social capital theory of crime.

Mean Streets

Cambridge Criminology Series

Editors:
Alfred Blumstein, *Carnegie Mellon University*
David Farrington, *University of Cambridge*

This new series publishes high-quality research monographs of either theoretical or empirical emphasis in all areas of criminology, including measurement of offending, explanations of offending, police courts, incapacitation, corrections, sentencing, deterrence, rehabilitation, and other related topics. It is intended to be both interdisciplinary and international in scope.

Also in the series:

J. David Hawkins (editor), *Delinquency and Crime: Current Theories*
Simon I. Singer, *Recriminalizing Delinquency: Violent Juvenile Crime and Juvenile Justice Reform*
Scott H. Decker and Barrik Van Winkle, *Life in the Gang: Family, Friends, and Violence*
Austin Lovegrove, *A Framework of Judicial Sentencing: Decision Making and Multiple Offence Cases*

Mean Streets

YOUTH CRIME
AND HOMELESSNESS

John Hagan
University of Toronto

Bill McCarthy
University of Victoria

in collaboration with Patricia Parker and Jo-Ann Climenhage

CAMBRIDGE
UNIVERSITY PRESS

40145789

PUBLISHED BY THE PRESS SYNDICATE OF THE UNIVERSITY OF CAMBRIDGE
The Pitt Building, Trumpington Street, Cambridge, United Kingdom

CAMBRIDGE UNIVERSITY PRESS
The Edinburgh Building, Cambridge CB2 2RU, UK   http://www.cup.cam.ac.uk
40 West 20th Street, New York, NY 10011-4211, USA   http://www.cup.org
10 Stamford Road, Oakleigh, Melbourne 3166, Australia

First published 1997
First paperback edition 1998
Reprinted 1999

Printed in the United States of America

Typeset in Baskerville

A catalogue record for this book is available from the British Library

Library of Congress Cataloguing-in-Publication Data is available

ISBN 0-521-49743-4 hardback
ISBN 0-521-64626-X paperback

Contents

Foreword: Measuring and Interpreting
Social Reality – the Case of Homeless Youth

Mean Streets is the first study of its kind, a careful examination of samples of homeless children, *in situ* – that is, on the streets of two Canadian cities, Toronto and Vancouver. Although "runaways" have been much publicized – even advertised – no previous study has systematically located children on the street and looked at their social worlds, comparing them with samples of in-home and in-school children, from the perspective of the children.

Mean Streets is also an all-too-rare combination of rigorous theoretical and empirical inquiry applied to a significant research problem. The problem is more complex than is implied in the book's title – that is, the relationship between youth homelessness and crime – though that surely is complex enough. John Hagan, Bill McCarthy, and their colleagues Patricia Parker and Jo-Ann Climenhage must first convince us that homeless youth are a sufficiently important population to warrant serious attention. They do that convincingly in Chapter One and in the book's Appendix, which I recommend reading in tandem.

Importantly, the two cities differ significantly in their approaches to handling homeless youth, with Toronto providing a more fully developed safety net for them and Vancouver relying to a greater extent on a crime-control model. Although law enforcement plays an important role in both cities, Vancouver youth, without the support services and shelters of Toronto's social welfare model, experience greater exposure to the traumas of street life and to criminal opportunities.

Extensive interviews of street youth and surveys of both street youth and youth in Toronto schools provide rich information on family and school backgrounds associated with youth homelessness. Interviews and field observations inform the nature of life on the streets of both cities. The research design of the study is imaginative, complex, and demanding. The focus throughout is on the young people, on their perspectives of family life and school experiences, on why some leave their homes – some flee, others are "kicked out" – and on life on the streets and in the parks, malls, abandoned buildings, and shelters of Toronto and Vancouver.

We learn a great deal about the extreme conditions experienced by young people while living away from family and other conventional institutions. The data are compelling that harsh, coercive, often explosive family discipline alienates children, sometimes to the point of driving them into the street. We learn of the seductions of street life, too, but most of all we learn of its privations and dangers and how it pushes young people toward crime as a means of securing basic necessities.

The book is replete with stimulating questions as well as answers. I am led to wonder, for example, about the relative merits of situational and group process perspectives in understanding differences between youth gangs and homeless youth (some of whom have been gang members, who when asked deny that their street "families" are gangs and take exception to the comparison). It appears that the microsocial level of explanation is less important to the explanation of behavior among the homeless than it is to behavior within gang contexts. Group processes seem less important to homeless youth. The gang situation lends itself to group processes in ways that most youth rarely experience. Conversely, foreground variables (related to the immediate street situation) such as those identified by Hagan and McCarthy (hunger, inadequate shelter, unemployment, and safety) clearly are less important to the explanation of gang delinquency than they are to street youth. They are almost certainly less important to the explanation of most youth crime than they are to crimes committed by homeless youth. Nevertheless, the authors make a strong case that, *in extremis*, foreground needs for food, shelter, and currency are fundamental to the explanation of behavioral adaptation.

Street life exposes both gang members and homeless youth to violence, however, as the discussion of "reciprocal violence" in Chapter Five makes clear. Clearly, also, the microsocial level of explanation is important to understanding the conditions under which some homeless youth are driven from their homes or choose to leave.

Ironically, these homeless youth often form street "families" that recreate familiar family roles and serve familiar purposes – safety, food, shelter, and protection, as well as social and emotional needs. The familial analogies invoked by homeless youth often appear, however, to reflect wishful thinking more than reality. Individual youth spend a lot of time wandering around, alone, searching for food, shelter, and some means of acquiring currency. And street families appear to be more transitory and even less cohesive than street gangs.

In this era of large available data sets, when we often settle for data less because they are appropriate to the task at hand than because they are available, this book is refreshing. Large data sets also carry the day often because they are more amenable to quantitative analysis than are field studies, yet Hagan and McCarthy provide ample and sophisticated quantitative analyses of their data. And surely no one would argue that scientific pursuit should be limited to data that are convenient, or that theory should be compromised by the difficulty of data production or analysis.

Hagan and McCarthy are to be congratulated for facing up to the complexity of their research problem, for daring to break new ground methodologically, and for doing the hard work necessary to fulfill their carefully thought-out research design. Moreover, they are successful in overcoming what is perhaps the most glaring weakness of disciplinary specialization: the insularity of theory and interpretation of data within narrow confines of specialized inquiry.

Criminology, long a captive of its special data sets and theoretical constructions, has emerged in recent years as a truly interdisciplinary specialization, with ties to all of the social and behavioral sciences. Though pockets of resistance remain, we no longer cringe at the thought that fundamental biological processes and other individual-level phenomena may be relevant to criminal and other forms of deviant behavior. Increasingly, we seek out the work of specialists in a variety of related disciplines, and we adopt comparative research designs and learn from inquiries in other cultures and societies. Again, Hagan and McCarthy are exemplary. More power to them, and good reading to all!

JAMES F. SHORT JR.
Washington State University

Acknowledgments

The research reported in this book has evolved over a period of more than ten years and has benefited from the contributions of many people. Joshua, Jeremy, Linda, Aja, Wyndham, Ana, and other family members provided the encouragement and understanding that research and writing demand.

Patricia Parker attended to all the details that a successful project entails. She helped prepare grant proposals, collect data, draft reports, and prepare the final manuscript. Her skills at organizing are unmatched, and her support kept us going through difficult times.

Over the years, many colleagues at the universities of Toronto, Victoria, and North Carolina at Chapel Hill listened patiently to the trials and tribulations of our research and offered invaluable advice. They include Ron Gillis, Bruce Arnold, Rosemary Gartner, Fiona Kay, Glen Elder, Clay Mosher, Bob Hagedorn, John Simpson, Alan Hedley, Morgan Baker, Cecilia Benoit, Mikael Jansson, Zheng Wu, and Arne Kalleberg.

Several people helped us collect the survey and interview data for the second study. Jo-Ann Climenhage undertook the arduous task of overseeing the interviewing of Toronto youth, and Jordie Allen-Newman helped interview youth in Vancouver. Several others helped us collect our data, and we are grateful for the efforts of Brian Cameron, Tracey-Ann Van Brenk, Gary Sherman, Tina Sahay, Claire Burnett, Claire Opferkuch, and Miriam Russell, who helped gather the Toronto data; and Tanis Abuda, Gordon Behie, Sara Eliesen, Doug Klassen, Rose Labrador, Mary Olita, and Chris Schultz, who assisted in Vancouver.

The various parts of this manuscript were written in several locations. We thank the universities of Toronto, Victoria, and North Carolina at Chapel

Hill for providing us with working environments that allowed us to develop the ideas central to our work. We are also indebted to the secretarial staff in each place: Dagmara Suszek, Karen Chong-Kwan, Carole Rains, and Shea Farrell provided invaluable assistance in the preparation of the manuscript. These institutions also provided financial support, as did the Social Science and Humanities Research Council of Canada. Our point of view, opinions, and findings do not necessarily reflect the official positions or policies of these institutions.

Alfred Blumstein and David Farrington responded enthusiastically to an early draft of our work. Jeff Fagan and Mark Fleischer also read drafts of our manuscript and gave us important feedback on several areas. The criticisms and encouragement of these colleagues were influential in helping us to improve the quality of this book. We also thank Elizabeth Neal, Eric Newman, and the production staff at Cambridge University Press who helped us put the finishing touches on this work.

Some of our chapters are rewritten from materials published elsewhere. We are grateful to the publishers for allowing us to use those materials in this work. Specifically, we thank the London School of Economics for "Streetlife and Delinquency," *British Journal of Sociology*, 1992, 43:533–61; University of Chicago Press for "Mean Streets: The Theoretical Significance of Situational Delinquency Among Homeless Youth," *American Journal of Sociology*, 1992, 98:597–627; and Academic Press for "Getting into Street Crime: The Structure and Process of Criminal Embeddedness," *Social Science Research*, 1995, 24:63–95.

In our Appendix we refer to the various social service agencies that supported this project. These agencies provided us with interview space, helped us establish connections with youth, and were enthusiastic advocates of our research. Agency staff gave us help and guidance and kept our spirits up when the data collection was difficult. The staff members are too numerous to list here, but we thank them for their kindness and support. Although their efforts greatly enhanced the success of our research, their contributions are most evident in the lives of the youth who leave the street.

Finally, we are deeply indebted to the youth who, in spite of their hardships, gave their time and effort to complete our surveys and talk about their lives. In telling their stories of childhood, family life, school years, and the street, these youth shared their secrets, fears, and dreams. We hope that these accounts will help change the ways we view and care for young people, on and off the street.

Tables and Illustrations

Tables

Maps

Figures

Street and School Criminologies

THE DEPICTION OF SOCIAL EXPERIENCE is most revealing when it considers people in extreme circumstances. The homeless youth who live on the streets of our cities confront desperate situations on a daily basis. Often without money, lacking shelter, hungry, and jobless, they frequently are involved in crime as onlookers, victims, and perpetrators.[1] Yet, unlike homeless adults, who are more visible casualties of the cumulative toll of living on the street, homeless youth are difficult to distinguish from their better protected peers. Their youthfulness frequently obscures the seriousness of their problems. Fictional and media accounts rarely or sufficiently document the experiences of these youth, who are often overlooked in academic writing and research about the urban poor.

North American criminology also neglects street youth. Despite the adversity of street life and the prevalence of crime, contemporary criminology concentrates more extensively on youth living at home and attending school. This focus limits the study of more extreme social and economic situations, implying that the influence of adverse backgrounds is exaggerated and that problems of crime are sufficiently represented by the experiences of more ordinary young people.

In this book, we begin to address this neglect of street youth.[2] We use observational, survey, and interview data gathered in two of the largest cities in Canada, Toronto and Vancouver, to document the family and school histories, living conditions, and, in particular, criminal experiences of youth who live on the streets. Our purpose is to bring into theoretical view the ways in which the background and developmental experiences of homeless youth and the foreground conditions of urban street life influence involvement in crime. Our approach draws on several criminological traditions, including strain, control, differential association, and labeling theories. These orientations can be effectively integrated, even though they are sometimes treated as incompatible.

Throughout this book, we make extensive use of our respondents' victimization and offending histories. These personal accounts are often detailed and revealing, so we use pseudonyms to protect our respondents' identities. We begin with Janet, whose experiences illustrate a degree of involvement in crime that is disturbingly common among street youth.[3]

Janet left her rural home in a maritime province at the age of 14 after her stepfather hit her "one time too many." She spent some time at her cousins' home and on the street in a city "back East" before heading to Toronto in search of her older sister Kathy. Kathy was selling hallucinogens, marijuana, and small amounts of other drugs from her downtown apartment. After a quarrel about one of her sister's "acid parties," Janet left Kathy's apartment for the street. The following discussion began when we asked Janet about her involvement in crime since leaving home:

JANET: When I was 14, that's when I started doing crack. I got the money from my friend. I was kind of watching out for her, taking licence plate numbers.

INTERVIEWER: She was hooking?

JANET: Yeah, and she'd give me half her money to go buy rock. . . . I was staying in hotels with my friends, partied all the time, and that's when I started doing coke. . . . I tried everything. I tried needles. . . . I was so scared it wasn't funny. . . . I go up there, and like there's two big bags of coke there. I said give me one of the syringes and like, I said to somebody else, like go ahead, do it. And as soon as they were doing it, it was, oh God. You feel like rubber.

INTERVIEWER: Did you end up with a lot of tracks?

JANET: No, I don't have any marks there, only little scars. I did it in my neck, in my legs. It's a good buzz, but anyway its too expensive. Crack was better, but I went down from 129 pounds to 100. I was so skinny. I'm 137 now. I smoke my pot, and that's it.

INTERVIEWER: What made you decide to stop crack?

JANET: It was when I went to jail. That's what happened.

INTERVIEWER: What did you go to jail for?

JANET: Assault causing bodily harm, I almost killed this girl. . . . I was on acid. I was 16. . . . Assault with bodily harm with a deadly weapon.

INTERVIEWER: Was that the only time ?

JANET: No, then I was in for stolen, stealing cars and everything else . . .

credit cards, and cash and stuff. . . . I was charged with so many different charges; twenty-two car thefts, and, ah, three armed robberies.

INTERVIEWER: What were they?

JANET: This, ah, 7-Eleven store, we went there with a knife and buddy had his gun and ran after us. . . . Then we had like, uh, it wasn't a real gun, it was like, uh, one of those starter pistols. . . . And this one woman, she thought it was real, so I just, pow up in the air. Stupid woman. . . . But I wouldn't do that again.

INTERVIEWER: What made you change?

JANET: I don't know. I guess talking to lots of people about it and then being in jail. No way I want more. I got beat up in there twice. . . . But then I beat up people, too. I beat up this one chick the first day I got in there.

Janet's extensive offending history is not unusual among the youth we interviewed, but it is not generalizable to all street youth either. Some street youth report no involvement in crime, and there is more to these young lives than crime.[4] Nonetheless, for Janet and many others, the street is a downward spiral of deviance, danger, and despair. The adversity of urban street life and the prevalence of crime among youth who spend their days and nights on the streets would seem to be an important focal point for crime research; yet contemporary criminologists continue to neglect the experiences of this group.

Criminologists of the Streets

The early part of this century was characterized by a pervasive anxiety about the life of impoverished urban neighborhoods and the dangers they posed for young people. Responding to this concern, the first North American criminologists investigated the harsh class conditions of distressed low-income communities. Often collaborating with street workers and social agencies, these sociologists of the streets explored whether the rapidly building forces of urbanization, immigration, and industrialization were exposing the youth of growing cities to criminogenic conditions. The street seemed a natural place to study these youth, especially as they gathered on street corners and in gangs.

Initially, this work was more descriptively detailed than analytically rigorous, more socially engaged than scientifically grounded; but this gradually changed. Some of the best early work was represented in the Chicago school of sociological criminology. In 1923, Nels Anderson's *The Hobo* detailed the lives of homeless men and their criminal as well as noncriminal involvements.

In the same year, W. I. Thomas's *The Unadjusted Girl* described the experiences of young women who left home and often worked as prostitutes on the streets of Chicago. Continuing this tradition, Fredrick Thrasher (1927) made contacts with street groups and interviewed them about their membership and activities for his classic book *The Gang*. In *The Jack-Roller* (1930) and *Brothers in Crime* (1938), Clifford Shaw provided detailed ethnographies of life on the street and involvement in crime. Edwin Sutherland and Harvey Locke (1936) also produced a little known book in the Chicago tradition, titled *Twenty Thousand Homeless Men*.

None of these studies are about street youth per se, but each is an effort to understand a life away from home that often involves young people who spend much of their time on the street actively involved in crime. This interest in urban street life extended well into the second half of the century, as reflected in the field research of William Whyte's (1943) *Street Corner Society* and Elliot Liebow's *Tally's Corner* (1967). It is also evident in James Short and Fred Strodtbeck's (1965) use of street workers in their work, *Group Process and Gang Delinquency*, and in Gerald Suttles' (1968) participant observation study, *Social Order of the Slum*. This tradition continues today in ethnographies and participant observation studies that focus on criminal and gang activities in distressed American neighborhoods depicted, for example, in John Hagedorn's (1988) *People and Folks*, Mercer Sullivan's (1989) *Getting Paid*, Joan Moore's (1991) *Going Down to the Barrio*, Felix Padilla's (1992) *The Gang as an American Enterprise*, Philippe Bourgois' (1995) *In Search of Respect*, and Mark Fleisher's (1995) *Beggars and Thieves*. However, urban anthropologists, rather than criminologists, are mostly responsible for revitalizing the study of street crime in these impoverished communities, and mainstream criminology has paid little attention to these works.[5]

Criminologists' neglect of recent field studies is in part attributable to new urban ethnographers' tendency to study exclusively people who are involved in crimes or gangs, thereby limiting comparisons between offenders and nonoffenders. These small and highly selected samples do not lend themselves to methods of quantitative analysis, which have become a mainstay of the criminological research enterprise since the development of systematic social survey methods at midcentury.[6] From the 1950s onward, attention to sampling, measurement, and sophisticated multivariate analyses has increasingly dominated criminological research. As criminology has become more self-consciously scientific in its methods, its imperatives have changed: Criminologists have abandoned the streets, turning to self-report surveys and the study of school youth.

School Criminologists

Armed with their new self-report methodology, criminologists moved into the schools of North America (and later other countries) to collect detailed information about family, education, community, and adolescent experiences. These self-report student surveys offered many advantages: They demonstrated that common forms of delinquency were measurable in anonymous studies of school populations; they allowed researchers to study large samples; they facilitated the systematic measurement of variables that could be tested for their role in the causation of delinquency; and they eventually provided a paradigm for classic contributions to theory testing in criminology (e.g., Hirschi, 1969; Matsueda, 1982).

This new methodology also raised questions about the relationships between class and delinquency and crime (e.g., Tittle, Villemez, and Smith, 1978; Weis, 1987; Jensen and Thompson, 1990). Self-report survey researchers questioned the taken-for-granted association between crime and poverty – a relationship evident in densely descriptive ethnographic studies, as well as in the measures of poverty and crime that sometimes tautologically and ecologically confounded areal studies of crime and delinquency. They rightly disentangled the concepts, insisting on independent measures of class and crime that provided building blocks for testing explanations based on class circumstances.

There is no doubt that the development of self-report methodology marked a major advance in modern criminology. The issue we take with this approach is not that self-report methodology is flawed but rather that its use is too often restricted to junior and senior high-school students. The neglect of other youth groups has transformed and, to some extent, misdirected the nature of criminological investigations. Three substitutions have characterized this transformation: (1) schools replaced the streets as sites for data collection; (2) parents' socioeconomic status superseded class backgrounds and more immediate class circumstances as presumed exogenous causes of delinquency; and (3) delinquency supplanted crime as the behavior to be explained.

In some ways, these changes enhanced the scientific standing of criminological research, but they also distanced self-report studies from the conditions and activities that stimulated attention to youth and crime in the first place. More accurate sampling frames can be established for schools than for the streets, but street youth are more likely than school youth to be involved in delinquency and crime. Student self-reports of delinquency are less prone to some of the biases found in official record keeping, but the common indiscretions that students report are less likely to be the crimes that concern citizens. Also, although it is true that parental status can be indexed (with attractive measurement properties for persons regularly employed in conventional occupations) independently of the adolescent behaviors that researchers seek to explain, the status continua underlying these measures assume that parents have occupations to be measured. Moreover, these measures are not directly linked to the experiences of the youth whose behaviors are being explained (Greenberg, 1977).

Overall, these substitutions made self-report survey research more systematic, but they also produced several unintended results: less theoretically relevant characteristics (i.e., status versus class) are now used to explain less serious behaviors (i.e., common delinquency instead of crime) of less criminally involved persons (i.e., students rather than street youth). Although the analogy can be overstated, there is a parallel between studying crime among students and studying AIDS in this population. Even though serious crime and AIDS are relatively rare among school youth, minor forms of delinquency are common, and students are exposed to the risk of HIV infection. Useful research, therefore, can be done on minor delinquency and exposure to HIV infection among students. However, it is hard to imagine medical researchers neglecting the investigation of AIDS among higher-risk groups (e.g., intravenous drug users and sexually active youth) or arguing against investing research resources in these populations. Similarly, youth living on the streets of our cities have increased risks of involvement in several illegal activities and represent an important avenue for studying crime. Unfortunately, homeless youth remain an underutilized supplement to a school-based criminology.

Homelessness, Runaways, and Street Youth

Social science interest in the homeless in North America diminished in the years following Edwin Sutherland and Harvey Locke's (1936) study, *Twenty Thousand Homeless Men,* and other classic contributions from the Chicago school (e.g., Anderson, 1923; Zorbaugh, 1929). In the 1980s, several influential scholars recognized this oversight and revived large-scale social surveys of the homeless (Snow and Anderson, 1987; Rossi, 1989; Wright, 1989). Shlay and Rossi (1992) identify at least sixty local and national primary data investigations undertaken since academics rediscovered this population; yet this resurgence rarely involves attention to youth. Instead, contemporary knowledge of the lives of homeless youth is largely limited to photojournalism (e.g., Craig and Schwarz, 1984; Goldberg and Brookman, 1995), oral histories and case studies (e.g, Artenstein, 1990; Weber, 1991), and a handful of small surveys (Janus, McCormack, Burgess, and Hartman, 1987; Kufeldt and Nimmo, 1987; Whitbeck and Simons, 1990, 1993).

Social scientists' neglect of homeless youth may have resulted from tendencies to conceptualize narrowly such youth as runaways and to concentrate on the origins of leaving home rather than on the consequences of being on the street. North American researchers have typically presumed that, in most cases, prematurely leaving home was an adolescent behavior associated with a desire for independence from parental authority; these researchers have also implicitly assumed that most runaways would return home shortly following their departures (see Adams and Munro, 1979; Liebertoff, 1980). The remaining runaways – those who left home more than once or twice or who stayed away for lengthy periods – were treated as a distinct group of youth thought to suffer from more serious psychological problems ranging from simple depression and anxiety to severe maladjustment, mental instability, and pathological personalities. Particularly dominant in the 1940s, this approach remained influential through the 1970s (see Armstrong, 1932, 1937; Robins and O'Neal, 1959; Levanthal, 1963, 1964; Jenkins, 1969, 1971; Stierlin, 1973; Olson, Liebow, Mannino, and Shore, 1980; Edelbrock, 1980).

Toward the end of the 1970s, several writers (e.g., Walker, 1975; Wolk and Brandon, 1977; Brennan, Huizinga, and Elliott, 1978) noted that research from the individual pathology perspective often ignored the stressful environments that frequently pushed youth from, or provoked youth to leave, their family homes. Building on a handful of studies that examined the psychological profiles of the parents of runaways (e.g., Foster, 1962; Robey, Rosenwald, Snell, and Lee, 1964; Rosenwald and Mayer, 1967), the structure of their families, and parent–child relationships (e.g., Hildebrand, 1963, 1968; D'Angelo, 1974; Shellow, Schamp, Liebow, and Unger, 1972; Wolk and Brandon, 1977), these writers offered integrated theories of why adolescents run away (Brennan et al., 1978; Nye, 1980). These theories emphasized the social context of leaving home, particularly the role of the family, school experiences, and relationships with peers.

More recent works have focused explicitly on family physical and sexual abuse as important determinants of leaving home (Farber, Kinast, McCoard, and Falkner, 1984; Garbarino, Wilson, and Garbarino, 1986; Janus et al., 1987; Kufeldt and Nimmo, 1987) and on differences between youth who have run from their families and those pushed or thrown out by uninterested parents (Adams, Gullotta, and Clancy, 1985; Janus et al., 1987).

Notwithstanding these contributions, few studies have explored the experiences of youth after they arrive on the street. The available studies (Minehan, 1934; Howell, Emmons, and Frank, 1973; Brennan et al., 1978; Janus et al., 1987; Kufeldt and Nimmo, 1987; Whitbeck and Simons, 1990, 1993) reveal that youth who leave and stay away from home encounter many of the problems that are well-documented and extensively studied among homeless adults (Momeni, 1989; Rossi, 1989; Wright, 1989; Blau, 1992; Burt, 1992; Snow and Anderson, 1993; Jencks, 1994). Like their adult counterparts, homeless or street youth experience unemployment, poverty, hunger, lack of shelter, criminal victimization, sexual harassment, trouble with the police, and solicitation into crime (Kufeldt and Nimmo, 1987; Whitbeck and Simons, 1990, 1993).

Street Youth and Crime

Recent figures indicate that approximately 100 million children and adolescents live on the streets of cities worldwide (UNICEF, 1989). Although conditions obviously vary, homeless youth are a growing presence and represent an important and sizable proportion of the adolescents living in high-risk settings of both developed (Wright, 1991) and developing nations of the world (National Research Council, 1993, p. 182; also see Aptekar, 1988; Wright, Wittig, and Kaminsky, 1993; Campos, Raffaelli, and Ude, 1994). An estimated two-fifths of the world's street youth live in Latin America (Barker and Knaul, 1991), with a majority of these youth living on the streets of Brazil (Campos et al., 1994). In the United States, recent figures suggest that the street youth population has reached one and a half million (Shane, 1989) and for much of the past decade in Toronto – one of the locations of our research – annual estimates of the number of street youth have ranged from 10,000 to 20,000 (Janus et al., 1987; Carey, 1990).

According to Campos et al. (1994), Brazilian street youth can be separated into two groups: those "on" and those "of" the street. Campos et al. (1994, p. 319) observe that youth "on" the street work at street-based jobs and return to their families at night or on weekends, whereas those "of" the street have fragmented family ties, sleep in street locations, and often engage in illegal survival strategies. Both kinds of youth are a prominent part of Latin American city life (Aptekar, 1988), whereas in developed countries, youth "of" the street cause more frequent concern. Our research concentrates on the latter, but it varies from much of the work in this area by focusing on issues of survival on the street, including involvement in crime.

Although early investigations suggested that street youth were no more delinquent or criminal while on the street than were their homebound counterparts (see Shellow et al., 1972; Gold and Reimer, 1974), more recent studies concur with social workers' reports and media portrayals that indicate otherwise.[7] In a study using data on youth from Colorado and from a national sample of adolescents, Brennan et al. (1978) find that 33 percent of runaways admitted stealing after leaving home (15 percent indicated that they stole objects worth $50 or more) and 20 percent reported selling drugs. Brennan et al. (1978) note that these activities were positively associated with the length of time spent away from home and the number of previous departures.

In a more recent investigation of 489 runaway youth in Edmonton (Canada), Kufeldt and Nimmo (1987) indicate that 71 percent of runaways reported being encouraged by others to participate in crime while on the street; moreover, 49 percent admitted involvement in unspecified illegal activities. Whitbeck and Simons (1990, 1993) report comparable findings in their study of 156 homeless adolescents and 319 adults in a midwestern U.S. city. They find that 43 percent of homeless youth shoplifted on the street, 33 percent sold drugs, 32 percent committed a break and enter, and 9 percent worked in prostitution. Whitbeck and Simons point out that for each type of crime, homeless youth report significantly greater involvement than their adult counterparts.

Several smaller and more qualitatively oriented studies also document the link between life on the street and involvement in crime (e.g., see Silbert and Pines, 1982; Palenski, 1984). For example, Palenski (1984) interviewed 36 New York City youth who left home and took to the streets. He notes that among these youth illegal behavior usually is not preferred but rather is adopted as a response to demands of being on the street:

> What often occurs is that young people abandon the runaway preoccupation for any set of alternative acts that will bring money, security or approval for the moment. This marks the onset of illegal behavior in that drugs, sex and petty theft are not supports to the runaway episode but options in themselves. (p. 133)

We have found further evidence that criminal involvement is not simply more prevalent among street youth but also more frequent and serious. In the first of the two Toronto samples analyzed in this book, we find that 46 percent of the homeless respondents made drug sales, 49 percent stole goods valued up to $50, and 27 percent broke into homes or businesses (McCarthy and Hagan, 1991). The respective percentages of 32, 13, and 13 reported in Hindelang, Hirschi, and Weis's (1981) Seattle-based community study are substantially lower, despite the latter study's stratification to overrepresent adolescents with police contacts. Even lower proportions are reported in studies of the school samples that have become common in criminology (e.g., see Hirschi, 1969; Elliott and Ageton, 1980; Paternoster and Triplett, 1988).

Data on the frequency of offending are less commonly reported in the school literature, but the information available indicates that street youth are disproportionately repeat offenders. For example, in a study of over fifteen hundred eleventh-grade students, Paternoster and Triplett (1988) report that among offenders, the median frequency of petty theft is three, and for smoking marijuana, it is ten. In the first Toronto street youth sample (described in more detail later), the median frequency of *more serious theft* (over $50) while on the street is eight, and for *selling hard drugs*, it is ten.

Criminologists increasingly recognize the importance of samples that include frequent and serious offenders (Piliavin, Thornton, Gartner, and Matsueda, 1986; Wolfgang, Thornberry, and Figlio, 1987; Sullivan, 1989; Matsueda, Gartner, Piliavin, and Polakowski, 1992; Inciardi, Horowitz, and Pottieger, 1993), and although street youth constitute a relatively small proportion of all adolescents, they are involved in a substantial and disproportionate amount of crime. Yet the youth in our samples range from those who are repeat, almost daily, offenders to those with little or no criminal involvement. The challenge of our work is to examine this variation to understand better the causal forces that lead many street youth to crime, as well as the direction that their involvement takes. First, however, it is important that we clarify our operational definitions of some key terms: youth, homelessness, and crime.

Youth

There is little consensus about the period of life generally referred to as *youth*. Although the journal *Adolescence* is devoted to studying aspects of the "second decade of human life," it regularly publishes studies of young persons past the age of 20. Similarly, research on runaway and homeless youth considers individuals of various ages. For the most part, these definitions reflect the characteristics of the research setting. Studies that survey runaways charged in court typically limit their samples to youth legally considered juveniles (e.g., those younger than 18 or 19). Likewise, those that sample youth who use hostels and other social services usually replicate these agencies' age restrictions. Typically, age limits for these services range from 16 to 24 years of age (Liddiard and Hutson, 1991).

Our approach is somewhat different. Life course research (Elder, 1975) reminds us that one of the defining characteristics of youth is its intermediary status between childhood and adulthood. Youth is a period of transition that is especially challenging and problematic on the street and is often prolonged to an age when youth in different circumstances would be considered adults. In selecting our sample, we used Starr's (1986) definition, which encompasses the period between puberty and adulthood. Starr notes, "whereas this time span varies by socio-economic status and career lines, the majority experience youth roughly between the ages of 15 and 24" (1986:324). To explore fully the effects of age, we also include it as a variable in our analysis.

Homelessness

Many studies of runaways use a typology to differentiate youth (see English, 1973; Stierlin, 1973; Brennan et al., 1978). Earlier we noted the distinction drawn by Campos et al. (1994) between youth who are "on" and "of" the street. Other researchers demarcate runaways, throwaways, the homeless, street youth, societal rejects, system kids, and those who leave abusive family environments (e.g., Gulotta, 1978; Gutierres and Reich, 1981; Adams et al., 1985; Garbarino et al., 1986). In selecting our sample, we did not differentiate among street youth. Instead, our selection criterion focuses on the experience common to all these youth: the lack of a permanent address. They may have run away (i.e., left home without parental consent), or they may have been forced from their home (i.e., parentally rejected "throwaways"). They may have been on the street for only a short time, or they may have adopted the street as their home. Some may be legally living on the streets, whereas others may have fled from group homes or detention centers; they may have outstanding warrants for their arrests or, because of their age, be legally prohibited from living independently of their families. These differences notwithstanding, we define youth as living on the street once they leave home and are without a permanent place of address.[8] This definition intentionally does not incorporate reasons for leaving, nor the length of time away from home. Instead, it focuses on street life in a more inclusive way. To assess more fully the effects of living on the street, we include a measure of the length of time youth have been without a permanent residence in our analyses.

Crime

Many sociological investigations of deviance dwell on frequent delinquent acts such as truancy, minor vandalism, petty theft, joy riding, and fist fighting (see Hirschi, 1969; Hindelang, 1979). These common activities may be most pertinent for adolescents who are attached to, or controlled by, institutions of the larger society. However, these behaviors are less salient in the lives of those who have left home and live on the street. As noted earlier in this chapter, many contemporary studies point to positive relationships between living on the street and minor and more serious crimes, including break and enter, robbery, assault, and drug- and sex-related offenses. We investigate an array of crimes and give particular attention to minor and more serious theft, prostitution, drug selling, and assault.

Some researchers argue that crime and delinquency are more general than specific and thus are best measured by global scales (Hindelang et al., 1981; Gottfredson and Hirschi, 1990); others disagree, maintaining that law violators specialize (Sutherland, 1947; Clinard and Quinney, 1973; Smith, Smith, and Noma, 1984; Tittle, Jackson, and Burke, 1986; Blumstein, Cohen, and Farrington, 1988a; Allan and Steffensmeier, 1989). To encompass these divergent perspectives, we give distinct as well as combined attention to the offenses noted previously.

The Streets of Two Cities

The research reported in this book is built around two studies: a 1987–88 cross-sectional comparative examination of street and school youth in Toronto, and a 1992 summer-long panel study of street youth in Toronto and Vancouver. These studies were undertaken in a purposeful sequence. The earlier cross-sectional Toronto study was planned first to establish the relationship between research based on school and street populations. The 1992 summer-long panel study of street youth in Toronto and Vancouver was subsequently undertaken to examine effects of variation in city context on street youth and crime, and to explore developmental processes that lead to continued involvement in street crime. The two cities are introduced here.

Toronto. Once called Hogtown, Toronto is English Canada's most cosmopolitan and important city. According to a recent newspaper editorial in

Canada's national newspaper, the *Globe and Mail*, it is the "engine that drives Canada." Located at the literal and metaphorical crossroads in the transportation network of a vast nation, Toronto is strategically placed in the eastern central wedge of Canada, which juts into the heartland of the United States. Thus, it is the linchpin that connects Canada as the largest trading partner of the United States. These features make Toronto a city of great energy. More than any other place in Canada, it is the place where fortunes are made and lost, and also where affluence rubs most closely against economic adversity and desperation.

Although Montreal was the earlier financial center of Canada, Toronto underwent a period of rapid economic growth during the postwar boom in the middle part of this century. In the ensuing years, Toronto's skyline has been a metaphor for its growth. It includes the world's tallest free-standing structure, the CN Tower; the futuristic Skydome Stadium; an architecturally celebrated City Hall; and a stunning array of bank towers that flank Bay Street, Toronto's symbol of corporate power and affluence. Not coincidentally, Toronto is Canada's leading financial center. All of Canada's major banks and many of its major corporations, insurance companies, and brokerage houses have head offices in Toronto. Ontario accounts for 50 percent of the manufacturing productivity of Canada, and Toronto employs close to half of the manufacturing workers in Ontario.

Toronto is one of the most ethnically diverse cities in North America, and much of its prosperity has been fueled by immigration. In recent years, more than a third of all Canada's immigrants have chosen to live in the Toronto area; they contribute to a growing metropolis that has increased from approximately one million people in 1950, to over two million in 1970, and close to three million in 1990.

Despite its affluence, Toronto was not immune to the recession of the early 1990s. In this period, the official unemployment rate rose to historically high levels of 12 percent, welfare caseloads increased markedly, and foodbanks served hundreds of thousands of people. It is estimated that between 1990 and 1992, Toronto lost over 175,000 jobs. In the restructured economy that has emerged from the most recent recession, Toronto's labor force has become more polarized between high-wage employment in its financial sector and low-wage service sector jobs in the retail, tourist, and food industries. Toronto is today a focus of fears about urban malaise and misfortune symbolized in a preoccupation with the prospect of becoming "Manhattanized" and in growing concerns about homelessness and crime.

Urban folklore about Toronto's bountiful opportunities draws youth to its downtown business district from the surrounding neighborhoods, suburbs, and nearby cities, as well as from more remote communities and rural settings. For many youth, particularly those from the maritime provinces, "going down the road" represents a frequently traveled search for opportunity that often leads to Toronto.

Toronto's downtown street scene encircles the architecturally imposing Eaton Centre. As the adjoining map indicates, this extravagant mall spans several city blocks, on Yonge Street between Queen and Dundas streets (see Map 1.1). Surrounding this shopping and tourist site are several major theaters, sports complexes, music halls, and a wide-ranging mix of restaurants and shops, including boutiques, department stores, and video arcades. This downtown area attracts a great number of pedestrians and, unlike many U.S. cities, tourists and shoppers walk these blocks late into the evenings of most nights. Three sites of prostitution border these blocks: One, in the Church and Jarvis street area, is known for female prostitution; a second, near Isabella and Sherbourne, is frequented by transvestites and is sometimes called "Tranny Town"; and the third, "Boys' Town," is popular for male prostitution and covers several blocks surrounding Grosvenor.

Several factors have encouraged the ongoing street life of this area. Although street youth are frequently escorted off the premises by security officers, the Eaton's mall – and several smaller indoor shopping centers in the vicinity – provide a place to meet, hang out, and escape inclement weather. The bustling pedestrian traffic, both in the malls and on the adjacent blocks, provides further opportunities for panhandling, seeking information, and establishing new relationships. As well, the density of the daytime population in this area facilitates anonymity, allowing youth who have fled parents, group homes, or probation orders to drift inconspicuously in a current of people, cars, and shops. The pace of the street also facilitates drug sales, with extensive marijuana and acid dealing on Yonge Street itself, and active crack and cocaine markets on several adjoining blocks.

The concentration of street youth in this area is further encouraged by its proximity to several storefront agencies and hostels that provide services for homeless youth. For example, the two largest youth hostels that accommodate homeless youth are located in the Allan Gardens area, approximately twenty minutes' walk from Eaton Centre. This area also contains several smaller parks and abandoned buildings where street youth hang out and seek shelter.

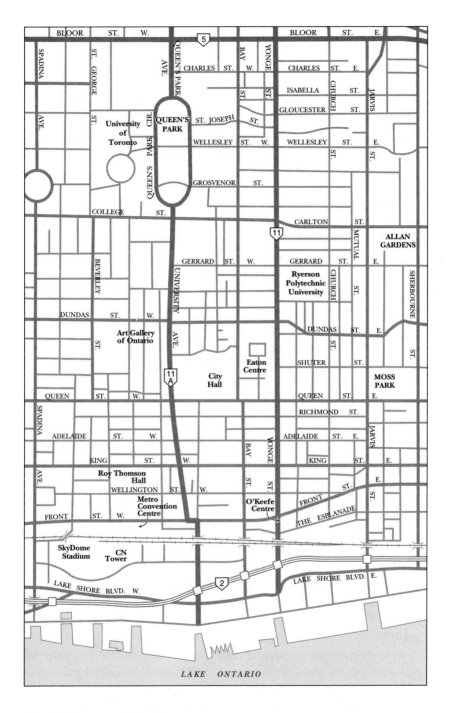

Map 1.1 Downtown Toronto.

Vancouver. Whereas Toronto dominates eastern and central Canada, Vancouver is Canada's "San Francisco." A picturesque and busy port on the southwest coast of British Columbia, Vancouver boasts a scenic location bordered by the Pacific Ocean, snowcapped mountains, and lush forests. Vancouver is the third largest city in Canada and has grown rapidly in recent years to over a million and a half people. In addition to a large number of First Nations peoples, and Canadians of British and European origin, Vancouver also is home to a sizable Asian–Canadian community and pockets of other ethnic groups.

Historically, Vancouver has dominated Canada's western economy, in part because it is Canada's trading link to the Pacific Rim. Prairie oil and grain, British Columbia lumber and minerals, and manufactured goods from central Canada all pass through Vancouver on their way to western Pacific destinations, while Asian imports also move through this port on their way to central and eastern Canadian markets. Unlike most Canadian cities, including Toronto, Vancouver's economy did not shrink over the last decade but instead experienced a robust and sustained growth. However, Vancouver also has its share of poverty and a growing street population. Its temperate climate attracts a transient population, including young people, chronic substance abusers, and aboriginal people from rural reserves.

Street life in Vancouver is concentrated in two areas centrally located on the adjoining map of the downtown peninsula that leads to Stanley Park (see Map 1.2). The first, the Granville Mall area, includes several streets where youth hang out in front of stores, a municipal art gallery, and several small shopping complexes. Drinking and panhandling are common, as are the use and sale of marijuana and acid. The sex trade is prominently located in this area, including Vancouver's "Boys' Town," on the blocks near Drake Street, and one of the main sites for female prostitution, along Richards Street, also borders the Granville Mall. Relative to Toronto's Yonge Street, there is less tourism in the Granville area, and the shops and businesses attract a smaller group of customers. Although there is a steady flow of people in the day and early evening, this slows to a trickle at night.

A number of social service agencies are located in the Granville Mall area, including the main site for youth assistance, a provincial government child-care office, on Drake Street. These agencies offer important services for street youth, but there are no hostels for youth under the age of 19; moreover, of those agencies that offer shelter for those aged 19 and over, none provide services that separate young people and adults. Thus, youth

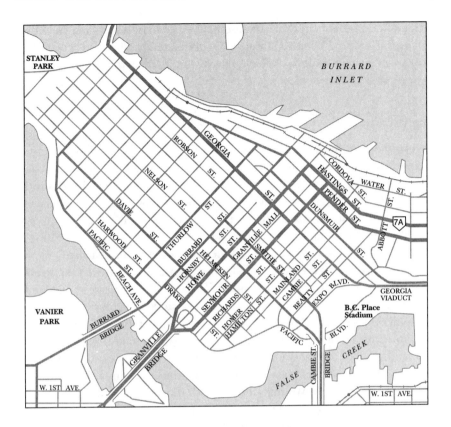

Map 1.2 Downtown Vancouver.

frequently seek shelter in the vacant buildings scattered throughout the Granville Mall area.

The second area of Vancouver's street life is centered around Hastings Street and the downtown "East Side." This part of the city has a continuing history as a haven for street alcoholics and drug addicts. Characterized by single-room-only hotels, the public consumption of alcohol, a sizable heroin trade, noticeable levels of crack use, and high levels of interpersonal violence, this area attracts what social agency workers refer to as the "hardcore" homeless. Prostitution also occurs in this area, but the workers and clients are disproportionately drawn from the population of heavy substance abusers.

A salient difference between Vancouver and Toronto involves the availability of social services for street youth. Toronto's rather well-developed social welfare bureaucracy plays a significant role in providing a social safety net for these young people. The absence of this safety net for street youth in Vancouver plays a major role in a part of the analysis that is presented in Chapter Five of this book.

Analytic Strategy

We begin our study of street youth in the following chapter with a mixture of quantitative and qualitative data that we use to document the family backgrounds, school experiences, and everyday activities of youth living on the streets. We describe the background and foreground class conditions and experiences of urban street life, and the ways these shape the daily lives of homeless youth. In particular, we detail how street youth spend their time in the legal and illegal pursuit of food, shelter, money, and pleasure.

We next consider the process of leaving home and taking to the streets. As a theoretical starting point for our empirical work, we propose that family class background and its connections to erratic and explosive parenting, parental rejection, and family disruption can be given simultaneous consideration in an integrated model that also considers school experiences in explaining youth homelessness. Our approach combines control and strain theories and highlights class circumstances that we emphasize at several junctures in this book. We regard the elaboration of this class-based model as a crucial step in understanding the causal process through which particular youth enter the street population.

We subsequently broaden our focus on class to include a concern of early criminologists that is too often ignored in contemporary research: the relationship of offending to sudden or situational adversity. We suggest that harsh street experiences of hunger, lack of shelter, and joblessness reflect the immediate class conditions that confront many street youth. An ethnomethodologist sensitive to class experiences would probably characterize these adverse life circumstances as forming the "lived world" of street youth. We investigate whether and how these foreground class conditions influence street crime apart from background activities and circumstances.

In the following part of this book, we examine how street youth's individual developmental backgrounds, and the distinctive social environments of Toronto and Vancouver, influence different kinds of street crime. Research on crime can often be distinguished in terms of its tendency to attend to what are sometimes called *ontogenetic* (internally developed) as opposed to *sociogenic* (externally imposed) causal forces. The former type of research emphasizes individual differences, whereas the latter work tends to focus on variations in opportunities and social environments. The location of our research in two cities, and our attention to different kinds of criminal activity – from theft, drugs, and prostitution to criminal violence – provide an important opportunity to distinguish the influences of these different kinds of causal forces.

We move next from the broad contours of street experiences in Toronto and Vancouver to a more detailed consideration of the influence of social ties in the formation of crime networks. Our position is that street youth tend not to be the asocial, unskilled offenders that recent sociological, psychological, and economic theories often imply. Drawing on insights of differential association theory, we concentrate on the social embeddedness of these youth in relationships that transmit skills and knowledge about street crime. We argue that these associations constitute a type of "criminal capital" that is as important in the world of street crime as analogous resources are in more conventional vocational settings.

We then consider a unique aspect of adolescent street life: the formation of quasi-family structures. Many of the youth in our research report that they belong to street families. They argue that these family groups play an important role in their day-to-day survival, helping them to gain access to food, shelter, and other necessities, as well as mitigating some of the harsh daily realities of street life. These quasi-family relationships provide companionship and a sense of belonging, and street youth suggest that they help to allay feelings of despair, isolation, and loneliness. We give particular attention to the impact of street families on the emotional and psychological well-being of their members, as well as to the effect of street families on offending.

Then we consider the consequences of arrest. We explore the possibility, implied in recent work, that adverse family backgrounds interact with police sanctions to increase trajectories of criminal involvement. Building on recent innovations in labeling theory, we suggest that family abuse represents a type of negative stigma that can encourage feelings of shame in its victims. Spiraling chains of shame can culminate in accentuated forms of deviant and destructive behaviors. Police responses to these behaviors may further stigmatize victims of abuse, encouraging defiant and life course persistent involvement in street crime.

In our final data analysis chapter, we move from factors that encourage homelessness and offending to experiences that facilitate leaving both the street and a life of crime. We suggest that the demands and effects of employment can redirect homeless trajectories by providing youth with access to individuals, groups, and related opportunities that can enhance their social resources. Employment also places street youth in a state of dissonance and can draw them away from their street networks. We investigate this possibility by analyzing the effects of employment on participation in several street activities, including crimes committed with street friends.

The final and perhaps most challenging task undertaken in this book involves an attempt to articulate an integrated theoretical framework for studying the involvement of street youth in crime. We recognize that most youth never become homeless and that much adolescent crime is not committed by youth on the street. Nevertheless, the diversity of youth who end up on the street, and the adversity they experience, provide a challenging context in which to develop a versatile theory of crime. Our effort, generally conceived, is to use our findings to reconceptualize inductively the notions of strain, control, embeddedness, criminal capital, and labeling within a larger theoretical framework. This theoretical approach uses the concept of social capital to connect the influences of background, developmental, and foreground variables on the movements of youth into, and away from, street crime.

As noted earlier, the material presented in this book was developed in a cross-sectional study undertaken in Toronto in 1987–8, and a 1992 panel study in Toronto and Vancouver. The appendix to this book details the procedures we used to collect and record these data. It includes an account of the extensive investment in field work that was necessary to develop the quantitative and qualitative data that ground our research. The appendix also addresses several important methodological concerns about sampling, data analysis, and panel attrition.

Taking Criminology Back to the Streets

From the classic gang studies by Thrasher in the early part of this century, to work by Short and Strodtbeck in the 1960s, the study of youth on the streets of our major cities was once central to sociological criminology. These contributions have been eclipsed by a criminology that studies adolescents who attend school and who rarely are involved in serious crime. However, the recent rise in homelessness throughout the developed and developing nations underlines the seriousness of problems of contemporary street youth. These youth are exposed to highly criminogenic conditions, both in their backgrounds and in their current living situations. Not surprisingly, they report considerable involvement in several types of street crime. Yet street youth are not a significant focus of contemporary criminology. This book is an argument for returning to the street and renewing attention to its implications for understanding crime.

Street Youth and Street Settings

TO UNDERSTAND STREET LIFE and its connections with crime, it is important to examine circumstances that lead youth from their families, as well as their lives on the street. A sense of these background and foreground experiences emerges from interviews we conducted with street youth. In these interviews, street youth describe their pasts and provide insights into experiences and events that lead to leaving home. These interviews also offer an introduction to the pleasures and problems of street life, including companionship and the availability of drugs and alcohol, as well as the difficulties of finding shelter, safety, food, and money. Many of these stories are disturbing, but they add a penetrating personal dimension to our understanding of the life histories of street youth and the daily situations they encounter.

In this and following chapters, we draw on nearly one hundred of the more than two hundred interviews we conducted with street youth in the third wave of our summer panel study. We present background details or experiences and a pseudonym to distinguish among the many young people with whom we spoke. This sociobiographical information is introduced to develop a composite picture of street youth that parallels the personal narratives often provided for smaller numbers of subjects in qualitative studies.

We provide a background to the interviews by drawing first on descriptive statistics from our initial study of 390 street youth in Toronto. This purposive sample was developed between the springs of 1987 and 1988 and involved surveying youth in shelters, drop-in centers, city parks, and on street corners in downtown Toronto. Although we cannot be certain that our initial Toronto sample fully represents the population from which it is drawn, data from social service agencies and independently produced samples of street youth yield comparable results (see Janus et al., 1987; McCarthy, 1990).

Our confidence in the initial Toronto sample is reinforced by similarities to the 482 youth interviewed in the Toronto and Vancouver panel study undertaken during the summer of 1992. To avoid unnecessary repetition, we only report descriptive statistics from the initial Toronto study here. The Appendix to this volume provides additional information on the several data sets analyzed in this book and contains a detailed record of the extensive field work involved in our research. There are, of course, some differences between the data sets and cities, and in Chapter Five, we discuss specific ways in which Vancouver street youth differ from those in Toronto. However, our present concern is to provide a broad overview of the backgrounds and experiences of street youth.

Backgrounds to the Street

A statistical snapshot of Toronto street youth first reveals that the street scene is disproportionately but by no means exclusively male. The street youth of Toronto are about two-thirds male and one-third female, and the males are on average one year older than the females (18.1 versus 17.1 years old). The gender and age composition of this population may be the result of females encountering greater dangers and difficulties on the street and therefore leaving it earlier.

As we note in further detail in the following chapter, between a quarter and a third of all street youth came from families that frequently experienced unemployment. A larger proportion of these youth left families that had been disrupted, with less than a third of the Toronto street youth (30 percent) having lived with both biological parents at the time they left home. Another quarter (24 percent) lived in reconstituted families with a step- or common law parent. The next most common family arrangement involved either an unattached mother (18 percent) or living in a foster or group home (17 percent). The majority of respondents also reported that they had lived in more than one family situation, usually in families reconstituted after divorce and remarriage.

Most street youth (87 percent) reported that their parents or guardians used physical discipline in the home, and more than half (60 percent) indicated that, on at least one occasion, they had been hit with enough force to cause a bruise or bleeding. We did not probe specifically for indications of sexual abuse; however, an open-ended question about the reasons for leaving home revealed that 14 percent of females and 6 percent of males reported that they were victims of sexual abuse. Many family settings were further characterized by parental alcohol and drug abuse and, in a significant number of cases, parental criminality.

Youth in the Toronto street sample also had considerable difficulty in school. The modal youth had a ninth-grade education, and one in five of these young people had no more than an eighth-grade education. One-fifth of the sample indicated that they "always" or "often" had problems understanding school material, and a similar proportion indicated that they frequently had conflicts with their teachers.

Family Life

These descriptive statistics only begin to hint at the many reasons that motivate youth to take to the streets. The most frequent explanations given by youth include problems of incompatibility with family and stepfamily members, disrupted and dysfunctional families, neglectful parents, coercive and abusive parents, parental rejection, and problems in school that often produced further conflict with parents. However, these phrases are too abstract to capture meaningfully the impact of the experiences and events that lead young people to the street. A better way to gain a sense of the backgrounds of members of our sample is to turn to the respondents' own descriptions of their experiences.

Our interviews in the panel study included a series of open-ended questions asking respondents about their home lives and street experiences. The youth we spoke with offered a range of reasons for leaving home, and their accounts suggest the complex interweave of factors and events underlying their departures. For example, Mary, who came from an actively religious, professional-class family, found it hard to isolate a single factor or incident that led her to leave home. She suggested that leaving home represented a culmination of forces that had troubled her relationship with her parents over a long period of time. Leaving was difficult both to do and to explain:

> You can't always sum it up in one reason. . . . It's taken us – we've been in here like over an hour – to get around to how it was when I actually left, and the reasons why I left. It's like that with a lot of people. You think, oh, it's gotta be one thing and that's why you left. It could be a combination of things, and it

doesn't always happen just at once. Then again, nothing ever does, nothing's ever really that simple.

As we suggested earlier, many of the families these youth left were dysfunctional by almost any definition. Parental use of alcohol and drugs were common, as were neglect and abuse. The former are typified in Sebastian's home life. Born in the British Isles, Sebastian had lived with his mother, father, and later his stepfather in homes on the east coast and in southern Ontario. He told us that he first left home at 16; when asked why, he replied:

My parents threw me out. . . . They're drug addicts. Hash, weed, coke, crack – everything. I didn't want to leave but they just threw me out. I had a huge fight with my dad. We'd fight 'cause I'd go, "quit drugs," and he would go "no" . . . I'd go, "quit drinking." He'd say "no." So we just argued about that most of the time. And one day he goes, "I think its about time you leave, get on your own." So I just left.

Sheneika's home life was equally turbulent. She was 13 when her abusive stepfather deserted the family and her mother turned to drugs:

My mom had some hard times. Lot of, lot of hard times with drugs, and 'cause once my, my dad left – he, he's actually my stepfather – once he left, he um, cleaned up the bank accounts and took off. So it left her with nothing. So she had to loan, and she was just so fed up she spent all the loan money on cocaine.

As Sebastian's and Sheneika's stories illustrate, problems of parental substance abuse rarely occurred in isolation from other problems. Respondents frequently described alcohol- and drug-using parents who were neglectful of familial responsibilities and whose involvement in family life was inconsistent and often explosive. The interconnections between parental substance use and erratic and frequently violent parenting are well represented in Robert's childhood.

Robert grew up in a middle-class home in an affluent part of Toronto. He contemplated leaving home on several occasions but waited until he was 16, when he could legally leave his dysfunctional family:

Both my parents were alcoholics, and I had a younger sister and older brother, and, uh, it just got to a point . . . I mean, we used to get beat up at least four or five times a week. It got to a point where we'd hide and just wait for them to find us. And I just decided when I was 16, I mean, I knew, I mean, I could run away before I was 16, but I always, you know . . . and, uhm, finally I just couldn't take it anymore.

Another respondent, Jeremy, also described physical abuse that began in childhood and that was connected to parental substance abuse. His parents separated when he was 7, and he bounced between them before moving into a series of foster and group homes and then to the street:

> When I was 12, I was sent home from school, and my mom said, "You're out of here" and I said, "What do you mean?" and she goes, "You're going to live with your father again." I said, "Oh shit." So I went down to my father's. My dad was an alcoholic, and he always abused me – physically. He'd punch me and stuff like that – throw me up against the walls. And like one night we were going at it, and I turned around, like he punched me a couple of times. I turned around and got a baseball bat out of the bedroom, and I hit him in the head, and then he got back up, and he started pounding on me big time. Well, the cops came and they took him, and they said "You can go live with your mother, right?" My mother had already said, "We don't want you," so I said, "Okay, I'm going to go to my mother's" and [instead] I went out in the streets. I was living on the streets for about two weeks.

Although abusive parenting frequently coincided with substance abuse, we emphasize that other parents also used force in their interactions with their children. Mary, who we introduced earlier, ran away from a home in which alcohol and drugs were condemned, but, as Mary's description of the following incident illustrates, her parents did not abstain from violence:

> I was talking with a friend on the phone and my father didn't like her. As soon as I hung up the phone, he got up and, you know, he grabbed me by the neck, and like just sort of pushed me into a wall, and I was like "Oh, my God."

We should emphasize that male parents were not the only ones to use force. Research (Straus, Gelles, and Steinmetz, 1980) documents that female parents also use force, and the experiences of many of our respondents replicate these findings. Thomas was 5 when he and his four siblings were taken from their home by child-care workers. His alcoholic parents had abandoned them. He spent the next two years in several foster homes before being adopted. According to Thomas, things went well for the thirty-day trial period in his new home; however, things deteriorated once this period ended and he was officially adopted:

Basically my [new] mother was very abusive. She came from an abusive background herself; my dad was quite passive actually. So when she realized that yelling didn't work on my father, or on me, she resorted to physical violence . . . anything from her hand to her fist, a belt, wooden spoons, or else, anything she could get hold of, she would throw at us.

Several respondents also spoke about difficulties that arose when step-parents or parents' "boyfriends" or "girlfriends" moved into their homes. In some cases, the problems they describe are commonplace: the disappointment that accompanies family breakdown and the difficulties of accepting new parents. Mat was shaken by his parents' divorce, and his comments capture his disillusionment and resentment toward his parents' new partners:

Basically, like when I turned 16, it wasn't anything like what I expected from when I was a kid. It turned out to be not such a, a warm place as it used to be, you know. . . . My mother and father got divorced when I was 16, and that was a big, a big, um, um, deal. I first went to live with my mother, then her boyfriend moved in and, you know, things stopped from there. It wasn't really arguing, it's just that I couldn't, you know, it's pretty hard to watch your mother with someone else . . . so I went with my father for a bit, but, well, [it was] the same situation. He had a new wife or a new girlfriend or whatever.

Descriptions of the dynamics of blended families often indicated relationships that were either severely strained or openly abusive. Complaints of rejection and unfair treatment were common, as illustrated by Jamie's experiences with her mother's partner. Jamie explained that she first left home in the dead of winter at four in the morning when she was 14. When we asked why she chose this inopportune time to leave, she replied:

I was sick and tired of my parents, well actually, it was my stepfather. He was being – he wasn't even my stepfather, he was my mom's boyfriend – he was being a total asshole. So, I just said fuck it and left. Uhm, he treated me differently because I was not his child, and his two children were angels and I was the shithead.

The introduction of stepparents also led to more severe problems that are well documented in the research on blended families (e.g., see Wilson, Daly, and Weghorst, 1980; Wilson and Daly, 1987). Ross's experiences are typical and reflect an abusive volatility that is consistent with the descriptive statistics presented earlier about the parental use of force with children. Ross explained that he first left home when he was 13, fleeing from a stepfather's physical abuse:

> INTERVIEWER: What type of things would happen?
>
> ROSS: He'd . . . uhm, punch me across the kitchen, uhm, come after me with a baseball bat, uhm, use a shotgun with rock salt on me. It's not lethal, but it stings because it goes into your skin and melts in your skin, you know how you get salt on an open cut, it burns. He got a whole shotgun barrel of it, right, and it goes right into your skin, and it stings for hours. Uhm, I used to come home, and I'd do some little thing wrong, like any 11- or 12-year-old would do, and I'd get a backhand, and then I'd be suddenly flying into the fridge.
>
> INTERVIEWER: Like what sort of little things?
>
> ROSS: Uhm, dropped the milk. That's the one time I remember. I held the bag of milk and dropped it, and it burst open, and the next thing I know I'm flying against the wall. . . . I don't know what happened, and then I look up and I see my stepfather there with the back of his hand all red with my blood. . . . It was only me. . . . I had a little brother – he never hit him at all, . . . I was picked on. I'm, uhm, a child from another marriage. . . . I wasn't his real son.

Like Ross, Lauren also fled from a violent home. Her stepfather frequently beat her mother, who in turn struck her. Lauren's stepfather also hit her, but less frequently than her mother, and as the following account reveals, it was her mother's use of force that was the deciding factor in her decision to leave home:

> I wasn't getting along with my mother. She likes to hit. She broke my jaw, and I told her I'm not taking it no more, so I just left. My mom freaks out about anything. I didn't do well in school, so I got a broken jaw. So I said I'm leaving. They're [mother and stepfather] too wild anyway. They're violent people, and they're alcoholics, and my sister does a lot of drugs. So I don't want to be in that.

In many cases, the youth we interviewed were not the only victims of violence. Consistent with patterns documented elsewhere (Straus et al., 1980), violent parents were often also abusive partners. This was clearly the case in Jamie's family. Jamie described several instances where her stepfather attacked her mother, noting that, basically, her mother "was beaten for like, well shit, I think 14 years." She later recalled that on one occasion he also tried to shoot her.

As is often the case in dysfunctional families, the abuse that characterized Jamie's family was not limited to her stepfather. Violence pervaded most or all of the relationships in her family. Jamie reported that she and her sisters had been struck by almost every family member:

> I've been beaten by guys, my brothers and mom, my dad, been beaten by all of them, so like, you know.

In some cases, the final incident that precipitated youth leaving their violent homes was not their own victimization but their intervention in violence that involved other family members. Kyle's experiences reflect this type of conflict. He recalled that his stepfather first beat him and his siblings when he was 6. In the ensuing years, his stepfather frequently assaulted him, his brothers, and his mother, usually in a drunken rage. He finally left when, in his words, he "finally got enough courage to actually stand up to him." He added:

> My stepdad was very abusive to my mom, and I got involved. Like I stood in front of her, and I said, "You're not hitting her, you gotta hit me first." And he hit me, and then he went to beat her up, and I called the cops. . . . They took him away for two weeks. But my mom dropped the charges, she accepted him back in, and then I said to her, "You either choose between me or him," and she chose him.

Sexual abuse was also a factor in the backgrounds of some of the youth we interviewed. Although we did not probe deeply for accounts of sexual abuse, they surfaced nonetheless. Sheneika is a typical case. When we asked her why she left home, she quickly replied, "Because my father was an idiot." We asked her to tell us a bit about him, and she said:

> Well, my father, he's actually my stepfather . . . I guess he figured that whatever he did at home would not, would not have any bearing on me and he used . . . used to sexually assault me a lot. And uh, I got fed up with it, and once I turned 13, I started running away.

Sheneika then closed discussion of this topic, as quickly as she had introduced it, with the following remark: "I know it's not my fault. These things happen, and they shouldn't have happened, but it, it did."

Other youth spoke in greater detail about their sexual victimization. Korrine grew up in a small, coastal village. Her parents separated shortly after her birth, and her mother had a series of short-term relationships with substance-abusing, violent men. She told us that she ran from her home several times before finally moving to the streets when she was 15:

> The first time I left I was 13. Just to get away from my mom and a lot of the guys that my mom had interactions with. There was a lot of sexual abuse, mostly my mom's boyfriends, my uncle, a couple other guys in the family. I had to get away from them. I told my mom about this one guy about four years ago, not at the time [it was happening]. I don't know, I just had to get out of there. It didn't feel good to stay there, but I didn't have any sisters so I didn't think it would happen to anybody else. And then my little brother told my mom that the same uncle that raped me, raped him. I was shocked.

Like Korrine, Simon also ran from a family in which a sexually abusive family member preyed on his siblings. Simon's home life involved a further problem that was not uncommon in the backgrounds of victims of abuse: a nonabusive parent implicitly or explicitly condoning an abuser's acts. We first met Simon in 1986 when he was working in Boy's Town. Sixteen years old, Simon had left his urban Ontario home three months earlier. In 1992, when we undertook our second study, Simon was again working the street. In the ensuing six years, he migrated to and from the street several times, and returned less than a month before our interview. When we asked why he first left home, Simon candidly replied:

> I left because I was sexually abused and physically abused by my stepfather. I repressed a lot of it, but it came out when I broke up with a girlfriend of mine, because I couldn't have sex with her, and she was on my case, which sounds strange that a girl would be on someone's case, but she was always on my case to have sex with me and I didn't want to have sex, and when we would try, I couldn't rise to the occasion. When we broke up, I was walking home, crying, and everything came back to me. It was like a huge wave. I went home, and I told my sister and found out my stepfather had also abused her, and I sort of had a nervous breakdown.

In a later point in our conversation, Simon returned to his experiences, describing his mother's response:

> Then we confronted our mother about what had happened, and she didn't believe us. And then my stepfather came home, and he confessed, and my

mom didn't want the police involved. And my mother wanted to continue her marriage with him, you know. So then I left.

In other situations, attempted abuse was the instigating factor in a youth's flight from home. In these situations, youth were usually in their teens and better prepared, psychologically and sometimes physically, to defend themselves from potential abusers. This scenario is captured in Jamie's description of the last time she left home. She had returned home after her first flight the previous winter and had endured her stepfather's physical mistreatment for several months. The event that she details below was the decisive factor in pushing her out of her home permanently:

When I was 15, 15 going on 16 I think it was, yeah it was, I was 15 going on 16, my stepdad and I got into a fight, and he tried to kiss me, like French kiss me, and I got fucking pissed off, and I gave him a shot in the head, and he put me up against the wall, and he started choking me, and we go into like such a big fight, my mother had to wrap a telephone cord around my throat to get me off of him. And then I said, "Look," I said, you know, "Why did you fucking do this to me? He's the one who hit me, he's the one who did this."

As in the earlier cases of youth who fled from homes in which family members were the victims of violence, some youth left home not as a result of their own sexual victimization, but because of the victimization of siblings. When we asked Brendon why he left home, he responded,

That's easy. I was kicked out. I was kicked out because my stepfather, I was 13, and my stepfather raped my two sisters, and I took a baseball to him and put him in the hospital, and my mother didn't believe that he did that and kicked me out of home. That's basically it. I tried going back, but I was never allowed.

Many youth stayed in foster or group homes prior to living on the street. In some cases, child-care workers removed youth from families that were unsafe. In others, parents contacted social services when they were unable to care for their children or when conflicts between youth and parents became unmanageable. The first scenario was noted earlier in our introduction to Thomas's experiences. The second situation is illustrated by Randall's home life. When Randall was 8, his father deserted his mother. He and his brothers lived with their mother for several years until their family changed again with the introduction of a stepfather, an experience he described as follows:

I was in a single-parent family. Then I had a stepfather who would do a lot of things . . . and my mom took us, after a long series of things, she finally gave us to social services. I went to some group homes, and then at 8 I was adopted.

Cicely's background typifies the third type of family circumstance. Like Randall, she grew up in a single-parent family; however, her conflicts with her mother originated much earlier:

She always had something against me. Like even when I was born, she was going to put me up for adoption and everything. She left me in the hospital and all that. And then, you know, when I turned 12, like, she put me in a group home. I was in there for a year; then I got out and went to foster homes.

School

Problems in school also figured prominently in the lives of these youth. For some, school was a forum for academic success, a place to socialize with peers, and an avenue for connecting with supportive, caring adults. Yet for the majority, school represented a more difficult world characterized by problems understanding school material, conflicts with teachers and principals, and troubles with other students. These problems were usually tied to, and precipitated by, conflicts at home. This interconnection is illustrated by Travis's comment about difficulties he had in school. Travis did not know his father and had two stepfathers by the time he was 10. According to Travis, his second stepfather's frequent and violent outbursts made it difficult to attend and feel comfortable at school:

I was, my stepdad was beating me regularly, and my mom knew about it, but she didn't say anything about it . . . and I just said that's it, I can't handle it. It was embarrassing for me. School was embarrassing for me because I always came in with bruises and black marks or a black eye or something, you know. Everybody's looking at me. I come in and like, like I never fit in.

Juan's troubles at school also originated with problems at home; however, he argued that disinterested teachers compounded his difficulties. Juan left school during the tenth grade but hoped to return and finish high school and attend college. He worried, though, that college classes would resemble those he attended in high school:

They teach the class, and they don't really care about it, if the students learn, or what. They should be more friendly. 'Cause, um, I think I had a lot of potential to be a good student, but I guess I never was exploited, right? Like my potential wasn't exploited. . . . And at home I never really had support either, because my father didn't want to, but 'cause he, like, he didn't go to school either, right? So, he didn't know.

Other youth also spoke about disinterested and inadequate teachers, although several also cited more fundamental and more structural problems with the school system. Dorian was in the ninth grade when he ran from his rural west-coast home. He had little desire to return to school, arguing that the structure of the educational system – its regimentation and systematization – made it all but impossible for him and many other youth to be successful:

Not all kids learn the same way. They can't take input or, you know, retrieve it, you know. But in school everybody's supposed to learn this one way, and they can't – it's only geared for a stereotypical group. And it just don't work. Kids don't have enough time to compute stuff, and you know, it's all tried to be rushed. You know, some kids can't just whiz through it, some are considered slow, mentally handicapped, stupid. I've had teachers tell me that, "You're stupid," you know. Fuck off, kill 'em. Can't do that though, it's illegal.

Other youth suggested that their anger toward school was fueled by their dislike of the controls, demands, and rules that characterize educational institutions. Cassandra dropped out of school in the ninth grade. She later returned but after a few weeks quit again. When she indicated that she had little interest in continuing her education, we asked why. She replied:

I hate it. They try to conform you to be something you're not. They want you to be a "yuppie." I got along with some students, but it depends on the crowd. I was kicked out twice, the last time in May of this year for lack of attendance and bad attitude. I don't like people telling me what to do.

Owen echoed Cassandra's dislike of school. He recognized that his indifference contributed to his problems with teachers and other school authorities, but he saw little possibility of changing:

Technically I have grade 10 but credit-wise I don't even have grade 10. It's just boring. I can't sit there in the class. . . . It just bored me, and then I'd tell the teacher off; they'd start talking back to me . . . and so I'd really tell them off. And they wouldn't like that too much so the vice-principal got to know my face very well. The first year there they had me in a behavioral class, which is for people with, not necessarily a learning disability, they just don't want to learn, bad attitude, you know. The next year they put me in another class, but when I sort of got into high school, things just sort of fell apart.

The disinterest in education common to many youth is further captured in a remark made by Albert. Albert had finished the eighth grade in a small village in northern British Columbia before his family relocated to Vancouver. Since the move, his attendance at school was inconsistent, and he was expelled several times during the ninth grade before he quit in the spring of that year. He saw no reason to return to school, noting that it provided little return for the effort it required: "School is bogus. Its like working for free; it's just a job you don't get paid at."

For many youth, problems with school material and teachers were augmented by difficulties socializing or coping with other students. Fourteen-year-old Crystal reported that she stopped going to school in the eighth grade when her Vancouver classmates alienated her for rejecting the behaviors, attitudes, and symbols of the clique that dominated her classroom (i.e., black T-shirts advertising heavy metal bands and blue jeans):

> I plan on going back to school, but I've been away for awhile. If I go back, I go back to grade 8. I liked it when I was younger, but things went wrong in Junior High. Everyone was a rocker, and I wasn't. Everything was bad.

She then added:

> I had a lot of disagreements with teachers and other students, uh, a lot of name calling and everything else. The kids can be hateful.

Robin's experiences were even more traumatic. Robin grew up in a middle-sized prairie city. At 14 he went "punk," getting a blue Mohawk and a pair of Doc Martens and piercing his ears, nose, and eyebrow; these changes were not well received by his teachers or other students:

> When I was in school, the teachers didn't have any other scapegoat except me. They looked at me because I had funny hair, and they didn't want an antisocialist, like myself, coming into the picture an' fuckin' their school up. They were telling all the kids in the school that the way I dress is wrong, and the kids beat the shit out of me for it.

Problems with school agendas, teachers, and other students simply exacerbated the problems that many youth had at home. This interconnected chain, with one set of conflicts influencing those in another area of life, is reflected in Jake's description of the events that led to his simultaneously quitting school and leaving home:

> I left when I was 16 years old. Me and my mom, uh . . . the friction was, uh, getting too bad between the two of us, right? Uh, anything, anything would trigger an argument, you know, especially anything to do with school. If I got up late for school or something, it's like, "Get up for school!" It's like, you get up for school, you got to go to a place where your principal doesn't like you, teachers don't like you, you know, and the teachers that do like you, give you the passing grades. And it's just like, "Oh, God, why do I even get up in the morning?"

Eventually Jake stopped getting up in the morning and, like the other youth in this study, took to the streets.

Although the preceding accounts represent the difficult backgrounds of most of the youth we interviewed, not all respondents fled from dysfunctional or abusive environments. Some youth reported that they had good relationships with their parents, and others had not experienced any problems in school. Several of these youth were on the street by choice, and some were there because of a lack of economic resources. Others indicated that there were conflicts in their homes but that they, rather than their parents, were the source of these difficulties. A comment by Roberto typifies the backgrounds of these youth:

> My parents, they saved up quite a lot of money for me and stuff, and I ended up blowing it all . . . I had a drug problem. . . . I came home drunk and stuff and, I don't know, my parents didn't like to see me like that, so they got into a fight . . . and, uhm, I just left.

Valerie told a similar story. When she was 15, her parents sent her to a foster home after she had stayed out on the street for several weeks with a friend. She moved through several foster homes and, just after turning 16, quit school and took to the street. Valerie noted that her relationship with her parents soured during a period of several months when her use of drugs escalated, and her parents eventually asked her to leave:

> I was getting really fucked up at school. I wasn't going, so there wasn't any point in staying. I was doing a lot of drugs, and I was always high, so I could never make it.

Kirk also attributed his problems to his involvement in deviant activities. He started hanging out on the streets of Toronto when he was 15. In the summer of that year, he left home for three months. When he returned, his parents told him he was no longer welcome because he refused to abide by their rules:

> I was hangin' around, I was naive. I was hangin' around, um, bad influences on myself, toward myself. I never really thought about, you know, "Should I do this with them, or should I go here with them." . . . I just didn't, 'cause I wanted to experiment; you know, live the other lifestyle that people live: the wild side. I was a real wild child. So I had to be on my own. Drugs, alcohol, women and partying, coke dust, hash . . . I was experimenting.

Even though many youth mentioned their problems with drug and alcohol use at home, only a small minority singled out these behaviors as the only source of difficulty in their families; instead, most had more troubled backgrounds that centered around problems of familial neglect and abuse. In contrast with another time or place where most street youth may simply have left home in search of new experiences and adventure, the backgrounds described by youth in our study reflect more desperate circumstances and experiences. It might be tempting to believe that these accounts are simply justifications or excuses for leaving home, but when we consider the descriptions of street life that follow in this and later chapters, it is difficult to accept the notion that most youth would choose this lifestyle without some sense of dread, desperation, or despair about returning home.

Our research indicates that these youth typically traded difficult situations at home and school for conditions on the street that, at best, could be described as different in their forms of adversity. This reality is captured in one of Brenda's comments. She fled from upper-middle-class parents whose use of force, pressure to abandon vocational goals of becoming a social worker, and verbal attacks culminated in a major quarrel. When we asked her why she tolerated the adversity of street life rather than returning home, she replied:

> It has been seventeen years of bullshit. And, ah, I mean, I kept on giving them chances, and I kept on going back because I didn't have any money, and I finally just got to the point where like, fuck it, money is not the important thing. If I have to starve once again and starve for the rest of my life in order just to live, I will.

The Street Lives of Homeless Youth

The majority (60 percent) of the youth in our research had left home on fewer than three occasions, and only about one-quarter (26 percent) had left home five or more times. More than two-thirds (70 percent) had not traveled beyond the borders of their home province, yet more than one-half of these youth (52 percent) had been living away from home for more than a year (less than 15 percent having been on the street for less than a month). Thus, although most of these youth had not traveled far from home, the majority had been on the street for some time. They were, therefore, often in need of shelter, and they pursued a variety of solutions to this problem.

Many youth reported that when they first left home, they initially stayed with sympathetic relatives – a divorced parent, uncles and aunts, grandparents, and particularly older siblings. Others sought refuge in the homes of friends. In some cases, the parents of friends were receptive to the difficulties that the youth was experiencing and readily offered shelter. In the absence of such hospitality, some youth relied on their friends to surreptitiously provide them with a place to sleep. The latter is evident in Sheryl's experiences. When she was in her early teens, Sheryl and her family emigrated from the Caribbean. She had few relatives in Canada, and when her parents told her to leave their home because they disapproved of her relationship with a "boyfriend," she and her boyfriend found temporary shelter in the house of a friend.

> SHERYL: Like when we first got kicked out, we didn't really know where we were going to go or anything. I was scared. We mostly stayed awake, and then we'd go to one of my friends' houses in the day and go to sleep. It's like we were up all night and sleeping all day.
> INTERVIEWER: Why did you only go there in the day?
> KIRSTEN: 'Cause that's when their parents were at work, and we could stay there until they was coming home.

However, the resources of friends and relatives are finite and easily "burned through," and many youth quickly found themselves without shelter. This pathway to the street is reflected in Susan's description of her first homeless experience. Susan left her home with an abusive boyfriend who had threatened to harm her family if she did not move into his apartment. They soon separated after a particularly vicious assault, and she began her search for a place to stay:

And, uh, I stayed at a friend's house for a couple of days, and then it's just like, I don't know, I just walked around. I stayed, uhm, actually there was a storage room that I stayed in for about three months. I just went back there every night.

As Susan's account suggests, spending nights walking and hanging out is a common initiation into life on the street, but it usually provides little or no opportunity to sleep. Jeremy, whose foster and group home migration to the street was described earlier, sought out alternatives that offered some opportunity to rest:

I mostly didn't sleep the first couple days. Then I got to a bridge, and I just slept underneath the bridge. Then I kept on walking, sleeping at night in people's sheds and stuff like that.

Other youth began their street careers in all-night diners or fast-food shops. David, an immigrant from the Philippines, told a variation of a story we heard frequently about attempts to sleep in restaurants and similar settings:

Wintertime. December, yeah, hard to sleep, and actually I went to the donut shop after. At least twice I slept there. But the second time I slept, the owner called the cops, and they kicked me out of there.

Similarly, another youth, Winston, recalled spending his first nights on the street in a different but equally popular all-night establishment that temporarily solved several problems:

I was sort of, uhm, you know, them coin laundries, the laundry mat? for awhile I used to go there. It was open twenty-four hours. I used to stay there. I stayed for about two weeks . . . there was like a sink there so I got up to, you know, have a little shower.

Perry's solution was less accommodating and therefore more transitory:

It was like two in the morning, we were walking around until about four o'clock, and there's this little parkette, and we slept on a hill there. And the grass was freezing. It was uncomfortable, and I hated it.

Youth who are on the street for extended periods often turn to "squats" or abandoned buildings as places to escape inclement weather. As the following comment suggests, "squats" vary in quality but are often an improvement over the street. Santori had considerable experience with squats and had lived in several empty houses, vacant stores, and abandoned buildings in the downtown core. She offered this assessment:

> Um, you get some good ones, uh, some unfurnished apartments that are like, just vacant. Uhm, sometimes places that are being torn up. Usually, like in a boarded up place, if you're careful, you can stay there for about a month to two months.

However, locating a squat often involves a considerable investment of time. Doug, who had a background in construction that gave him some familiarity with building sites, emphasized that patience was required to find a squat that was not only empty but safe from owners, neighbors, and in particular, the police:

> You walk around during the day and stuff and see what, who's hanging around where, you know. Uhm, like some buildings, some abandoned buildings still have their windows and doors and stuff, but there's just nobody inside them. So you want to stick around, watch for a bit, see if anybody walks in or out. Uhm, you want to scout for alarms and stuff, you know. And then at night you go in. Like during the day you look for a weak spot, you know like a board, broken window, something you know.

According to most respondents, sleeping in squats often demanded that street youth alter their behaviors and monitor those of others. Doug went on to note that successfully maintaining a squat required attention to the following kinds of issues:

> Not going in and out during the day, being quiet when you're in there, like just go in there and go to sleep, you know. Uhm, don't overexceed the people that go in, like only take your friends and people that you know [who] won't come in on acid or any other type of drug. They're going to be freaking out and, you know. Like they're going to be tripping, and they're going to be, you know, putting their heads through walls. I mean, it happens all the time, you know, "I feel no pain, watch."

Valerie, who had squatted in several cities, including Toronto, Vancouver, and several other smaller communities, noted that squatters also faced other problems, including discovery and eviction:

As long as you could find a squat, you think everything is fine, but you'd be there for a few days and then the police would shut it down, and they'd take all of your stuff, and you'd be on the hunt again. When they close the squat down, you're screwed, especially in the wintertime.

Alternatively, some youth resorted to other forms of shelter, including balconies, rooftops, heating vents, hotel lobbies, and businesses. The diversity of settings used for shelter is testimony to both the desperation and ingenuity of street youth. Jordy, who came to Toronto from Calgary via Vancouver, described a variety of possibilities he had explored:

Parks, right on the grass, if it's summertime. If it's wintertime, uh, abandoned buildings, sneak inside the mall. I've slept inside stores, there's clothes there and everything. Woke up in the morning, put on the clothes, and went up through the ceiling and out.

Probably the most creative solution to the problem of finding shelter, however, was reported by Thomas, who we noted earlier had left the home of his adopted parents for the streets of Toronto:

I had a knapsack on my shoulder and two small duffle bags. . . . I didn't really know what it was like to be in a big city . . . for the first couple weeks I just wandered around, put my stuff in a bus locker and, um, just wandered around. After a couple months' time, I ended up stealing a mattress . . . from the back of a truck. I lived under a bridge at Mt. Pleasant and Bloor. Um, I had a gas barbecue which I ripped off from someone's backyard. I got propane tanks every month basically, to keep me warm in the wintertime and to cook my food. Also . . . um, I had a friend, I had met people . . . and one of them just happened to work for Bell telephone. Well, he illegally tapped in and got me a phone for external use only. . . . All this under a bridge.

Of course, most street youth do not find such unique solutions to their housing problems. Instead, the difficulties experienced in finding shelter often lead to a kind of nomadic roaming pattern: typically, youth arrive on the street, stay outside for a few days – perhaps in parks, all-night restaurants or walking the streets – find shelter with friends in someone's apartment or a squat, move to a hostel, migrate to another hostel, and then begin the sequence again. This was the case for over half (51 percent) of our respondents, who reported that they had used at least three different types of shelter since arriving on the street. As Valerie noted, the instability and transience that characterizes this recurring search for shelter is a source of continuous strain:

> The worst thing was not knowing where you were going to sleep. Sleeping in a storefront or on the street. Who knows what's going to happen to you?

Respondents also spoke about the lack of basic necessities with which one has to cope when living on the street. Richard came from a family where drinking and fighting were commonplace. Despite the difficulties of the street, Richard eventually concluded that it was preferable to his home environment. In the following conversation, Richard explains some of the techniques he used to obtain clothing needed to survive on the street in winter:

> Well, clothes, there's places you can go and get free clothes, you know. But you got to handle, settle with hand-me-downs. But, you know, every once in a while, you have to go "shopping."

Even basic hygiene is a problem on the street. Many places commonly used for shelter, such as squats and parks, are dirty, and for the most part, showers and laundry facilities are unavailable or unaffordable, making it difficult to stay clean and healthy. These problems are reflected in a comment made by Paul. Paul arrived in Toronto after leaving Newfoundland in search of work; unable to secure permanent employment, he occasionally slept in a parking lot that he described as follows:

> There was a bunch of shopping carts there full of stuff, and that's all the real hard-core kids that got their shopping carts full of junk and stuff, and they, and that's the best parking lot, they just park all their stuff there for the night ... that'll tell you what kind of a place that is. I mean, you're apt to come out a little bit itchy in the morning, you know what I mean?

Many youth clearly were distressed by problems of basic hygiene on the street. Jeremy, who we introduced earlier, reported that he "went to the swimming pool a couple of times and had a shower there. And, I don't know, sometimes I grabbed showers at friends'," but he added that "most of the time I really didn't shower a lot."

Sean was in a worse predicament. He left his physically abusive father when an uncle offered him a ride from Montreal to Toronto; once there he immediately headed for a youth hostel, which placed him in a group home. He lived in the group home for a year and a half before being asked to leave because of his age. Without relatives or other connections, Sean headed back to the youth hostel but was soon kicked out for missing his curfew. In recalling the next few weeks of his life, Sean emphasized his anxiety about not being able to wash:

> I was outside in June. It was really rough . . . I had dirty clothes . . . I mean some days I would, I would smell, you know. Not because I'm a dirty person, it's just because sometimes it's just rough. . . . I was sleeping in front of Evergreen [a drop-in center] some days, two, three days in a row actually. And sometimes I went in the park near the Eaton Centre . . . I don't know if it was a danger to my life, but uh, some old guys tried to come and pick me up, you know . . . sex and stuff like that.

Janet, whose migration from the maritime provinces to Toronto was described in Chapter 1, noted that the absence of facilities made it difficult to stay clean, and she ranked this aspect of her experience among the worst parts of street life:

> Well, the nights and everything and when you . . . have your period and you have to use toilet paper . . . I had to clean my clothes like underwear and stuff everyday, washing it at Evergreen [a drop-in center] and blow dry it under those things.

Youth who slept in parks or alleys or in front of buildings had other difficulties, including harassment by business owners and residents. They were also more frequently arrested, and they had higher risks of being the victims of theft or assault. Jordy learned from his earlier stays in Calgary and Vancouver to protect himself in a variety of important ways:

> Well, you've got little parks that are in back alleys and stuff like that, but those are more risky. I wouldn't sleep back there. I like sleeping where it's really well lit, so that if anybody's going to wake me up, it's a security guard. And when I slept in the park, I always slept with a couple of friends, because too many stories of people getting woken up in the park and getting beaten up.

As this comment suggests, staying on the street exacts a considerable emotional and psychological toll. Another youth, Jack, had at an earlier point in his life run away from his rural New Brunswick home to live in the woods, but this did not prepare him for the trauma of his first nights on the streets of Toronto. Recalling his initial shock at having to find a place to sleep on the street, he said:

> Having to sleep on a bench, that was bad. I cried; I couldn't believe it. [I said to myself] this is not happening, you know?

For many youth, hostels are an important respite to the problems that accompany living on the street. Most hostels provide shelter, food, counseling, and access to social services, including health care, social assistance, job training, and legal services. Martin had recently immigrated from the Caribbean and initially lived with an older brother. Their relationship deteriorated when Martin objected to his brother's use of force in disciplining him, and he eventually headed for the street. When we asked him about hostels, he expressed a common, though certainly not universal, sentiment, which mixed a sense of relief with appreciation:

> It was good. It was like my own place, you know . . . they'd give me my supper, breakfast, lunch. It was great.

Other respondents spoke favorably about the counseling services provided by agencies. For many youth, agency workers were the first adults they trusted, confided in, and considered friends.

Nonetheless, several youth pointed out that hostels also have their disadvantages. A prominent concern was the lack of privacy and personal space. Richard noted, "in . . . hostels . . . you never have your own cozy room, right? You've got to split it with other people." Hostels also have limited resources and restricted hours of operation that, according to some respondents, indirectly encourage youth to hang out on the street. This sentiment is evident in Franklin's assessment of hostel policies:

> In a hostel you get kicked out in the morning, right? Like at 8:30, they say, "We, we don't care what you do, just come back at four." So you walk around, and you find places where people hang out, and you talk to them, you know, 'cause they know you're in the same situation, and they gotta pass the time, the time somehow. So, you just, meet different people, and everybody's in the same situation.

Restrictions on the length of stay at individual hostels also create problems as youth have to search for alternative accommodations. We described earlier Jack's shock at spending his first night on the street trying to sleep on a bench. After entering a hostel, Jack had to cope with the anxiety caused by hostel policies:

> [The worst part is] the actual stress of worrying about when you have a time limit, that you have to go to another hostel soon. What happens if these hostels have no bed? The actual fact that you have to pick up your life and move somewhere else, and get used to the new scene, the new rules. And actually just the stress of going, here again and just, thinking, "When am I going to get out of here?"

Time limitations, as well as shelter rules (e.g., curfews and prohibitions) often resulted in "shelter hopping," a pattern common among new as well as experienced street youth. Sean described a common peripatetic pattern of movement between shelters:

> Beverely Lodge, that's where it started . . . then I went to Covenant House, yeah. I went, I stayed there twenty to twenty-one times after the first time. So, I just like, got kicked out for seven days, go to Seaton House, go to another house, you know, hop, hostel hopping, I guess.

Respondents also commented on the characteristics of some hostels, noting that they are not always clean or safe. Susan left home because her parent's disapproved of her boyfriend. Together they headed to the street and shortly thereafter moved into one of the coed hostels; however, Susan was not prepared for the conditions she encountered:

> I was in the hostel, and it was not pleasant . . . it was just so disgusting. People were stealing from my room. I mean, you only get so much to start with, which isn't hardly enough, and people are stealing it.

Theft is a common problem in hostels, particularly in those that have a diverse client base. Lisa was cruelly abused by a boyfriend who had encouraged her to leave home. She later fled from him and moved to a local hostel; however, she was further victimized and lost most of her possessions:

> Just like, you know, you'd carry your stuff around with you, and other people would steal it. Like, or you'd put it down somewhere for like, two seconds, turn your head, and it was gone. . . . Especially in hostels, a lot of my stuff got stolen in hostels.

Richard also expressed indignation about thefts at hostels, noting that although he frequently stole, he never robbed from other hostel residents:

Even, like I mean, stealing off of people in hostels makes me sick. Like, I mean, I couldn't steal off someone who is in the same position as I am, because you know, I know how hard it is. When you got clothes, minimum clothes, and then somebody comes in to shoot the shit, and they like, just grab it you know . . . that really sucks.

Other problems with residents, particularly older, more desperate members of the homeless population are evident in the following accounts of experiences in hostels that served all ages. Again, Richard provides an account of hostels that serve the older homeless:

It's hard to get a good night sleep . . . because you got people gabbing, you know . . . and a lot of people do drugs, and they come in . . . and, you know, you're like "shut up, I'm trying to get some sleep." It's two in the morning, you gotta get up in another five hours.

Daniel also stayed at this particular hostel. He mentioned problems with older residents' substance abuse, drawing attention to the distinctions between street people that hostel policies fail to accommodate:

I don't like it, it was a dirty place. I wouldn't live there, man. I'd rather sleep on a park bench myself. It's disgusting, they drink aftershave there.

Sean's strong aversion to agency and shelter settings originated in an experience in a hostel that housed both younger and older males. Understandably, he dreaded "ending up" in a shelter for homeless adults, which he poignantly designates "the bottom of the line":

[It was] scary. I was just a kid, you know, 17 years old going there, you know, I didn't know what to expect. I mean like, they were pushing me around . . . you know, the ones that been on the streets for years . . . they asked me to take my clothes off, they wanted to steal my clothes. Like they were four against me.

Larry was less than five foot six inches tall and weighed less than one hundred fifty pounds; he was therefore quite reasonably worried about his safety in hostel settings. He reported one encounter that began with his simple desire to find a place to sleep for one night:

I walked there [to the hostel], and I fell asleep straight away, and, um, in the middle of the night . . . um, I wake up and there's two guys at my bed there.

One guy's trying to yank my boots off, and the other guy's undoing my pants. . . . Another night I was there, I saw a guy get his face cut open, because he refused to give another guy a cigarette. They like cut him from here right down, with the knife . . . and that's when I said, "Well, I'm out of here."

Not surprisingly, shelters that predominantly house the adult homeless are regarded as a last resort; for most youth, staying on the street is a preferable and, in their view, less dangerous option. However, the streets are by no means safer than hostels, and many youth reported being victimized on the street. Theft is particularly common, and regardless of where they find shelter, street youth are usually at risk. Santori had recently been evicted from a squat, and she was visibly shaken by this experience:

The day before was the worst day of my entire life. . . . We hadn't eaten in two days, and I lost everything I own . . . I lost my backpack, my bag . . . and just stuff that I'd like to keep. . . . I don't care about the clothes because they all can be replaced, right? But the writing and everything I cared about. I want that . . . I want it back, I just want it back.

Violence is also common on the street. Both females and males reported being attacked and beaten since leaving home, and for many, these experiences represented a continuation of the victimization from which they fled. Francine's experiences are a case in point: She ran from a physically abusive father and on the street was assaulted by several youth. She recalled that:

I got beat up four times since I've been down here. The last time because I was saying "Hi" to a girl's boyfriend, 'cause he kept on saying "Hi" and she beat me up really bad . . . both my eyes were like popped out, bloodshot, broken nose, bruises right along my jawline. Another girl kicked me, uh, uh, "below the waist," like kneed me below the waist. I got kneed in the face a few times, and I looked pretty bad.

Regardless of their inclination to use force before leaving home, the majority of the youth we spoke with said that street assaults or threats of assault left them with no choice but to use violence. Brad said that he was usually not inclined to start fights; however, he added that he was more than willing to use violence if the situation demanded it. He then illustrated his point by describing a recent incident:

Well, three or four days ago, I told this guy to move, he was a skinhead, and we kind of went at it. He smashed my head against the brick wall . . . about three, four times, and I smashed his against the wall. It all started because he gave me a bad attitude, that I asked him for a cigarette nicely and he gave me one of his bad attitude type things.

Other youth embraced violence more readily and frequently. When he first left home, Kirk lived for a time with a group of youth in a ravine near downtown Toronto. Living away from home, he quickly learned the skills necessary for surviving in a world where the ability to use force is frequently required:

It was pretty cool man, yeah, I got into a couple of scraps, learned about some, learned some fighting off some other people. How to fight, you know, my first fight ever, I was downtown, 15 years old, and I went to jail, and I finally kicked the shit out of someone that I wanted to kick the shit out of. . . . And I had all the buddies going, "Yeahhhh!" you know.

Santori also had an extensive history of using violence, as is evident in her response to a question about street fights:

Street fights? Oh yeah. None in Toronto. Oh, a couple that like, not like good fights, like blood and everything. But I've been in a couple. Just mainly with guys. Ignorant, stupid guys, not street people, just people that are completely ignorant and tell me to get a job or something. I punch them out.

These events are reported as commonplace on the street, and many youth respond by carrying weapons or staying in groups for protection. Morgan, a large, tough-looking youth, captures street youth's perceptions of violence as well as their own brutality in the face of perceived danger: "I'd slash somebody right up if I had to. . . . I have my switch blade in my pocket, you know." As is clear from Morgan's further observation, most youth who stay on the street for a considerable length of time accept violence as an inherent part of street life:

Yeah. Uhm, but it all depends really on the way you are, how stupid you are. Some kids don't last. Like, they get the shit beat out of them and they're gone.

Several respondents also reported that they had been sexually assaulted on the street. Assaults were perpetrated by both strangers and acquaintances, and they often occurred when youth were squatting or sleeping in public places (e.g., parks). Jake reported that he was raped soon after coming to the street:

When you come down on the street, you're young and you're gullible. I was
16. I was young and gullible, and I got raped, and it still haunts me.

Other assaults occur in connection with street crime, particularly prostitution. Leslie grew up in a public housing project in Toronto and had seen
a lot of the street scene before she left home. She subsequently entered the
world of street prostitution, but her previous experiences did not protect
her from sexual assault:

Um, I got raped when I was ah – when was that? – five, six days after my
sixteenth birthday. . . . He put a knife to my throat so I couldn't move, you
know, and it was sharp. I didn't move. I was fucked up. He kept me from, ah,
three o'clock in the morning until seven o'clock in the morning, and I finally
got away from him.

Sexual abuse takes other forms, and a common scenario involves demands for sex as "payment" for shelter or protection. Janet observed that
the expectation of sex makes street life considerably more difficult for
females:

It's [the street] harder on women than it is on men because you get worn out
so fast and everything, and then all they want is sex, sex, sex.

Many males were also victims of sexual exploitation. Several youth described situations in which they were exploited by adults who initially provided care but then expected sex in return. Summarizing his experiences,
Robert recalled that:

Well, I mean, being young, 16, I mean all of a sudden you have these men just
hovering over you, and it's like you feel special . . . 'cause they were treating
me nice . . . [but] uhm, I mean a lot of them would use me for sex . . . at the
time it was like these people cared about me. Uhm, they like me to stay at
their homes. They're buying me this, they're buying me that.

As these accounts make clear, living on the street leaves many youth
without adequate shelter and increases their risks of being victimized and
exploited. Anxiety and uncertainty characterize street life and, as Lisa's
remark suggests, leave many youth shaken and worried:

Just the things that we had to do . . . panhandling, stuff like that. It was scary,
not knowing where we were gonna sleep, not knowing who was going to hurt

us, or who didn't want to hurt us, or where we were going to be able to bathe next, or where we were going to get clothes or money or food, or a place to stay. . . . Just not being sure about anything was scary.

Searching for Food

The search for food is as open-ended and wide-ranging as the search for shelter. Some youth reported that they often bought groceries (3 percent), relied on friends from home (4 percent), or ate at fast-food restaurants (11 percent), and a quarter of the sample reported using all three of these methods. However, social service agencies are the most common single source of provisions, and a majority of youth (58 percent) reported using meal services in hostels.

Notwithstanding the provisions available in hostels and foodbanks, finding food is a recurrent problem. Most of the youth (76 percent) indicated that on at least one occasion they had gone an entire day without eating; moreover, more than half of the youth (55 percent) said they frequently went hungry. While Jeremy was bouncing between foster and group homes and the street, he would go to schoolyards to search for food:

Once, it was okay because like, I think, yeah, it was school time, one of the times, it was, right. And they go, uhm, everybody'd come to school with their lunch, and they'd be passing up half their lunch, and I'd be sitting there waiting for them all to get outside the school grounds. For the whole day I'd sit there.

As this account suggests, hunger often encourages street youth to do things that are foreign to most young people who, unlike street youth, would not consider collecting discarded lunches as a source of food.

Searching for Money

Street youth develop many means of making money, including work, panhandling, social assistance, and crime. In this discussion we consider the first three sources of income, leaving crime for more detailed consideration in later chapters.

The work experiences of street youth are predictably varied. More than a quarter (30 percent) of those surveyed had not worked since leaving home. Mary is typical of these youth; her parents had encouraged her to concentrate on schooling, and her subsequent lack of employment experience made it difficult to find any type of work:

I've never worked in my life. I want to get into a job-training program . . . so I can have some experience. 'Cause if I don't have experience, I'm not going to get a job, 'cause that means I'm not a credible person yet. You know, nobody can say anything about me.

Youth who had jobs while living at home had greater success in finding work on the street, but for many, employment was limited to temporary jobs in the minimum-wage, service sector. Glen had worked steadily before leaving home and had found several jobs on the street, yet most of these were temporary:

Uh, well, most of the time, the most work I've done here is just working through temp agencies; put out the work for the day and get paid at the end of the shift.

The exception for Glen was a relatively stable job as a busboy, but the low pay and working conditions discouraged him from making a long-term commitment to this position:

I got a job when I turned 17, at a steak house being a busboy and I hated it. . . . Just, I was getting something like four dollars an hour, for taking people's shit, you know.

Other youth described similar employment experiences. Randall had worked in several jobs and offered this assessment of working in the fast-food industry:

It's not that, you know, the job's strenuous, it's just extremely dull. It takes a lot of energy to keep up your motivation and just keep going. Like, when you're on a nine-hour shift and you have to sit there at the front counter and be polite to every single customer that comes up to you, and remember all the steps of serving the food, and getting it to them and making sure that everything is fine; it gets very exhausting, especially when you're on your feet all day. . . . Well, at least it's work experience. They pay you peanuts, though, and treat you like a subhuman. . . . You know, like McDonald's would have gotten a lot better, a lot better results from the workers if the bosses treated the workers like humans and if they paid them just a little bit better, even a dollar more an hour, it's going to make someone work a heck of a lot more than being paid minimum wage.

Randall provided another description of an employment experience common among street youth: "Like then there's telemarketing. I learned humility through that." Not surprisingly, nearly two-thirds (62 percent) of the youth who found jobs on the street were unemployed at the time of the survey.

For other youth, panhandling is a common source of income, and for those with a unique approach, it can provide a reasonable return. Sharon came to Toronto from Winnipeg and at one point raised enough money from student aid and welfare to rent an apartment briefly. However, most of Sharon's recent life was spent on the street, and she experienced some success panhandling:

> Um, God, I had like so many different lines. One night was funny. Um, I was down with a couple of friends. We were doing a "Three Stooges" thing, and I was panning for money so they could help us find our long lost brother "Moe." I made fifteen bucks in about five minutes, which is cool. Like everybody just thought this was like one hell of a line.

Gary was unusual in our sample: He had a sizable bank account that he emptied when he left home. This degree of planning perhaps reflects a way of thinking that led Gary to the Toronto financial district when he needed money:

> I used to put on a clean shirt and clean pants and comb my hair and walk down to King and Bay and say, "Listen, I'm trying to find a job." I'd even have a piece of paper, have a newspaper in my hands saying, "I'm trying to get to this place, it's way out in Scarborough [the suburbs], do you have a bus ticket?" And they'd usually give me a dollar, you know, so that was my way of panning.

However, panning was not always lucrative, and many respondents reported that they rarely made much money. When asked how much money he usually made, Gary replied: "I made enough to buy myself a packet of cigarettes and something to eat." Moreover, income from panning was far from consistent and could not be relied upon. In discussing her experiences, Francine noted:

> It depends, like in the winter, it's cold, and people realize street kids have no place to stay or nothing. So like in winter they give more. . . . In summer, it's, uh, not that good, because it's hot weather, and people think street kids can go to the hostels or drop-ins to get food and sleep.

Nancy pointed to a further difficulty with panhandling. Her middle-class, suburban home had not prepared her for the difficulties that characterize

street life, and she noted that resorting to panning forced youth to acknowledge the destitution of their lives:

> Like cause, you know, it really is hard to do that. To beg for money and stuff,
> when you're, like, really hungry and you just want a bit so you can get some
> food or whatever.

Street youth also turned to social assistance for support, and a majority of
our respondents (53 percent) indicated that they had collected welfare at
least once since leaving home. Although youth with a permanent address
were able to collect regular assistance, most Toronto street youth were
limited to one-time "emergency welfare" – a temporary form of social assistance for people in a crisis.

Hanging Out

When not searching for shelter, food, or income, street youth spend much
of their time "hanging out." Together with other youth, they congregate at
social service agencies, city parks, street corners, shopping malls, video
arcades, and other spots popular among youth. As well as a means of passing
time, hanging out with other street youth provides important information
about the street. Asked how he acquired information about street services,
Jack replied:

> Well, you learn all that in the street. When you live in a hostel, you find these
> places, people take you to these places. When you're hanging around the
> street and you got nothing to do [they say,] "Hey man, you want to go here
> and get a meal?" or "Oh, I need a haircut," and you say to them, "Oh, I know
> where you can get a haircut." You live on the street, you find out.

Hanging out also has other dimensions, one of which is its conduciveness
to "partying": the consumption of alcohol and drugs in groups. Partying is a
popular street activity; it is not reserved for special times or occasions, such
as evenings or weekends, but typically occurs whenever anyone has the
available means. Not surprisingly, reports of substance use among our
sample were very high, significantly higher than the level reported before
leaving home and higher than reported in studies of high-school students.
Once on the street, 80 percent of our respondents smoked marijuana, 55
percent took LSD or other chemicals, and 43 percent used cocaine (cf.
Hindelang et al., 1981).

The level of drug use is reflected in numerous accounts, one of which was provided by Santori, who, as we reported earlier, had been on the street for several years.

> I know a couple of guys that sell. So I'm like, that's how I get stoned every day. Like I'm not a total drug face, you know, the only thing I do is smoke pot and hash and do acid.

Roy also reported a lengthy history of drug use that began in his small northern Ontario hometown. When he arrived in Toronto, he became involved in male prostitution, and his drug use escalated:

> Now I really got into it big time there for like two or three years once I left home. Like I smoked it once in a while at school while I was living at home, but when I left home, from the day I got to the hostel until a year ago, I was like an everyday user. I smoked hash all day, we smoked grass all day, drank all day, um, got acid once in awhile, did coke once in awhile. I think I've done every drug at least once.

In addition to its conduciveness to substance abuse, hanging out on the street offers considerable opportunities for interacting with people involved in crime. These interactions offer a climate that supports criminal activities and provide a forum for learning "criminal" techniques and establishing connections with offenders. We explore these relationships in greater detail in subsequent chapters; for now, we simply provide one example of the support for crime that characterizes street life. Alan was heavily involved in both street theft and drug selling and had little patience for street youth who did not take advantage of the available opportunities:

> Like when I walk down the street and I see people panhandling for money, like, I turn around and I look at them, and I go, "Why are you sittin' here panhandling for money? Why don't you sell some drugs, or go rob someone or somethin', right? Why do you do have to, like, sit there and ask everyone walkin' by for some money?"

Street Life

The majority of youth in our research had been on the street for six months or longer; during this time, they often had gone without shelter, food, work, or money. The search for sustenance and security was a preoccupation for these youth, the more so because each day's search tended to end as it began, with these young people often remaining unfed, unemployed, and unsheltered. These circumstances were captured in the comments of Julia, who had been homeless in both Toronto and Vancouver:

> I remember bein' out there, out on the streets in the wintertime. And sleeping in abandoned buildings, you know, with the water leakin' all over the floor. The building's been condemned, you know. Freezing cold, no blankets, you know. Just – and the police hassling you, and, at the time I didn't even know where I could go for help, you know . . . and I was too young for welfare. It was just hard. Just hard. It's like, it's kinda hard to explain how you feel when you are out there. There's no, there's no words that would express the feelings you have. But the closest to it, I guess, would be severe outcast of loneliness. Just outcast and lonely and very unsafe.

Julia's experiences and those of other street youth are not uncommon; indeed, given what is known about adult homelessness, it is not surprising to learn that street youth confront all of the difficulties and dangers we have described. It is also not surprising that these youth report extensive involvement in the common crimes – robberies, thefts, assaults, drug selling, and prostitution – that capture the attention of the media and figure prominently in the concerns of citizens (see Rossi, Waite, Bose, and Berk, 1974; Warr and Stafford, 1983; Wolfgang, Figlio, Tracy, and Singer, 1985). What is startling is that criminologists have all but abandoned the street and street youth in studying crime.

In the next chapter, we take criminology back to its roots and explore the paths that lead youth to the street. We begin our analysis of street crime by focusing on class and family backgrounds that frequently provoke youth to leave their homes.

CHAPTER THREE

Taking to the Streets

MANY SOCIOLOGICAL THEORIES OF CRIME assume that adverse class conditions cause delinquency and crime. This class–crime connection is one of the central tenets of sociological criminology, from theories of anomie (e.g., Merton, 1938), social disorganization (e.g., Shaw and McKay, 1942), and subcultures (e.g., Cloward and Ohlin, 1960) to critical and Marxist traditions (e.g., Greenberg, 1981; Colvin and Pauly, 1983). Empirical evidence of this correlation is commonly found in studies of individual-level official data (see Hindelang et al., 1979; Braithwaite, 1981), as well as in studies organized around areal units, using police and court statistics aggregated into census tracts and neighborhoods (e.g., Chilton, 1964; Sampson and Groves, 1989). However, this association is often elusive in self-report surveys (Tittle et al., 1978; Weis, 1987; but see Braithwaite, 1981), leading some researchers to suggest that the effect of class on crime is weak or nonexistent and that criminologists should focus their attention elsewhere (e.g., Jensen and Thompson, 1990).

As we suggest in Chapter One, a possible source of the discrepancy between official and self-report survey findings is the latter's frequent reliance on youth who attend school.[1] The parents of these students typically have jobs, and their children usually live at home and receive relatively good care and protection. These defining features of school criminology unnecessarily restrict variation in class origins and conditions, as well as in developmental processes through which family, school, and street experiences influence criminal involvement.

In this chapter, we adopt an alternative approach to the conceptualization, measurement, and sampling of class and crime. We first elaborate the

55

mechanisms that link these variables, highlighting those involving family, school, and street experiences. We then apply this approach in a comparative analysis of school and street settings. A central argument of this chapter is that, apart from other dissimilarities, class differences in both family background and current living experiences distinguish school and street youth and must be taken into account in comparative analyses of crime among these groups; thus, the class-based approach we propose emphasizes that class conditions can be both background and foreground causes of crime.

Class as Background and Foreground

Class operates in the background of crime when, for example, it establishes the conditions and circumstances of parenting. Colvin and Pauly (1983) draw on the work of Kohn (1977) to develop this idea in their structural-Marxist theory of delinquency. Kohn reports that parents who work in tightly controlled and highly routinized work situations, characteristic of poorly paid and unstable jobs, use more severe forms of punishment in their interactions with their children. Extending this finding, we suggest that parents who experience economic and psychological strain associated with frequent and extended periods of unemployment are also more likely to use coercive control in their families. We propose that parental employment problems represent class-based background factors that, among other things, encourage family disruptions and erratic and explosive forms of parent–child interactions – patterns that lead to behavioral problems in childhood, at school, and later in adolescence.

Results of several studies support our position that parental economic problems can lead to the mistreatment of children and youth: Straus et al. (1980) provide evidence of a positive association between parental unemployment and parental violence toward children; McLoyd (1989) reports that family poverty increases the risk of harsh, inconsistent punishment; Patterson (1982) documents how family disadvantage and poverty lead to disrupted and coercive parental discipline; Sampson and Laub (1993, 1994) find that social assistance and low socioeconomic status (SES) are related to harsh and erratic parental discipline (also see Larzelere and Patterson, 1990); and Elder (1974) and Conger and Elder (1994; in particular, see Simons, Whitbeck, Melby, and Wu, 1994) report that family income loss and instability are linked to neglectful and volatile parenting.

The conceptual model we explore links parental background and developmental variables in the causation of crime and integrates dimensions of control and strain theories. Erratic and explosive patterns of parenting are emphasized respectively in control and strain theories of crime, although these exact terms are not necessarily or conventionally specified (e.g., Kornhauser, 1978). We regard both of these aspects of parenting as important; thus, although some theorists oppose the integration of control and strain traditions (Kornhauser, 1978; Hirschi, 1989), we argue that a union of these theories is a necessity (see Elliott, Huizinga, and Ageton, 1985; Messner, Krohn, and Liska, 1989).

Control theory is widely known for its focus on social bonds developed in families and schools. These bonds reduce crime and delinquency, which control theory otherwise suggests would be ubiquitous (Hirschi, 1969; Gottfredson and Hirschi, 1990). Our application of this theory attends to the consistent and constraining roles of families in keeping youth at home and uninvolved in crime; the converse of these processes can result in erratic parenting and situations in which parents are uninvolved, unattached, and neglectful of their children.

For the most part, control theory and school-based studies of delinquency emphasize a restricted range of indirect, noncoercive familial and school controls involving supervision and attachments. When control theorists extend their analysis to include direct coercive controls, they usually focus on a lack of parental discipline, inconsistent punishment, and parent–child rejection; less attention is given to more abusive parenting styles (Loeber and Stouthamer-Loeber, 1986). Even approaches that recognize the importance of parental violence often combine measures of abuse with indicators of less severe parenting styles such as demeaning or threatening parenting, thereby reducing attention to abusive behavior per se (e.g., see Larzelere and Patterson, 1990).

The literature on street youth and our interview data summarized in Chapter Two highlight these kinds of limitations in the scope of control theory. Such materials identify weak parental attachments, erratic parenting (i.e., neglect), and family disruption as common occurrences in the backgrounds of street youth, but these data further suggest the significance of explosive parenting (i.e., involving violence and abuse) and extreme forms of parental rejection (i.e., which results in youth often being "thrown or pushed out" of their homes). Whereas control theory can be extended to give attention to parental neglect, strain theory more easily allows consideration of physically violent parental abuse, and strain theory additionally emphasizes stressful family class experiences and their connection to parenting and crime.

The specific version of strain theory that we use focuses on the consequences of youth's efforts to avoid painful, aversive situations, especially at home. In an important series of papers that develop this version of strain theory, Agnew (1992; see also 1985, 1994, 1995) observes that familial strain originates when families act in ways that: (1) prevent youth from achieving goals; (2) remove, or threaten to remove, stimuli valued by youth; or (3) threaten or use negative or abusive behaviors. Our qualitative data suggest that many street youth leave families that are characterized by these three sources of strain, particularly abusive relationships. Braithwaite's (1989) theory of reintegrative shaming also emphasizes the strain caused by harsh, punitive parenting. In Chapter Eight we explore more fully the implications of Braithwaite's theory; here, we focus on the strain specified in Agnew's approach and its effects on leaving home and street crime.

Our interviews further reveal, as reported in Chapter Two, that street youth experience considerable conflict at school, particularly in their interactions with teachers and school authorities. These accounts suggest that limited school involvement and commitment (traditional control theory variables; see Hirschi, 1969; Wiatrowski, Griswold, and Roberts, 1981) and extensive school conflict (an indicator of strain; see Farnworth and Lieber, 1989) may intervene in a further developmental fashion between class and family experiences and the subsequent links these have with street life and crime.

A key aspect of our study involves redefining life on the street as a subsequent intervening cause of crime. This redefinition is a departure from treating life on the street as simply an episode of running away, and therefore as just one more indicator of delinquency; this approach has been a tradition in self-report delinquency research from Nye and Short's (1957) pioneering effort to Hindelang et al.'s (1981) important work. We diverge from this convention for two reasons: Many youth who take to the streets are old enough to do so legally, and most important, street experiences probably play an important causal role in the onset and persistence of criminal behavior. In particular, we propose that the adverse conditions that street youth encounter represent an intervening, foreground set of class circumstances that influence offending. In the following chapter, we explore in greater detail the effects of these more proximate class conditions; for now, we note that difficult, foreground class circumstances are manifest in many of the day-to-day problems that street youth encounter when they are, for example, hungry and without shelter, work, or money.

We now have introduced the fundamental elements of our initial model of street life and street crime. The resulting model, diagrammed in Figure 3.1, integrates strain and control theories: We treat parental unemployment and resulting family violence and school conflicts as sources of background and developmental strain, and we incorporate erratic parenting and school involvement and commitment as causal factors that are central to social control theory.[2]

Family class origins are often far removed in place and time from street crime. This distance is important, because when family class backgrounds operate indirectly through developmental processes to cause later behavioral problems, they do so from a location that makes their impact more diffuse and difficult to discern, and therefore less likely to be recognized. This is a point that criminologists too often miss in understanding the connection between class and crime.

Reclassifying Crime Research

School criminology traditionally operationalizes class in terms of interval or ordinal rankings of parents' occupational statuses (see Tittle et al., 1978). This approach to the measurement of parental occupational status was developed for purposes of operationalizing a prominent conception of American status attainment and mobility (Reisman, 1964; Sewell and Hauser, 1975) rather than for the more specific purpose of testing crime theories. However, these occupational measures bear little relevance to prominent theories of criminogenesis' emphasis on harsh class circumstances experienced by desperate and deprived segments of the population (see Matza, 1966; Hirschi, 1972; Hagan, 1992). As Farnworth, Thornberry, Krohn, and Lizotte (1994) note:

> Theories predict differences in delinquency between the lowest social class and higher classes, but the status attainment measures are better suited to identifying differences within the higher classes than in discriminating between upper and lower classes. (p. 36)

Tittle and Meier (1990) concur, observing that "it would make more sense to measure deprivation directly than to measure SES, which is a step removed from the real variable at issue" (p. 294).

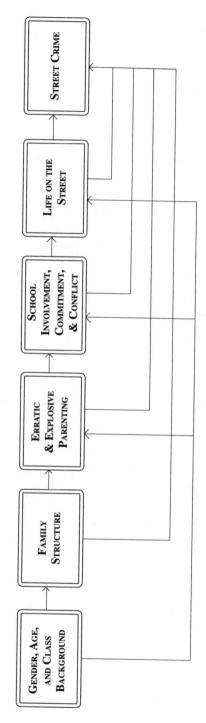

Figure 3.1 A conceptual model of street life and crime.

Wright (1985) explains the importance of this kind of reconceptualization, noting that definitions of specific classes can be understood as a particular form of proposition:

> All things being equal, all units within a given class should be more like each other than like units in other classes *with respect to whatever it is that class is meant to explain.* (p. 137)

The key to defining a class this way is to identify relevant linking conceptual mechanisms. For example, in economics or sociology, when income is the theoretical object of explanation, educational attainment – whether as an indicator of certification or skill transmission – is an obvious linking mechanism that must be incorporated in the measurement of class. In criminology, our theoretical objects of explanation – delinquency and crime – demand a distinct conceptual consideration of linking causal mechanisms. As noted previously, class background theories of crime are persuasive when they emphasize that difficult and demeaning class circumstances can lead through problems in parenting to delinquency and crime.

Recently, some self-report research has attempted to address the neglect of truly disadvantaged class backgrounds. These efforts have shifted attention from parental occupational measures to parental experiences of unemployment, which are more direct reflections of deprived class positions and conditions. Yet, with the exception of selected studies that concentrate on high-crime areas and produce samples with significant numbers of unemployed heads of households (e.g., Farnworth et al., 1994), school criminologists have not included many underclass families in their samples. Brownfield (1986) reports that efforts in school surveys to identify class circumstances in terms of parental joblessness reveal that "researchers have considerable difficulty finding and studying the disreputable poor" (p. 429). Nonetheless, studies that focus on parental unemployment more often find evidence of a relationship between class and self-reported delinquency (Farnworth et al., 1994).

More generally, the limited study of parental unemployment diminishes the likelihood of finding stable or substantial family class-of-origin effects on youth crime (Mueller, Schuessler, and Costner, 1977). Although this is significant in itself, there is the further concern, noted earlier, that the influence of class position is presumably indirect, operating through family and school developmental experiences that may all lead to more immediate class conditions, such as taking to the street, that more proximately and therefore more strongly influence crime.

Bringing Back the Street

In part, criminologists probably have abandoned street youth because of an uncertainty about issues of sampling on an endogenous or outcome variable such as being on the street. It is often preferable to design research with random samples of the general population or to stratify samples on the basis of exogenous variables. Random samples allow straightforward representation of the general population of interest; samples stratified on exogenous variables are only slightly more burdensome in that they require reweighting on the basis of sampling ratios of the exogenous selection variables. In contrast, concerns about the challenges of generalizing from samples selected on the basis of endogenous or outcome variables have resulted in a rule of thumb that advises against sampling on these variables.

This rule of thumb is good advice when the phenomenon that one wishes to study is well distributed in the general population or easily captured through selective sampling on exogenous variables. Although minor forms of delinquency are well distributed in the youth population, this is less true of rarer forms of social behavior, such as being on the street and involvement in serious delinquency and crime. It is precisely because street youth are highly involved in the latter that we separately sample and study them. When samples are selected on the basis of endogenous or outcome variables, such as living on the street or crime, the task of generalization becomes more challenging, but not impossible.

Sampling on endogenous or outcome variables poses two distinguishable problems of causal inference involving external and internal validity. The problem of external validity involves generalization to the broader population, whereas the problem of internal validity involves the specific group separated out for study. These problems are easily overstated, yet both need to be addressed. In this chapter, we focus on external validity; we discuss issues relevant to internal validity in Chapter Four.

We address the issue of external validity with a response-based sampling strategy (see Manski, 1981; also Xie and Manski, 1989). This approach involves sampling from the response population (i.e., street youth) and the remaining larger population (i.e., youth not on the street), and then bringing the samples together.[3] We demonstrate in this chapter that bringing such samples together in a meaningful way is not a major problem when the sizes of the response and larger populations are known.

When our data were collected, there were approximately 150,000 youth attending public and private schools in Toronto. "Expert estimates" of the Toronto street population from street youth agency workers ranged from

10,000 to 20,000 (Janus et al., 1987; Carey, 1990), suggesting a school-to-street ratio of approximately 12:1. In this analysis, we use a conservative estimate of 7,500 Toronto street youth, and we weight school-to-street youth at 20:1. In separately reported results, we verify that, because of the insensitivity of odds ratios to marginal distributions, introducing alternative weightings for our samples has limited consequences (see Hagan and McCarthy, 1992).[4]

We briefly discussed the development of the first Toronto street sample in the previous chapter, and we review it and our school sample in greater detail in the Appendix to this book. The comparison school sample was selected in the same year as the street study and surveyed 13- to 19-year-old students in three metropolitan schools serving heterogeneous parts of the city of Toronto.[5] The school sample includes 563 students and when combined with our street sample provides information on 953 youth. Separate descriptive statistics for the samples of street and school youth are provided in Table 3.1. These indicate that about two-thirds of the street youth are male, compared to about one-half of the school youth, and the former are on average about a year older than the latter (17.6 and 16.6). The age difference is not a result of sampling criteria because both groups were restricted to 13 to 19 years of age.[6]

Operationalizing Our Integrated Model

The measurement of class is complicated, because as we emphasized earlier, we need to consider both family class origins and the more immediate class conditions that youth experience. We operationalize class background with a modified version of Wright's (1985; see also Wright 1978; Wright and Perrone, 1977) typology – an approach increasingly popular in delinquency theory and research (Colvin and Pauly, 1983; Hagan, Gillis, and Simpson, 1985, 1987; Messner and Krohn, 1990; Farnworth et al., 1994). For this analysis, we measure foreground class conditions in terms of membership in the school and street samples; we elaborate on this operationalization in subsequent chapters.

We measure family class background with questions asking about parents' current employment or self-employment and employment or supervision of others. To make the operationalizations comparable, survey items about parents of street youth were referenced to "when you lived at home." The class categories we use separate employers, the petty bourgeoisie, supervisors, workers, and the surplus population or unemployed (see Table 3.1 for details). The supervisor category forms a large middle group

Table 3.1. Concepts, Indicators, and Descriptive Statistics for Analysis of Being on the Street

Concepts	Indicators[a]	School sample (563) X	SD	Street sample (390) X	SD
Gender	Dummy coded 1 for male respondents	.458	.499	.667	.472***
Age	Coded as years of age	16.632	1.326	17.597	1.457***
Class Background					
Surplus Population Workers	Dummy coded 1 for unemployed head of household	.021	.145	.074	.263***
	Dummy coded 1 for employed head of household who is not employer and does not supervise others	.291	.455	.262	.440
Managers	Dummy coded 1 for head of household who supervises but does not employ others	.510	.500	.482	.500
Petty Bourgeoisie	Dummy coded 1 for self-employed head of household who neither employs nor supervises others	.030	.171	.028	.166
Employers	Dummy coded 1 for head of household who supervises and employs others	.147	.355	.154	.361
Intact Family	Dummy coded 1 for two biological parents	.718	.451	.313	.464***
Erratic Parenting					
Maternal Instrumental Control	A scale (a = .776) constructed from items: "Does/Did your mother know your whereabouts/who you are/were with when you are/were away from home?"[b]	3.813	1.579	2.410	1.535***
Paternal Instrumental Control	As above for fathers (a = .776)	3.067	1.685	1.946	1.497***
Maternal Relational Control	A scale (a = .600) constructed from items: "Do/Did you talk with your mother about your thoughts and feelings?"[b] and "Would you like to be the kind of person your mother is?"[c]	2.147	1.456	1.585	1.428***
Paternal Relational Control	As above for fathers (a = .610)	1.671	1.371	1.379	1.412***

Explosive Parenting

Coercive Control	A scale ($a = .745$) constructed from items: "(Do/Did) your parents or guardians ever use physical forms of discipline "? and "(Have/Had) you ever been intentionally struck so hard by a parent or guardian that it caused a bruise or bleeding?"[d]	1.181	1.561	3.221	2.306***

School Involvement, Commitment, and Conflict

Homework	"How often (do/did) you do homework, projects, etc., after school?"[e]	2.490	1.129	1.703	1.329***
School Goals	"How much schooling would you like to get eventually?"[f]	3.654	.798	2.790	1.420***
Conflict with Teachers	"How often do/did you have trouble with teachers?"[e]	1.167	.942	2.097	1.267***

Serious Theft

Participation	A scale ($a = .627$) constructed from items of the form: "Have you ever [taken things from a car (tape deck, etc.); taken things from a store worth more than $50; used a bank or credit card without owner's permission; taken a car from someone you didn't know for a ride without owner's permission; taken things worth over $50 that didn't belong to you; broken into a house or building and taken something]?"[c] (1 = any delinquency)	.225	.418	.565	.497***
Frequency	Scale constructed from foregoing items (coded 1 to 50)	5.586	55.502	32.611	76.123***
Involvement	Scale constructed from foregoing items (coded 0 to 5)	.671	1.480	2.974	2.230***

[a] Past tense constructions are used in street sample; see text for further details.

[b] Never = 0, sometimes = 1, usually = 2, always = 3.

[c] Not at all = 0, in a few ways = 1, in most ways = 2, in every way = 3.

[d] Never = 0, once or twice = 1, sometimes = 2, often = 3, always = 4.

[e] Never = 0, rarely = 1, sometimes = 2, often = 3, always = 4.

[f] No more than you've already got = 0, more of high school = 1, high school graduation = 2, on the job apprenticeship or vocational school = 3, college or university = 4.

*** $p \leq .01$, t-test of means.

between the extremes of high and low positions emphasized in class theories, and we therefore use them as the comparison group in our analysis.

In order to construct a conservative measure of class, we use information on both parents (if present) and assign a class that reflects the position of the most advantaged parent. For example, we categorize a family in which one parent is a supervisor and the other a worker, as belonging to the supervisor class, regardless of the gender of the person working as a supervisor. Thus, surplus population families are limited to either a single parent who was unemployed or a household where both parents were unemployed at either the time of the survey (i.e., for school youth) or when the respondent last lived at home (i.e., for street youth). Only about 25 percent of the surplus population families had a single parent, so the effects of class of origin and family structure are not conflated.

As much of the popular literature and previous research notes, street youth come from all classes. Still, there is a notable difference in class backgrounds of school and street youth, with a greater proportion of street youth (7 percent) than school youth (2 percent) coming from surplus population families. Both figures reflect a low unemployment phase between two recessions in Toronto.[7] Of course, a much larger proportion of youth came from families that had experienced problems of unemployment at some point. Based on the two studies reported in this book, we estimate that about one-third of street youth left families that experienced significant employment problems in the past.[8]

The family structures of school and street youth also differ. We measure family structure in terms of intactness, in this case meaning the youth was last, or is now, in a family with two biological parents. These biological parent families are compared to all other kinds of families in our data. Street youth are less than half as likely as school youth (about 31 and 72 percent, respectively) to come from intact families.

We measure two dimensions of parent–child interactions: erratic or neglectful parenting and explosive or violent parenting. As noted earlier, erratic parenting involves inconsistency in parental attachment, supervision, and discipline; processes central to social control theory. Following convention, we measure erratic parenting with scales commonly used by social control theorists and researchers (Hirschi, 1969; Hagan, Simpson, and Gillis, 1989). Low scores on these scales reveal the erratic or inconsistent parenting central to our research. The specific scales we use include separate measures for mothers and fathers and distinguish two elements of parent–child relationships. The first measure of maternal and paternal relational control combines the following indicators: "Do/did you talk with your mother/father about your thoughts and feelings?" and "Would you like/have liked to be the kind of person your mother/father was?" The second measure of maternal and paternal instrumental control is based on questions that ask: "Does/did your mother/father know your whereabouts/who you are/were with when you are/were away from home?" The mean scores on these scales indicate that compared to parents of street youth, mothers and fathers of school youth are more consistently involved in the lives of their children.

Explosive parenting is operationalized through two measures of the use of force. These items ask: "Do/did your parents or guardians ever use physical forms of discipline?" and "Have you ever been/were you ever intentionally struck so hard by a parent or guardian that it caused a bruise or bleeding?" In the two-city study reported later in this book, we consider more detailed scales designed to measure parental violence toward youth and the latter's use of force against their parents. Responses to the two questions asked in our first study indicate that street youth were much more likely to have left families where parents used force, and on average scored more than twice as high as school youth on this scale.

We use three indicators to measure school involvement, commitment, and teacher conflict. We operationalize involvement with the following question: "How often do/did you do homework, projects, etc., after school?" Our measure of commitment focuses on school goals and asks, "How much schooling would you like to get eventually?" To assess school conflict, we use an item that inquires about problems with teachers: "How often do/did you have trouble with your teachers?" Street youth scored lower on homework and goals and higher on conflict than school youth.

The analysis presented in this chapter focuses on serious theft. Past work indicates that reports of serious theft are highly predictive of official crime, providing strong evidence of the construct and predictive validity of our measure (Hindelang et al., 1981).[9] Moreover, as our indicators demonstrate, the economic value of things stolen provides a convenient dimension for distinguishing the seriousness of infractions. We use six indicators to measure serious theft: taking things from cars (e.g., tape decks); taking things worth more than $50 from stores; illegally using a bank or credit card; taking a stranger's car without permission; taking things worth over $50 that belong to others; and breaking into a house or building and taking something. We asked school and street youth how often they had ever done these things, and we asked street youth how often they had done them since leaving home. Because life–time measures might confuse pre– and post–street-life activities, we limit our measure of street youth's involvement in crime to the period since leaving home. Our approach constitutes a conservative test of the effects of street life, in the sense that the reporting time is much shorter for the street youth than for the school youth.

We use three measures of serious theft in our analysis: participation, frequency, and a measure that joins these two dimensions. Participation is coded in a binary form to reflect whether any of the acts of serious theft were ever committed (0 = never; 1 = ever); frequency indicates how often (1 to 50); and involvement joins the previous measures in a scale (0 to 5) that collapses all scores above 5. The participation and frequency measures often are used to draw distinctions between prevalence and incidence in delinquency research (Blumstein et al., 1988a; Paternoster and Triplett, 1988). We include the involvement measure because it retains the full sample, allows variance on amount, and adjusts the distribution so that it is not extremely skewed. Findings for all three of these measures indicate that although the reports of street youth are confined to a shorter period, street youth are more criminally involved than school youth. The greatest absolute difference is in frequency of theft, with street youth scoring 32.6 on this scale and school youth scoring 5.6.

Taking to the Street

Our analysis begins with logit models of taking to the street. Logit models are used to analyze the odds or probability of an outcome, such as taking to the street, occurring. Each equation in this analysis is a weighted logistic response function that takes into account the overrepresentation of street youth in the combined sample. The analysis of school and street youth in this chapter is specifically designed for use with response-based samples.[10]

Variables leading to taking to the street are introduced in the sequence of their assumed influence in Figure 3.1, and the results of estimating each equation are presented in Table 3.2. Our first equation indicates the unmediated effects of gender, age, and family class background on taking to the street. We exponentiate the logistic coefficients to provide a more intuitive interpretation of the results (Alba, 1987). Doing so reveals that being male increases the odds of taking to the street by nearly 90 percent (i.e., $.628^e = 1.87$), while each advancing year in age increases these odds by nearly 75 percent. In addition, compared to being from a supervisor class family, being from a surplus population family nearly quadruples the odds of taking to the street. As the class theories predict, surplus population families are the only class category that significantly increases the odds of leaving home.

Table 3.2. Maximum Likelihood Logit Estimates for Models of Being on the Street

Independent variables	2.1		2.2		2.3		2.4	
	b	SE	b	SE	b	SE	b	SE
Gender	.628*	.333	.612*	.339	.412	.390	.040	.414
Age	.562***	.137	.549***	.138	.534***	.152	.535***	.157
Surplus Population	1.300**	.667	1.041	.707	.971	.788	.431	.925
Workers	-.021	.380	-.128	.391	-.290	.436	-.448	.467
Petty Bourgeoisie	-.143	.941	-.402	.951	-.157	.985	.362	1.032
Employers	.105	.453	-.050	.467	-.091	.510	-.156	.522
Intact Family			-1.729***	.339	-1.439***	.367	-1.552***	.396
Coercive Control					.797***	.154	.822***	.165
Maternal Instrumental Control					-.467**	.237	-.229	.250
Paternal Instrumental Control					-.579**	.225	-.429*	.238
Maternal Relational Control					-.181	.249	-.019	.258
Paternal Relational Control					.195	.269	.256	.279
Homework							-.244	.180
School Goals							-.430***	.157
Conflict with Teachers							.571***	.180
Intercept	-13.036		-11.839		-10.934		-10.444	
X²	30.181		58.933		110.250		136.120	

* $p \leq .10$
** $p \leq .05$
*** $p \leq .01$

The second equation in Table 3.2 introduces the family structure variable and indicates that youth from intact families are less than one-fifth as likely to be on the street as are youth from families lacking one or both biological parents. Family structure reduces to marginal significance the effect of being from a surplus population family (i.e., this effect is still significant at the .10 level if a one-tailed test is applied). The reduction in the size of the class effect, from 1.3 to 1.0, is also notable. These results suggest that youth from surplus population families are more likely to take to the streets because of class-based family difficulties and disruptions; however, other factors are also at work.

The third equation in Table 3.2 estimates the effects of parent–child relations. The strongest of these effects involves the measure of explosive, violent parenting: One point on this scale more than doubles the probability of being on the street. Meanwhile, two of the traditional measures of parental control also have significant effects: Both maternal and paternal instrumental control decrease the probability of taking to the street. On average, a one-point increase in the maternal instrumental control scale reduces the likelihood of taking to the street by about one-third, and a similar increase in the paternal instrumental control scale decreases the likelihood by about one-half. The combination of family variables in this equation also clearly reduces the effect of being from a surplus population family below any plausible level of significance. The effect of being from an intact family is also diminished, suggesting that youth from intact families are, in part, less likely to take to the street because they experience less violent and more consistent parenting.

The last equation in Table 3.2 introduces the effects of schooling. School goals and conflict with teachers have effects of predictably opposite directions, so that an increase of one point on the school-goals scale decreases the average likelihood of taking to the street by about one-third, while on average an increment of one point on the conflict-with-teachers scale increases this likelihood by about 77 percent. Both school variables reduce the effects of maternal and paternal instrumental control, indicating that parental instrumental control exerts much of its effect by enhancing commitment to school and minimizing conflict with teachers.

Overall, these results support our integration of strain and control theories. The findings indicate that males from surplus population families are more likely to take to the streets. Families that experience problems with employment are also less likely to be intact, and these families are more likely, as a result of the pressures on them, to use inconsistent and volatile styles of parenting, especially with their sons. These youth in turn have lower school goals and increased conflict with teachers, all of which increase the probability of taking to the street.

Modeling Serious Theft

We turn next to the estimation of models of serious theft *within* the school and street samples. Separation of the two samples at this stage temporarily holds constant the intervening role of being on the street and allows examination of distinct causal influences of family and school experiences on serious theft within the separate groups. Because we assume that family class backgrounds are mediated by taking to the street, we do not expect them to exert significant direct effects *within* the school and street samples; as we see later, they generally do not.

We estimate logit models of participation, tobit models of frequency, and ordinary least squares (OLS) models of involvement in serious theft for street (Part A) and school (Part B) youth. The results in Table 3.3 reveal considerable consistency, as well as some subtle and interesting differences in serious theft among school and street youth. The most consistent effects across both samples and models are of gender, homework, and conflict with teachers: On the street and in school, males, those who do less homework, and those more frequently in conflict with teachers are more prone to serious theft. With respect to differences between the samples, age and parents' use of force significantly increase theft in the school sample, whereas neither appears to do so in the street sample. Yet we know from our earlier analysis that age, parental violence, and the lack of maternal instrumental control increase the likelihood of taking to the street.[11]

The most interesting divergence between the various models involves the strength of the tobit coefficients in the street sample. The size of these coefficients anticipates the importance of taking into account the wide range of frequency in serious theft, a point that is developed a bit later. The results from the different models also reveal that the OLS model best summarizes the relationships evident in the three models. We estimate OLS models throughout much of the remainder of the book, although, as indicated next, we use alternative approaches where warranted.

Effects of the Street

The foregoing logit, tobit, and OLS models can now be used to estimate effects of taking to the street on serious theft. Although the following analyses may have a statistical foundation that is unfamiliar to many readers,

Table 3.3. Estimates for Models of Participation, Frequency, and Involvement in Serious Theft among Street and School Samples

Independent variables	Logit model of participation (0/1)		Tobit model of frequency (1–50)		OLS model of involvement (0–5)	
	b	SE	b	SE	b	SE
A. Street Sample						
Gender	1.042***	.263	9.763***	2.582	1.253***	.246
Age	.013	.086	1.119	.829	.024	.079
Surplus Population	−.528*	.465	−3.025	4.481	.432	.427
Workers	.031	.279	−2.935	2.698	−.004	.258
Petty Bourgeoisie	−.630	.701	−7.820	6.557	.086	.634
Employers	−.108	.324	−3.743	3.173	.215	.303
Intact Family	−.240	.251	−.443	2.423	−.216	.232
Coercive Control	.047	.098	1.323	.941	−.025	.090
Maternal Instrumental Control	−.063	.168	−3.575***	1.626	−.142	.155
Paternal Instrumental Control	.025	.171	−1.020	1.646	−.082	.157
Maternal Relational Control	−.487***	.168	−.632	1.499	−.123	.143
Paternal Relational Control	−.001	.157	−1.345	1.518	.033	.146
Homework	−.195**	.091	−1.511*	.892	−.335***	.085
School Goals	.079	.082	.482	.786	.144**	.075
Conflict with Teachers	.300***	.094	2.433***	.908	.258***	.086
Intercept	−.548		−8.353		1.783	
B. School Sample						
Gender	.816***	.249	.699	.598	.416***	.123
Age	.141*	.088	.183	.211	.081*	.044
Surplus Population	−.791	.924	−2.002	1.918	−.357	.397
Workers	−.114	.271	−1.422**	.645	−.134	.133
Petty Bourgeoisie	.012	.642	−1.580	1.632	−.228	.337
Employers	−.228	.348	.228	.815	−.198	.168
Intact Family	−.407*	.249	−.880	.630	−.187	.130
Coercive Control	.160	.130	.528*	.321	.121*	.066
Maternal Instrumental Control	−.160	.171	−.884**	.440	−.161*	.091
Paternal Instrumental Control	−.170	.160	.243	.388	−.042	.080
Maternal Relational Control	−.276*	.164	−.045	.392	−.091	.081
Paternal Relational Control	−.077	.177	−.185	.410	−.044	.085
Homework	−.365***	.111	−.846***	.271	−.188***	.056
School Goals	−.074	.136	−.303	.354	−.089	.073
Conflict with Teachers	.454***	.128	.855***	.328	.304***	.067
Intercept	−2.310		2.969		.268	

* $p \le .10$
** $p \le .05$
*** $p \le .01$

we summarize the results in an intuitive fashion to address important issues concerning the effects of class background and street experiences in producing crime.

In Table 3.4, we use the logit models for the street and school samples to estimate participation in serious theft, assuming that the two groups share identical compositional (i.e., background) characteristics.[12] This estimation is undertaken for low-, medium-, and high-risk populations. We simulate low- and high-risk samples respectively by substituting the means of the independent variables for the school sample (low risk) into the street and school logit equations, and the means of the street sample's (high risk) independent variables into the street and school logit equations. We construct a medium-risk population by using the mean of the two groups' means.

Simulating populations with varying levels of risk in the school and street equations modifies compositional assumptions about the respective samples. It is useful to do this because it allows us to estimate possible consequences of varying characteristics of youth who are included in the school and street samples. For example, when street youth characteristics are assigned in the school equations, it is possible to estimate the consequences of high-risk youth, like those on the street, staying in school. Alternatively, we can estimate consequences of low-risk youth, like those in school, taking to the street. By assigning the same risk characteristics across settings, we simulate an elimination of compositional differences between the samples, allowing us to estimate net effects of the school and street settings themselves. The medium-risk sample is of further value in estimating the consequences that might result from broadening our school sample to include youth such as dropouts who live at home and thus are neither in school nor on the street.[13]

In Table 3.4, we explore the effects of being on the street on participation in serious theft. Our results indicate that participation declines with an increase in background risk characteristics of the simulated populations of interest. For example, although low-risk youth are much more likely to offend if they are on the street (.356) than at home (.174), this difference is smaller but still substantial among medium-risk youth (.403 and .300), and again smaller among high-risk youth (.574 and .534). The implication is that high-risk youth are likely to participate at least once in serious theft whether they are in school or on the street, whereas lower-risk youth are significantly more likely to participate in a serious theft if they are on the street than in school. However, even if we upgrade the assumed risk potential of school youth to a middle level to simulate a broadening of the school sample to include dropouts who do not take to the street, while meanwhile lowering the assumed risk potential of street youth to the same level for purposes of comparison, the street estimate is still substantially higher.

The last column of Table 3.4 presents the results of applying a formula for conditional probability to estimate participation in crime in the combined street and school samples, within risk groupings.[14] The formula for conditional probability is used to integrate the two samples.[15] The resulting calculations use logit-based estimates of probabilities of being on the street from columns two and four. When the street sample contributions are integrated into the analysis, the results indicate very slight increases over the school sample estimates of overall participation.

A different pattern emerges in Table 3.5, which presents tobit-based estimates of the probabilities of delinquency at three levels of frequency within specified risk groups.[16] Here the effects of the street are apparent in all risk groups: The probability of low-risk youth being involved in twenty or more serious thefts is .204 on the street and .005 in school; at medium levels of risk, the comparison is .283 and .010, while for high-risk youth, the respective probabilities are .379 and .027. As expected, these probabilities are higher when estimated at lower levels of frequency, and lower at higher levels of frequency.

Still, throughout Table 3.5, the effects of street life on crime are quite apparent, and most apparent for high-risk youth. Since high-risk youth have the highest likelihood of being on the street (i.e., the same logit-based likelihoods estimated in the previous table), the combined sample estimates of the probability of serious theft (again derived by applying the formula for conditional probability) at different levels of frequency show the greatest increases over school-based estimates among the high-risk youth. For example, at a frequency level of 10, the high-risk school-based estimated probability is .221, while the combined estimate is .300, an increase of more than one-third. So, the relatively small proportion of street youth among adolescents contributes greatly to the estimated frequency of serious theft in the adolescent population. With risk characteristics set equal across settings, street life has pronounced effects on serious theft behavior. Thus, the omission of street youth results in underestimations of serious theft in the youth population, of the effects of the street, and of the factors that lead youth to the street.

A final way of articulating the effect of youth taking to the street on crime involves decomposing the difference in theft scores for street and school youth based on the OLS regressions presented in Table 3.2. Following Jones and Kelley (1984), we decompose the gap in involvement in serious theft

Table 3.4. Logit-Based Estimates of Participation in Serious Theft Within Specified Risk Groups

Population of interest	Participation within street sample (1)	Probability being on street (2)	Participation within school sample (3)	Probability being in school (4)	Participation within combined samples (1)(2) + (3)(4)
Low Risk [a]	.356	.008	.174	.992	.175
Medium Risk [b]	.403	.052	.300	.948	.305
High Risk [c]	.574	.234	.534	.766	.543

[a] School means.
[b] Mean of school and street means.
[c] Street means.

between street and school youth into three parts: the coefficients component, a compositional component, and an interaction term.[17] The first component is formed by the residual difference between groups, attributed to the effects of life on the street, taking into account the compositional and interaction effects that we consider next. This component is equal to the difference between what the actual mean involvement in serious theft of school youth is, and what the mean involvement of street youth is estimated to be, when we assume that street youth have the same compositional (i.e., lower-risk) characteristics as the school youth and that nothing else changes. The second, or compositional, component is the gap in involvement in delinquency attributable to differences in compositional (i.e., risk) characteristics evaluated at the level of influence that these characteristics exercise among school youth. This component estimates the amount by which the mean involvement in serious theft among school youth is suppressed compared to street youth as a result of the more favorable background characteristics of school youth. The third component is an interaction term formed by the interaction of differences in the composition and coefficients components.

These three components of the gap in mean involvement in serious theft between street and school youth are estimated in Table 3.6. They reveal that compositional characteristics account for nearly half of the difference

Table 3.5. Tobit Estimates of Probabilities of Serious Theft at Three Frequency Levels Within Specified Risk Groups

Population of interest	Frequency = 10			Frequency = 20			Frequency = 30		
	Street sample	School sample	Combined samples	Street sample	School sample	Combined samples	Street sample	School sample	Combined samples
Low Risk [a]	.363	.156	.158	.204	.005	.005	.096	.001	.001
Medium Risk [b]	.461	.198	.212	.283	.010	.010	.147	.001	.009
High Risk [c]	.571	.221	.300	.379	.027	.110	.280	.002	.067

[a] School means.
[b] Mean of school and street means.
[c] Street means.

Table 3.6. Decomposition of Difference in Serious Theft Scores for Street and School Youth Using OLS Regressions of Involvement Scores on Gender, Age, Class Background, Parenting, School Commitment, and Conflict

Coefficients component	Composition component	Interaction component
1.320	1.040	-.109
(58.64%)	(46.20%)	(-4.84%)

Computed Difference: 2.257

Actual Difference: 2.303 [a]

[a] Discrepancy attributed to accumulated round error.

in mean theft involvement between groups, and that more than half of this difference remains attributable to experiences on the street (coefficients component). Compositional differences between school and street youth are a reflection of the factors and experiences that lead to being on the street, and street experiences in turn further contribute to involvement in crime.

Linking School and Street Criminology

The results reported in this chapter support the view of many sociological theories that harsh class background experiences cause crime; however, they also suggest an important and usually neglected effect of more immediate class experiences, such as those that characterize street life. Our findings demonstrate that youth from surplus population families are more likely to take to the streets, and that the experience of street life itself increases serious theft. These findings are not apparent from our school or street samples considered separately; this is consistent with past research and with predictable effects of limiting variation in background and foreground class conditions. Studies of adolescents attending school characteristically involve relatively stable parents who are less likely to have the employment problems that contribute to seriously disadvantaged class backgrounds.

School samples also provide limited variation on more immediate, intervening class conditions that transmit indirect effects of parental class backgrounds and other variables on crime.

Our findings simultaneously encourage the integration of control and strain theories. These findings indicate that youth from surplus population families are in part more likely to be on the street because of difficulties and disruptions in parenting. Youth from disrupted families are more likely to take to the street, and the effect of family disintegration is transmitted through erratic and explosive parenting. Neglected and abused youth are in turn less likely to be committed to schoolwork and more likely to be in conflict with teachers. So both control and strain variables are important factors in youth taking to the street; and, of course, street life itself brings both release from parental control and new kinds of strains for these youth.

In this chapter, we emphasize the question of whether studying street youth alone poses an external validity problem, that is, a problem of representation and generalization to the larger adolescent population. In addressing this issue, we present evidence that the problem actually cuts in two directions, in that samples of neither school nor street youth alone can fully inform us about the influence of factors like parental class background on offending. By combining these kinds of samples, we demonstrate that disadvantaged class backgrounds of parents can lead through family disruption and other problems to the increased likelihood of youth taking to the streets, and that the street in turn is a foreground cause of crime. Our findings encourage the joining of street samples with school samples to enhance the external validity of both kinds of data in research on class-based aspects of theories of crime and delinquency.

We also note, however, that the issues of external and internal validity of school- and street-based studies are distinct. Thus, school and street samples can be used independently to study important causal processes that lead to offending in each population. Indeed, some of the results presented in this chapter are consistent with this position. This is so in spite of the fact that, as we have shown, school and street samples are quite different in composition. We further address the internal validity of using street samples alone to study causes of crime in the following chapter.

The causal processes portrayed in Figure 3.1 explicitly assume that street youth are very different from school youth. Furthermore, when we fully take these background differences into account by assigning street characteristics in our school analysis, we find that the simulated high-risk school youth are about as likely as street youth to participate in serious theft. However, high-risk youth in school are much less likely to engage in frequent serious theft than such youth on the street. The implication is that adverse foreground street conditions significantly alter the likelihood that high-risk youth will engage in frequent serious theft. One might say that on the street, serious theft activity moves from a level of innovation to avocation. To understand better serious and frequent thieves, then, we need to explore further the conditions and experiences of youth who take to the street.

To this point, we have treated street life as something of a black box. We have not explored how specific aspects of the foreground experiences of street life, identified qualitatively in Chapter Two, cause delinquency. Rather, our goal has been to demonstrate cross-sectionally that there is a background causal process that leads to being on the street, and that the street itself is productive of serious crime. In the following chapter, we begin to open the black box of street life by systematically examining the impact of hardships encountered on the street.

Adversity and Crime on the Street

IN CHAPTER TWO, we describe the conditions that characterize homelessness and present evidence of the hardships that many youth encounter while living on the street. In Chapter Three, we demonstrate that street youth report disproportionate involvement in serious theft, an activity that we suggest partly follows from their homeless circumstances. In this chapter, we build on these findings. We explore in greater detail the effects of homelessness and argue that the destitution and desperation that characterize street life constitute important foreground class conditions that figure prominently in the genesis of street crime.

We also address a key issue of internal validity noted in the previous chapter. This concern involves the extent to which sampling street youth alone can pose problems in establishing causal processes that lead to crime. There are numerous threats to internal validity (Cook and Campbell, 1979), but the problem of restrictive sampling, or sample selection bias, often is neglected (see Berk, 1983, p. 386). In our research, the issue is whether samples of street youth constitute groups with unique attributes that might bias assessments of causal processes. Since subsequent chapters of this book are based exclusively on analyses of our Toronto and Vancouver street data, it is important to establish that explorations of such samples by themselves can validly reflect causal processes, such as the experience of destitution, that affect youth on the street. In this chapter, we present evidence that this is indeed the case.

Destitution and Crime

The idea that crime is significantly influenced by people's immediate, desperate class circumstances was once a fundamental tenet of criminology. Early European criminologists, including Russell (1847), Fletcher (1849), and Bonger (1916), argued that a sudden, devastating change in economic position was a prominent cause of crime, and they therefore linked crime and delinquency to sudden increases in food prices and the rapid disappearance of jobs. Sellin (1937) adopted a similar situational perspective in pointing to the unanticipated onset of unemployment to explain changes in crime rates during the Great Depression. However, this emphasis on situations of destitution and desperation did not endure or prosper. Instead, theoretical attention to problems of daily survival declined, as if the relative prosperity of post-Depression society had eliminated situational desperation as a cause of crime and delinquency. Sociological theories of criminogenesis shifted their attention from the foreground to the background of criminal experiences.

Four characteristics of contemporary criminology deflect attention from the foreground role of current class circumstances in the causation of crime. We describe two of these factors in earlier chapters. The first is the institutionalization of self-report studies of students who live at home, and the declining interest in the effects of less protected settings like the street. The second arises from the failure of these studies to find evidence of a class–crime connection and involves criminologists' subsequent dismissal of, or disinterest in, the causal significance of class conditions.

The third feature is the tendency to discount foreground causal factors theoretically and instead focus on background and developmental variables. Modern criminologists' neglect of foreground situations is evident in a number of theories: Strain theories locate the motivation for crime in cumulative frustrations arising from background structural inequality (Merton, 1938); learning theories concentrate on long-term exposure to the behavior and attitudes of deviant others (Sutherland, 1947); control approaches focus on the failure of family and school experiences to develop self-control or social bonds (Hirschi, 1969); and labeling explanations concentrate on successive stages of stigmatization (H. Becker, 1963, 1964). Each of these traditions assumes that crime and delinquency are predetermined by background experiences and developments that cumulate over time; this is one reason they focus on the formative years of childhood and adolescence.

Admittedly, some theorists in these traditions give limited attention to foreground, situational circumstances. The vocabulary varies, but consideration is sometimes given to pressures, inducements, or motivations for crime, variously described as situational, mechanistic, dynamic, endogenous, or contemporaneous. However, these factors are usually not given extensive consideration. For example, in an early and influential statement, Sutherland (1947) acknowledges and then minimizes the significance of situational effects by asserting that although desperate situations can contribute to crime, the primary definitions of these situations are determined through differential exposure to competing norms. Thus, he argues that "while a person could define a situation in such a manner that criminal behavior would be the inevitable result, past experiences would, for the most part, determine the way in which [s]he defined the situation" (Sutherland, 1947, p. 77).

Briar and Piliavin (1965), and more recently Gottfredson and Hirschi (1990), arrive at similar conclusions, although these authors argue respectively that it is the lack of commitment to conformity or self-control that determines whether situational circumstances will lead to crime. So the predominant view, even among those who acknowledge the effect of situational conditions, is to assign them a secondary role in the causation of crime and delinquency.

The fourth and final factor involves inclinations of those who recognize situational effects to emphasize inducements, opportunities, or attractions to crime, to the neglect of equally immediate and often desperate class conditions. For example, Gibbons (1971) suggests that external motivations for crimes can arise from opportunities accompanying "criminogenic conditions." According to Gibbons, "in many cases, criminality may be a response to nothing more temporal than provocations and attractions bound up in the immediate circumstances" (1971, p. 271). Katz (1988) echoes this view, arguing that traditional theories neglect the "seductions of crime" that involve attempts to maximize pleasure or satisfaction in intensely felt situations. As with Gibbons, Katz's emphasis is restricted to particular foreground factors: the sensual attractiveness of situations that seduce people to offend. This argument is more persuasive in circumstances that present opportunities or temptations for crime than in those that pose problems of day-to-day survival; focusing on the former instead of the latter underestimates the impact of desperate situations.

Given the four tendencies we have outlined, it is not surprising that situations posing problems of survival and well-being are given little attention in theory and research on crime. The challenge we confront is to reintroduce classical concerns with foreground circumstances of desperation and destitution into contemporary theories. We alluded to this challenge in Chapter Three, when we noted that Agnew's (1985, 1992, 1994, 1995) strain theory and Hirschi's (1969) control theory can be extended to include the strains and lack of social control that characterize street life; here we argue that the traditional class theories' focus on more distant class backgrounds should be extended to include foreground experiences.

Regardless of their particular orientations, theorists interested in class – from classical (e.g., Marx and Weber) to more contemporary scholars (e.g., Wright and Freeman) – recognize that people isolated from, or only episodically involved in, a society's economic system represent the most disadvantaged class. For the most part, theorists focus on groups whose exclusion is long lasting: slaves, the lumpen proletariate, the disreputable poor, or the underclass. There is much research on the problems that accumulate for the individuals and families in these groups and their consequent effects on society. However, less attention is directed toward situations where the exclusion is more episodic. This can occur when people suddenly become unemployed, lose their livelihood, become bankrupt, or are "cut off" from a previous source of income. Similar circumstances often are involved when youth leave or are "thrown out" of their homes. The results may be minor in situations in which individuals can find alternative sources of shelter and support. However, for other less fortunate people, such situations can be disastrous, exposing them to great economic difficulty, if not destitution. This situational adversity can include a devastating array of foreground class conditions.

The qualitative material presented in Chapter Two indicates that many street youth's involvement in the legal economy is marginal and episodic: When employed, most work in the service sector or in jobs that are temporary. So when these youth become unemployed, the severity of their loss of income can erase their few prospects for independently obtaining food, shelter, and other necessities. Moreover, the use that these youth make of social assistance is limited and inconsistent, and few can count on economic support from family or friends. Not surprisingly, these youth report that they often are without money, food, or a place to sleep.

Regardless of their family class backgrounds, street youth often confront these foreground class circumstances. This situational adversity has several implications for strain and control theories of crime: Sudden destitution increases the motivation to offend, if only as a way of satisfying subsistence needs of food, clothing, and shelter, and it weakens or reduces ties to and involvement in conventional organizations and institutions, thereby diminishing the potential social costs of offending.

Adversity and Street Crime

As noted in Chapter Two, much of street life involves the search for money, food, clothing, and a place to sleep. When we asked how they obtained these necessities, respondents referred to employment, social assistance, panhandling, hostels, food banks, friends, and occasionally family; they also spoke about crime. Many youth talked about their offending as an important, and often their only, source of income. They noted that they also used crime as a more direct means of satisfying immediate and often pressing needs. The latter is evident in several accounts that describe acts of theft that were a part of the search for food. These thefts include stealing from supermarkets and convenience stores, doing a "dine and dash" at restaurants (eating and bolting without paying), "bun runs" (stealing from delivery trucks), as well as other ploys. The techniques of this urban foraging for food vary, but they frequently include an emphasis on swiftness and stealth. The latter are captured in a conversation we had with Jeremy. In Chapter Two, we noted that Jeremy sometimes obtained uneaten lunches from schoolyards; he also described another survival strategy:

> INTERVIEWER: So what else did you do for food?
> JEREMY: Food, I'd always like . . . you know those little Chinese markets?
> INTERVIEWER: In Chinatown?
> JEREMY: Yeah. They've got the food out front. You grab it and run. All the
> time.

Keith also relied on shoplifting from convenience stores as his main food source. After completing a jail term for assault, Keith ventured to Toronto rather then returning home. There he and several other youth formed a street family. According to Keith, he and the other youth in this group depended on a popular chain store for food:

> We went to the 7-Eleven to eat. We stole food from the 7-Eleven all the time. That's all we ate, just the food we stole from the 7-Eleven.

In other situations, the theft of food was less spontaneous and reflected some forethought and planning. In Chapter Two, we described the resourcefulness displayed by Thomas in making use of a gas barbecue. When Thomas told us that he used his gas barbecue for food as well as heat, we asked where he got his food. He replied:

> There's a Mr. Grocer [supermarket] in the area. I decided to walk in there with a nice heavy jacket on a few occasions and acquire whatever I needed.

Thomas continued, noting that, in general, he relied on theft as his main source of income:

> Um, average day would be wake up in the morning, uh, leave, lock up and basically look for money, any opportunity to break into a car, a house, whatever.

Jeremy, Keith, and Thomas had considerable street experience; however, as the following comment reveals, street neophytes also resort to theft as a means of getting food. Lindsey left home after an argument with her father escalated to shouting, banging doors, and throwing things. Neighbors called the police, and an officer escorted Lindsey to the city's main youth hostel, where she stayed for a month or so. Several weeks before our interview, Lindsey had been "kicked out" of the hostel for using "hostile language"; since then she had alternated between walking the streets at night and staying in a friend's apartment. We asked her what she had been doing for food during this time, and she answered:

> My friend's friend said, "If we've got no food, let's shoplift some." So we did that quite a lot. Um, you'd go in, you'd bring a bag or whatever, and you'd just start shoving stuff in . . . you know, the staples to keep living on.

Another newcomer to the street, Nancy, mirrored Lindsey in her attitudes and experiences. Nancy made it clear that she disliked street life and most of the people she encountered. She objected to drug use, found prostitution abhorrent, and was critical of many elements of street youth's lives (e.g., hanging out, partying). She admitted to some involvement in crime on the street, but she emphasized that her participation was limited and was a direct result of the adversity she encountered: "The only thing I've ever done is stealing, just shoplifting once in awhile. If I'm hungry, I will shoplift food."

As we noted at the start of this discussion, street youth also use theft as an indirect means of dealing with a shortage of food. A typical approach involved stealing and then selling the stolen goods. This pattern is evident in Jake's description of his most recent offense:

> I broke into a school. I broke into a school that I used to work at, in the daycare, and I stole two Nintendo systems. I needed to. I had to make money.

She ["girlfriend"] was starving; I was starving. My mom couldn't exactly help me. We had a long time to wait for our checks [social assistance] to come. They didn't even show up. So, I, um, broke into school, and I stole the two systems, and I sold them. It gave us enough money just to get by.

Food and money for food were not the only necessities that street youth obtained through theft. Most youth were ill prepared for living on the streets and lacked the rain and winter clothes necessary to stay dry and warm in inclement weather. In Chapter Two, we describe how youth also lost their clothes when, for example, they were stolen and when they were evicted from squats. Victor and other members of his street family responded to clothing-related problems in the same way they dealt with other difficulties on the street:

Um, basically we'd get in trouble, doing whatever we could to make money to clothe the family.

When asked to elaborate, Victor explained:

Stealing. From wherever I could find something to make money from. It wouldn't really be choosing, it'd just be on a spur of the moment. If I saw something that I'd figure I could make money off of, I was into it. I don't know, just kind of picking up a purse.

Other youth also described stealing to clothe themselves. Gary remembered one occasion when he and a group of streets friends were hanging out at the city bus terminal. They noticed that packages and other freight were frequently left unattended, offering a convenient and a timely opportunity for theft:

My friend, he just walked over and grabbed a box and walked off like he should be, like he's supposed to have this box in his hand. And there's eleven brand new sweaters in there. So we all got brand new sweaters. We were all warm that winter.

Youth who preferred squats and the streets to shelters, or who were no longer welcome at hostels, faced other difficulties when the weather turned cold and damp. Lisa described an occasion when she took advantage of an opportunity to obtain bedding for herself and fellow squatters, thereby providing everyone with some protection from the cold:

I went to the hospital once, because I was really, really sick, and I stole a bunch of hospital blankets, so we had sheets and blankets. [In the day I stored them] in a locker . . . the lock was broken, so you could stick the key in whenever you want, and you didn't have to put money in.

Although theft appeared to be the most common criminal solution to the search for necessities, it was not the only solution: Street youth also turned to other crimes as ways of making ends meet, particularly prostitution. Like several youth working in the sex trade, Tyler reported that he often asked customers to "treat" him to a meal. He was usually turned down; however, he was occasionally given a hurried trip through a fast-food drive-thru, and several repeat customers had taken him to restaurants or given him food after taking him to their hotels, apartments, or homes. More often, though, as the following experience indicates, he used the money he earned to pay for his own meals:

I was with a "date" last night . . . and today – I hadn't eaten in two days – and I had a bit of extra money so I had two grilled chicken burgers, large onion rings and fries, a milkshake and a milk. Then I had an ice cream and another large onion rings.

Tyler's description of his experiences with one of his "regular" customers suggests that, in other situations, he exchanged sex directly for necessities:

He [date] likes to do seven or eight balls [of crack] a day with me, and he said, "Do you want to go and get more?" And I said, "No." And so we didn't. And, uhm, uhm, he bought cigarettes. Like I "pull one" for free, and he spends his money on cigarettes and food, or pot and a fifteen pack. But I always get at least cigarettes.

Many other youth also described the connection between need and prostitution. In most cases, these youth tied their entry into the sex trade to a time when they were particularly destitute, lacking the basic essentials necessary for survival. This pattern is evident in the experiences of two respondents who we met in agencies that provide services for youth involved in prostitution. According to Deirdre, she started working in the sex trade after spending several months on the streets of Vancouver:

I met a man, and he decided to tell me what to do, and that's where I was, so, I didn't really care at the time 'cause I had no money, I had nowhere to live.

Crystal related a similar experience, saying that she started working the streets of Toronto after being thrown out of her family home when she was 14. At this age, she could not legally take advantage of the Toronto hostels, and she refused to move to a foster or group home. Summarizing her life situation at that point, Crystal explained, "there was nothing to help me, and I had to turn to prostitution to survive."

For other youth, involvement in the sex trade was more episodic, occurring in times of extreme need when they believed they had no other economic recourse. The experiences of two youth, Sean and Sharon, typify these situations. Sean's experiences came to light when we asked him if he'd ever run into any problems on the street. He replied:

Well, I don't know if it was a danger to my life but, uh, some, a couple of old guys tried to come and pick me up, you know, for my, you know, sex and stuff like that. I didn't agree with, I didn't like that.

He then added:

It was hard, because I, but like I used to, uh, hook a little bit, not really every day, but 'cause sometimes I needed the money to get through.

Sharon described a similar experience:

Um, well, I never actually went out with the intent of doing that, but there was like a few times that I'd gotten offered by guys to like, give them a hand-job or whatever for a few bucks, so I took up the offer a couple of times. 'Cause it's like, well, I had no money, and this was easy enough to do.

According to most youth, noncriminal means of meeting their needs simply could not match the returns provided by crime (see also Freeman, 1996; Snow and Anderson, 1993, Chap. 5). Social service agencies offered some necessities (from food to shelter, depending on the city), and there were some opportunities for earning money (i.e., from employment to panhandling), but according to many street youth, these paled in comparison with the returns that could be gained through crime. This view is reflected in one of Tyler's comments on the differences between youth who responded to street life by working in the sex trade and those who chose other, legal activities:

I'm a young urban professional . . . like I go out, I make some money. . . . I mean I don't sit there and panhandle and get all of maybe twenty bucks a day. I get all of twenty bucks a half-hour. . . . So, uhm, I'm a "yuppie" street person in a sense. . . . I can afford to live, and they're literally surviving. We are all really just surviving, because none of us know how to live. All we know how to do is survive, except we survive a bit easier.

Sheneika echoed this sentiment:

Ho's [whores] don't go day in and day out looking for a place to live. We have a place to live. Whether it be a hotel room or not, we have a place to live. We have food all the time. We always have cigarettes, we always have everything. Because we have money. When you are living on the street, it's a different story.

The comments of Sheneika, Tyler, Sharon, Sean, Gary, Thomas, and others demonstrate the tendency of street youth to link their involvement in crime to the adversity they encounter on the street. Indeed, many youth argue that crime only became an option when the conditions on the street became unbearable and they saw no other viable response to their adversity. But do these accounts accurately depict a causal relationship between adversity and crime? Or are these simply justifications constructed to excuse or rationalize illegal acts? In the next part of our analysis, we explore this issue, adding to our model of crime measures of the foreground class conditions that characterize street life; specifically, we examine the relationship between offending and being without food, shelter, and employment.

Three Kinds of Street Crime

In this chapter, we extend our focus on serious theft and introduce two further measures of street crime: theft of food and prostitution.[1] We focus our attention on these crimes for two reasons. First, we want to consider separately minor and more serious street crimes. Theft of food is a common form of crime that relates very clearly to needs on the street. Whereas theft of food might be considered a minor form of delinquency, however, serious theft and prostitution are not. The potential economic returns combined with the costs of detection clearly separate serious theft and prostitution from theft of food and other status offenses or crimes of mischief commonly used to measure delinquency among high-school youth. These distinctions are made clear in the public rankings of these activities on crime seriousness scales (Rossi et al., 1974; Wolfgang et al., 1985) as well as in conversations with street youth.

Second, we include theft and prostitution measures because they are likely to reveal gender-specific patterns, with situational difficulties more likely to cause male involvement in theft and female participation in prostitution. That is, strains of the street are most likely to exert effects along previously observed lines of gender specialization in crime (see, for example, Harris, 1977; Steffensmeier, 1980a, 1980b, 1993).

Our first outcome measure asks, "Have you had to steal food since leaving home?" with responses coded from never (0) to most of the time (3).[2] Our second measure, serious theft, parallels the scale introduced in Chapter Three and includes responses to items asking how often the respondent did the following since leaving home: (1) took things worth over $50; (2) took things from a car (tape deck, etc.); (3) took things from a store worth less than $50; (4) used a bank or credit card without the owner's permission; (5) took things from a store worth more than $50; (6) took a stranger's automobile; and (7) broke into and took things from a house or building. We measure involvement in prostitution with a single item: "How often have you had sex for money since leaving home?" Descriptive statistics for these items indicate that the average youth on the street had stolen food and worked in the sex trade on at least one occasion and had committed a more serious theft three times.[3]

Explanatory Variables

We use three measures to capture the current or foreground class conditions that characterize street life. Our first indicator measures hunger and is based on a question that asks how frequently the respondent had spent entire days without food while on the street (coded from 0, for never, to 3, for most of the time). Our second measure focuses on access to secure and stable shelter and uses information on the living conditions that youth experienced since leaving home. This item has four categories ordered in increasing levels of risk and decreasing levels of security: from (1) living exclusively with friends or relatives, through (2) staying in public hostels and shelters, and (3) living on the street as well as in hotels, to (4) staying on the street, in hostels, and in hotels. The latter kinds of private hotels may be especially hazardous in exposing street youth to sites of ongoing criminal activities (e.g., drugs and prostitution); moreover, the last category probably comes closest to reflecting the nomadic pattern of street life described in

Chapter Two. Our final indicator is unemployment since leaving home. We use this information to categorize youth as continuously employed since leaving home, employed since leaving home but unemployed at the time of the survey, or continuously unemployed since leaving home. Descriptive statistics for these three variables reveal that the average street youth had gone hungry at least once or twice; had been employed since leaving home, but was unemployed at that time of the study; and had slept on the street as well as in public hostels.[4]

The models we estimate in this chapter include the background and developmental measures of strain and control discussed in the previous chapter. We introduce measures of background class position, parental use of force, family disruption (i.e., the absence of two biological parents), and paternal and maternal relational and instrumental control, and we add a single item tapping family sexual abuse (coded 1 for reported problems in the survey that involve sexual mistreatment) for special consideration in relation to prostitution (see Simons and Whitbeck, 1991). We also included measures of school involvement, commitment, and conflict.

These variables represent a wide range of concepts, but it is still possible that we have misspecified the causation of crime in some way, and this could result in spuriously attributing causal significance to the situational difficulties we have emphasized. To guard further against this, we include several omnibus controls; these include the length of time on the street (i.e., the length of time at risk), the number of times the respondent has left home (previous street experiences), and criminal support at home (the number of home friends arrested) and on the street (the number of street friends arrested). Given the relationship between past behavior and offending (Gottfredson and Hirschi, 1990; Nagin and Paternoster, 1991), we also add measures of the respondent's participation in crime and delinquency while at home. These items are comparable to the measures of street crime discussed previously. We measure serious theft and prostitution at home with items parallel to those used for the period on the street. Our study did not include a question that asked specifically about the theft of food at home, so instead we use a two-item scale measuring minor theft. This scale combines questions that ask how often the respondents took things valued at less than $5, and between $5 and $10.[5] Controls for crime at home may be important because compared to more conventional youth, street youth have more extensive criminal backgrounds (e.g., Brennan et al., 1978; McCarthy and Hagan, 1991).[6]

The Analysis

We first present bivariate relationships between our explanatory variables and the three dependent measures of street crime. We then separately estimate three OLS regression models for each measure of street delinquency: Model 1 introduces the measures of foreground class circumstances while taking into account the other street variables; Model 2 adds background and developmental variables; and Model 3 combines street, background, and developmental factors. To the extent that our measures of immediate class conditions have measurable direct effects on theft of food, serious theft, and prostitution – independent of time on the street, delinquent associations, background differences of strain and control, and offending at home – it would seem methodologically conservative and substantively justifiable to regard these situational class conditions as important foreground causes of street crime (Hirschi and Selvin, 1967).

We then incorporate the Toronto school sample introduced in the previous chapter into a second, supplementary part of our analysis. We do this because, consistent with arguments of both strain and control theories, the background factors that influence crime on the street encourage youth to leave home in the first place. This implies that the error terms for leaving home and street crime may be correlated, and this may lead to specification errors in the estimation of causal effects in the street sample. This possibility of misspecification is the threat to internal validity that we introduced as the problem of sample selection bias at the outset of this chapter.

Foreground Effects of Situational Adversity on Crime

Table 4.1 contains bivariate correlations between explanatory variables and outcome measures of theft of food, serious theft, and prostitution. These correlations indicate that the strongest and most consistent associations are with two foreground measures of hunger and shelter, and two street control variables – length of time on the street and arrests of street friends. In contrast, our third situational measure, unemployment, is significantly related to only one indicator of street crime, prostitution. There is also evidence of gender specialization in street crime: Gender is positively related to theft of food and serious theft, and negatively associated with prostitution. This indicates that, as expected, males are more likely to steal while females are more likely to work in the sex trade.

The bivariate correlations also reveal several significant associations between strain and control variables and street crime, but the pattern of rela-

Table 4.1. Bivariate Coefficients for Theft of Food, Serious Theft, and Prostitution (N = 390)

Independent variables	Dependent variables		
	Theft of food	Serious theft	Prostitution
Age	−.048	.026	−.008
Gender	.160***	.180***	−.096**
Surplus Workers	−.001	.017	.048
Workers	−.039	−.018	−.123***
Petty Bourgeoisie	−.034	−.082*	−.062
Employers	.075	−.022	.031
Intact Family	−.003	.010	.034
Maternal Instrumental Control	−.135***	−.162***	−.042
Paternal Instrumental Control	−.026	−.040	−.075*
Maternal Relational Control	−.011	−.092**	−.004
Paternal Relational Control	−.029	−.046	−.064
Coercive Control	−.019	−.021	.105**
Sexual Abuse	−.003	−.038	.129***
Homework	−.276***	−.236***	.101**
School Goals	.027	.035	−.030
Conflict With Teachers	.171***	.251***	.018
Home Friends Arrested	.212***	.252***	−.039
Minor Theft at Home Scale	.308***	.319***	.011
Serious Theft at Home Scale	.303***	.461***	.011
Prostitution at Home	−.008	.036	.184***
Unemployed	−.034	−.045	.103**
Hunger	.369***	.262***	.194***
Shelter	.169***	.164***	.230***
Number of Times Left Home	.086**	.036	.203***
Length of Time on Street	.128***	.251***	.227***
Street Friends Arrested	.197***	.394***	.168***

* $p < .10$
** $p \leq .05$
*** $p < .01$

tionships is less clear. Both measures of theft are negatively related to maternal instrumental control and homework, and positively associated with conflict with teachers, home friends arrested, and theft at home. In comparison, prostitution is positively related to sexual abuse, coercive control, prostitution at home, and unexpectedly, homework. It is also negatively associated with a worker class background and paternal instrumental control. Gender also influences these crimes, with males reporting more involvement in theft and females indicating greater involvement in prostitution. Notwithstanding these effects, situational variables are at least as (if not more) prominently associated with street crime as background and developmental variables, even though these foreground situational variables are rarely measured in crime and delinquency research; furthermore, gender appears to channel involvement in street crime.

We begin our multivariate analysis with the models of theft of food in Table 4.2. Model 1 introduces the three measures of situational adversity (unemployment, hunger, and shelter) and three street control variables (length of time on the street, number of previous street experiences, and street friends arrested). Although all these measures except unemployment are significantly related to theft of food at the bivariate level, hunger alone has a substantial and statistically significant effect on theft of food when they are introduced together.

We introduce background and developmental variables alone in Model 2. Of these 18 variables, 4 have significant effects: Theft of food decreases with commitment to homework, increases with number of home friends arrested and with minor theft at home, and is more common among males. In Model 3 we combine street, background, and developmental variables. With the exception of gender, the foregoing effects remain significant, and the effect of hunger increases slightly. Two additional variables are also significant in the combined model: Theft of food is positively related to employer class background, and negatively associated with age. Overall, these models suggest that hunger does not simply mediate effects of background or developmental variables on theft of food on the street; rather, hunger accounts for much of this theft in its own right.

We turn next to Table 4.3 and the models of serious theft. When we introduce street variables in Model 1, hunger again has a substantial and significant effect. In addition, theft is also positively related to the absence of secure shelter and two street control variables: the length of time on the street and the number of street friends arrested. Model 2 considers background and developmental variables alone. Like theft of food, serious theft is negatively related to homework, and positively associated with the num-

Table 4.2. OLS Regressions of Theft of Food

Variables	Model 1 b	Model 1 SE	Model 2 b	Model 2 SE	Model 3 b	Model 3 SE
Age			−.038	.032	−.058*	.032
Gender			.183*	.102	.154	.097
Surplus Workers			−.146	.171	−.117	.162
Workers			−.051	.105	−.028	.098
Petty Bourgeoisie			−.204	.258	−.275	.246
Employers			.182	.124	.278**	.117
Intact Family			−.035	.094	−.084	.089
Maternal Instrumental Control			−.037	.036	−.024	.034
Paternal Instrumental Control			.019	.036	.033	.033
Maternal Relational Control			.021	.032	.025	.030
Paternal Relational Control			−.024	.033	−.001	.032
Coercive Control			.006	.019	−.004	.018
Sexual Abuse			.201	.182	−.046	.174
Homework			−.137***	.035	−.141***	.033
School Goals			.028	.031	.043	.029
Conflict With Teachers			.043	.036	.006	.034
Home Friends Arrested			.066**	.029	.058*	.030
Minor Theft at Home Scale			.087***	.019	.079***	.018
Unemployment	−.068	.059			−.092	.057
Hunger	.293***	.150			.301***	.048
Shelter	.050	.045			.058	.046
Number of Times Left Home	.002	.003			.001	.002
Length of Time on Street	.005	.008			.009	.008
Street Friends Arrested	.050*	.029			−.012	.031
Intercept	.028		1.016		.859	
Adjusted R^2	.139		.181		.256	

* $p \leq .10$
** $p \leq .05$
*** $p \leq .01$

ber of home friends arrested, conflict with teachers, and theft at home. Serious theft is also less common among youth from families belonging to the petty bourgeoisie.

When we introduce the background/developmental and street variables together in Model 3, most of the previously reported effects are relatively unchanged. Exceptions are that home friends arrested and conflict with teachers lose significance. In contrast, both hunger and lack of shelter remain significantly related to serious theft on the street; so, as with hunger and theft of food, these foreground factors operate in their own right and are not simply products or mediators of background or developmental variables.

Our analysis of prostitution provides further evidence of the role of street effects. Table 4.4 indicates that two situational measures and two street control variables are significantly associated with prostitution in Model 1 – unemployment, shelter, time on the street, and number of times left home. In contrast to models for theft, the significant bivariate relationship between hunger and prostitution decreases to nonsignificance.

The results in Model 2 reveal that prostitution is also related to a number of background variables – sexual abuse, prostitution at home, and a family background in the working class. With a few exceptions, the foregoing effects remain essentially unchanged when we add background and developmental variables to a model with street variables (see Model 3). The only substantial differences are the emergence of a significant relationship between prostitution and street friends arrested and the decrease in the size and significance of the effect of sexual abuse. Thus, although we introduce twenty-one control variables, two foreground variables – unemployment and shelter – retain their sizable, direct, and significant effects on street prostitution.[7]

A Further Test

Our results suggest that the adverse conditions and circumstances encountered by street youth are prominent foreground causes of involvement in crime. Up to this point, however, we have considered only youth who are on the street, thus ignoring the process of their getting there that we emphasize in the previous chapter. The final part of our analysis brings the process of taking to the street back into the picture by reincorporating the Toronto school sample; this process also allows us to address the main threat to internal validity – sample selection bias.

Sample selection problems arise in situations in which the members of a

Table 4.3. OLS Regressions of Serious Theft

Variables	Model 1 b	SE	Model 2 b	SE	Model 3 b	SE
Age			.017	.077	−.125	.077
Gender			.163	.249	.015	.236
Surplus Workers			−.404	.410	−.232	.384
Workers			−.071	.250	.072	.234
Petty Bourgeoisie			−1.414**	.616	−1.074*	.583
Employers			−.259	.296	−.031	.278
Intact Family			−.067	.224	−.129	.211
Maternal Instrumental Control			−.062	.085	.014	.081
Paternal Instrumental Control			.090	.085	.069	.079
Maternal Relational Control			−.099	.077	−.093	.072
Paternal Relational Control			−.040	.080	.015	.076
Coercive Control			.008	.045	−.015	.042
Sexual Abuse			.142	.437	−.508	.414
Homework			−.173**	.083	−.192**	.078
School Goals			.092	.073	.094	.069
Conflict With Teachers			.182**	.085	.125	.081
Home Friends Arrested			.195***	.070	.061	.071
Serious Theft at Home Scale			.383***	.049	.360***	.046
Unemployment	−.141	.144			−.183	.135
Hunger	.270**	.121			.288***	.113
Shelter	.225*	.116			.221**	.108
Number of Times Left Home	−.002	.007			−.006	.006
Length of Time on Street	.061***	.019			.072***	.019
Street Friends Arrested	.467***	.071			.289***	.073
Intercept	.503		1.145		1.914	
Adjusted R^2	.196		.220		.350	

* $p \leq .10$
** $p \leq .05$
*** $p \leq .01$

Table 4.4. OLS Regressions of Prostitution

Variables	Model 1 b	Model 1 SE	Model 2 b	Model 2 SE	Model 3 b	Model 3 SE
Age			.015	.082	.015	.084
Gender			−.165	.261	−.288	.249
Surplus Workers			.159	.436	.285	.413
Workers			−.622**	.268	−.494**	.253
Petty Bourgeoisie			−1.033	.664	−.486	.636
Employers			−.146	.318	.147	.302
Intact Family			.115	.241	.127	.229
Maternal Instrumental Control			.001	.091	.060	.088
Paternal Instrumental Control			−.081	.091	−.068	.086
Maternal Relational Control			−.008	.083	.006	.078
Paternal Relational Control			−.039	.086	−.025	.082
Coercive Control			.078	.048	.039	.046
Sexual Abuse			.998**	.468	.458	.449
Homework			.145	.089	.161	.099
School Goals			−.084	.078	−.062	.074
Conflict With Teachers			.107	.092	.024	.088
Home Friends Arrested			−.046	.074	−.120	.077
Prostitution at Home			.671***	.177	.578***	.167
Unemployment	.301**	.143			.286**	.147
Hunger	.124	.119			.083	.123
Shelter	.361***	.115			.330***	.118
Number of Times Left Home	.020***	.007			.020***	.007
Length of Time on Street	.076***	.019			.070***	.021
Street Friends Arrested	.114	.070			.173**	.079
Intercept	−1.317		1.071		−1.328	
Adjusted R^2	.135		.090		.180	

* $p \le .10$
** $p \le .05$
*** $p \le .01$

sample are not selected independently of a study's dependent variable. In these contexts, membership in a group (e.g., street youth) and in the resulting sample may reflect underlying characteristics that distinguish group members from the rest of the population (i.e., all youth). In our work, certain attributes may be responsible for street youth's selection into the street population and may be related to their involvement in crime. Berk (1983) cogently describes this problem, noting that it is a concern for most social science research:

> To summarize, whenever one has a nonrandom sample, the potential for sample selection bias exists. Examples are easy to construct. Studies of classroom performance of college students rest on the nonrandom subsets admitted and remaining in school. Studies of marital satisfaction are based on the nonrandom subset of individuals married when the data are collected. Studies of worker productivity are limited to the employed. (p. 391)

He further notes that even a random sample does not eliminate concern about sample selection bias:

> Suppose one has a random sample of all felony arrests in a given state in a given year. The random sample of felony arrests is a nonrandom sample of all reported felonies in that state in a given year. The reported felonies are a nonrandom sample of all felonies committed. . . . In principle, therefore, there exists an almost infinite regress in which at some point sample selection bias becomes a *potential* bias. (p. 392)

There are several techniques available for addressing sample selection problems (Berk, 1983; Stolzenberg and Relles, 1990; Winship and Mare, 1992), and we use the most common: Heckman's two-stage estimator.[8] The first stage of constructing this estimator involves establishing a weighting ratio that is then used to estimate a dummy endogenous variable that constitutes the sample selection variable (i.e., membership in the street versus school sample).

As noted in Chapter Three, our conservative estimate is that over the approximate year of the study, for every twenty youth in school in Toronto, there was one youth on the street. We use this ratio to reweigh the samples in proportion to their representation in the general youth population of Toronto (see Manski and Lerman, 1977; Xie and Manski, 1989). Using the 20:1 ratio described in Chapter Three, we estimate a probit equation of taking to the street like that estimated in the previous chapter (see Table 4.5).

Table 4.5. Bivariate Regression Coefficients and Probit Estimates for Models of Leaving Home

Independent variables	Bivariate coefficients		Probit estimates	
	Unweighted	Weighted	Coefficient	SE
Age	.325***	.153***	.266***	.076
Gender	.206***	.089**	.044	.215
Surplus Workers	.128***	.074***	.606	.461
Workers	−.033	−.014	−.112	.233
Petty Bourgeoisie	−.006	−.003	.105	.552
Employers	.009	.004	.020	.279
Intact Family	−.400***	−.189***	−.606***	.196
Maternal Instrumental Control	−.405***	−.187***	−.087	.072
Paternal Instrumental Control	−.324***	−.142***	−.076	.072
Maternal Relational Control	−.188***	−.083**	.001	.074
Paternal Relational Control	−.103***	−.046*	.041	.082
Coercive Control	.467***	.262***	.225***	.046
Sexual Abuse	.162***	.121***	1.089**	.556
Homework	−.304***	−.146***	−.026	.091
School Goals	−.362***	−.216***	−.206***	.065
Conflict With Teachers	.388***	.203***	.198**	.096
Home Friends Arrested	.481***	.268***	.264***	.077
Serious Theft at Home Scale	.325***	.163***	−.012	.047
Intercept			−5.937	
Chi-Square ($df = 18$)			1073.400***	

* $p \le .10$
** $p \le .05$
*** $p \le .01$

The second stage in applying Heckman's estimator involves transforming the predicted values from the probit equation into a hazard rate and entering them into OLS street crime equations. The differences that result from this "adjustment" can be interpreted as measuring the extent to which examining the selected street population alone raises problems of internal validity that undermine our modeling of foreground causes of street crime.

The results of our probit analysis of leaving home are presented in Table 4.5 and parallel those provided earlier in Chapter Three (see Table 3.2).[9] The adjustment based on the results of the probit selection equation is introduced by the inclusion of a hazard rate (lambda) in Table 4.6. The hazard rate introduces the composite influence of background variables on taking to the street into the substantive equations and, in the process, adjusts the remaining coefficients for the process of selection into the street sample. Again, our goal is to assess and adjust for problems of internal validity or bias that may result from selecting a sample of street youth as the basis for the OLS estimates of causal effects presented earlier. Simultaneously introducing the background social control and strain variables along with the hazard rate produces collinearity problems, so in this analysis, we include only the hazard rate.

The results of reestimating the newly adjusted substantive equations are presented in Table 4.6 and are consistent with those reported in this, as well as the previous, chapter. That is, the argument that strain and control background variables operate on crime through youth taking to the street is supported by the finding that the hazard rate is significant in the reduced equations (Model 1), and then nonsignificant in the full structural equations (Model 2) for all three dependent variables. However, there is no evidence here that estimating equations with street youth alone biased our analysis; instead, the findings from the substantive equations (see Model 2 for each form of street crime) reaffirm the influence of the situational variables. As before, theft of food and serious theft increase with hunger; serious theft and prostitution increase with problems of obtaining secure shelter; and prostitution increases with unemployment. These foreground class effects are all significant and substantial and therefore increase our confidence in the internal validity of our main findings – that situational problems of sustenance and security cause street crime.

The Adversity of the Street

We began this chapter by noting that contemporary theories of crime dwell on background and developmental factors. This is reflected in an array of theoretical orientations that highlight childhood and early adolescent life experiences in the family, at school, and among similarly located peers. The backdrop to this orientation is a concern with predispositions and propensities to crime and involves an unanswered question of just how far into the

Table 4.6. OLS Regressions of Theft of Food, Serious Theft, and Prostitution, Correcting for Sample Selection Bias

Independent variables	Theft of food				Serious theft				Prostitution			
	Model 1		Model 2		Model 1		Model 2		Model 1		Model 2	
	b	SE	b	SE	b	SE	b	SE	b	SE	b	SE
Lambda	-.142**	.065	-.018	.063	-.590***	.167	-.124	.155	-.256*	.157	.042	.153
Unemployment			-.065	.058			-.118	.142			.299**	.140
Hunger			.293***	.049			.268**	.119			.144	.118
Shelter			.067	.045			.184*	.110			.329***	.109
Number of Times Left Home			.002	.003			-.002	.006			.020***	.006
Length of Time on Street			.005	.008			.060***	.019			.077***	.019
Street Friends Arrested			.050	.029			.461***	.072			.124*	.071
Intercept	.905		.056		3.746		.783		1.647		-1.331	
Adjusted R^2	.005		.148		.026		.205		.001		.141	

* $p \leq .10$
** $p \leq .05$
*** $p \leq .01$

background of individual lives such causes can be traced (e.g., White et al., 1990; Caspi et al., 1994).

Our goal here is to push criminological theory in precisely the opposite direction: toward foreground causes of delinquency and crime, beginning with the focus of this chapter on criminogenic situations.[10] Such situations were once central in the study of crime, for example, in Sellin's (1937) study of offending during the Great Depression and in the Chicago tradition of field research. This important tradition made street settings central to the collection of data and the organization of crime research. However, the emergence of the contemporary self-report paradigm had the unintended consequence of moving research away from the street and into the schools, and of shifting attention away from the criminogenic nature of situations in which disadvantaged youth often find themselves. The timing of this shift, in the late 1950s and 1960s, may be significant because this was a period of relative prosperity in North America, when it was perhaps possible to believe that conditions of the city were becoming more malleable and the prospects of the urban underclass more benign. Yet the 1980s and 1990s have made many citizens more sensitive to the harsh circumstances that often characterize inner-city life and the potentially criminogenic conditions of the street. Thus, it is important to return our research to these settings.

So far, our return to the street has included an elaboration of strain and control theories that spans background, developmental, and foreground factors. A key to this integration is a focus on class and other adverse conditions at home, in school, and on the street. This integration emphasizes that taking to the street and subsequent criminal activity are often responses to successive and causally linked sources of adversity – for example, when parental unemployment is connected to abuse and neglect at home, which leads to youth taking to the street. Our integration also acknowledges that absence of family and school ties can lead to the street, so that the presence of strain and absence of control both can lead to street crime. We see no contradiction in the integration of these theoretical orientations. Indeed, our perspective on strain is in some ways reminiscent of the focus on conditions of overcontrol and undercontrol found in early versions of control theory (e.g., Durkheim [1897] 1951; Nye, 1958).

Our findings support the foregoing kind of integration and elaboration of strain and control theory. This support is most apparent in the final stage of our combined analysis of separately sampled school and street youth. These analyses of theft of food, more serious theft, and prostitution include a composite variable that incorporates the process of leaving home. The composite variables support the premise that background and developmental variables directly affect taking to the street and indirectly influence theft and prostitution. In essence, these results indicate that the youth who are most likely to become homeless are also the most likely to engage in theft and prostitution while on the street. This is why, in our experience, analyses of street youth data that include considerable variation on such variables do not pose internal validity problems for the estimation of causes of street crime.

Meanwhile, the variables that provide foreground measures of the situational adversity encountered by street youth in our data exercise significant direct effects on street crime, apart from the mediating role they can also play. These effects vary somewhat by type of crime, but overall, we found that situational variables play a prominent role as foreground class conditions that cause street crime. This is true even when street variables are pitted against each other and with a wide range of background, developmental, and control variables, and when the sample selection effects discussed in this chapter are taken into account. Consistently, hunger causes theft of food; problems of hunger and shelter lead to serious theft; and problems of shelter and unemployment produce prostitution.[11] These effects of situational variables gain plausibility from the comprehensive range of control measures we have imposed.

Collectively, the kinds of foreground conditions we have included in models analyzed in this chapter reflect the problems that street youth often confront in meeting subsistence needs. Of course, not all street crimes are subsistence related; nonetheless, we have demonstrated that some are motivated by need. Beyond this, Freeman (1996) has suggested a "foraging" model of crime as a way of understanding how youth often mix broader wants and opportunities with subsistence needs in ways that combine choice with constraint in the causation of street crime. This approach importantly notes that although crime is often willfully predatory, it can also be subsistence motivated. These possibilities clearly are not mutually exclusive. For example, predatory criminal lifestyles may often evolve out of, and coexist with, experiences in meeting subsistence needs.

We now have taken the first steps in opening up the black box of street life and demonstrating the foreground class effects of conditions such as unemployment, hunger, and lack of shelter in causing street crime. The next step in our exploration involves considering how the circumstances of being on the street can vary across settings like those of Toronto and Vancouver, two cities that differ considerably in the support and attention they give to street youth.

The Streets of Two Cities

MANY SCHOLARS AND CITIZENS argue that we must look to individual differences as much as to social environments in order to understand the origins of social problems, including problems of the street. For example, Baum and Burnes (1993) maintain that problems such as homelessness and crime share common causes that have as much to do with the characteristics of the people involved as with the structural circumstances and social experiences they encounter. Gottfredson and Hirschi (1990) similarly suggest that a range of disvalued behaviors, from adolescents running away from home to adults engaging in force and fraud, have common origins in lapses of self-control.

The background and developmental differences that these theorists emphasize often are understood as deficiencies that derive from parentage and parenting. The psychological literature on human development encourages this orientation, suggesting that such deficiencies can lead individuals to congregate in particular environments. From this psychological or developmental perspective, problems of homelessness and crime are seen as more ontogenetic than sociogenic – that is, as being more internally than externally driven, arising more from individual differences than from variation in the social environments in which people develop (see Dannefer, 1984; Caspi et al., 1994).

Alternatively, sociologists and social psychologists who study the life course tend to focus on social structures, roles, and socialization processes. This tradition of research is inclined to view socially structured experiences as formative environments in which individual differences emerge and change, especially in the transition from adolescence to adulthood (Elder,

1975). In this and following chapters, we increasingly incorporate a life course perspective in our attention to foreground experiences of youth living on the streets. Street youth encounter many opportunities to become involved in crime; they also come into contact and conflict with criminal justice agencies that seek to control this behavior. We see these experiences as playing a formative role in the life course development of these youth. A focus on these foreground experiences tends to downplay developmental arguments premised on ontogenetic differences and instead embraces a more sociogenic view of the life course.

However, at a minimum, ontogenetic arguments possess sufficient political and ideological currency to be taken seriously, and empirically there may be much to be learned about the interrelationship of ontogenetic and sociogenic processes in life course development (Cairnes, 1986). The life course tradition is open to this possibility, noting that socioenvironmental factors can accentuate as well as initiate attitudinal and behavioral patterns (Elder, 1994). Rather than rejecting developmental premises, we suggest that it is important for criminologists to explore simultaneously ontogenetic and sociogenic processes of life course development. We investigate the likelihood that some types of street crime are more ontogenetic in origin, whereas others may be mostly sociogenic. Prominent theories of crime and other social problems such as homelessness rarely explicitly address this possibility.

It may be necessary to introduce added specificity and variety into our measures of street crime in order to explore how crimes vary in their ontogenetic and sociogenic origins. Accordingly, we expand our attention in this chapter to a range of street crimes, and we separate violence and prostitution for special consideration in comparison to nonviolent forms of offending. Included among the latter are measures of theft, drug use, and drug selling. Violent crimes represent more serious and specific challenges to the conduct norms that most citizens accept and endorse; thus, deep-seated ontogenetic forces often are invoked to account for the occurrence of these crimes. In contrast, prostitution and other nonviolent crimes are more ambiguous in content and meaning, and the strength of condemnation and control of these crimes is more variable across social settings. It therefore is more likely that the causes of these crimes are more sociogenic in origin.

The diverse backgrounds and experiences of street youth offer substantial variation in ontogenetic and sociogenic forces thought to be productive of different kinds of crime. Our analysis for this chapter focuses on the two waves of the Toronto and Vancouver panel study conducted in the second phase of our research. We provide a general description of these cities in Chapter One; now we discuss more specific differences in these cities' responses to problems of crime and adolescent homelessness. The policy differences in city-based responses to homeless youth are significant because they introduce an important source of sociogenic variation into our research.

Street Youth and Crime in Toronto and Vancouver

Throughout most of this century, Toronto and Vancouver have had considerably different experiences with street crime. Although Toronto's population has consistently been larger than Vancouver's, its crime rate typically has been lower. The variation between these cities prominently contributes to regional differences in crime rates between eastern and western Canada. As noted by Brantingham and Brantingham (1984), "these patterns have remained relatively stable over the past fifteen years at least, and the general bias toward progressively higher crime rates in the west has been visible in the criminal conviction data for at least sixty years" (p. 272). As frequently as these differences have been observed, they rarely, if ever, have been the subject of scholarly explanation.

Meanwhile, lay explanations of Vancouver's relatively high crime rate usually have an ontogenetic focus involving a history of self-selection. From this perspective, Vancouver's temperate climate, coastal geography, and seaport setting are thought to attract a less controlled (i.e., "rowdy") population given to a range of disreputable activities. In contrast, Toronto is widely known for its clean streets and comparatively safe neighborhoods (Jacobs, 1961). Hemingway (circa 1920, cited in Lemon, 1984, p. 323) once called Toronto "the city of churches," and *Fortune* magazine more recently observed that "squeaky clean Toronto . . . is pleasant to the point of somnolence."

The street youth of Toronto and Vancouver may both contribute to and reflect their respective urban conditions. That is, both ontogenetic and sociogenic forces likely play roles in generating differences between these two cities. Ontogenetic forces are especially likely to be identified in the family backgrounds and experiences of street youth. Perhaps most significantly, and as noted in earlier chapters, these youth often have family backgrounds that involve physical and sexual abuse (Farber et al., 1984; Garbarino et al., 1986; Janus et al., 1987). Although this abuse most often stems from parents, other family members may be involved, and this chapter addresses the point that youth themselves may be sources of violence against their parents (Agnew and Huguley, 1989).

The prospect of youth abusing parents suggests the possibility that individually based ontogenetic forces can play a significant role in the causation of crime among street youth. As well, many street youth may be involved in delinquency before they go on the street. It is conceivable that Vancouver's hospitable climate and coastal setting attract a less controlled population given to these behaviors from childhood. This "self-selection" explanation of the higher crime rate in Vancouver assumes self-sustaining and reinforcing problems that derive from individuals' ontogenetic background characteristics.

However, there are also striking differences in the ways that Toronto and Vancouver respond to their respective problems of street youth and crime, and this divergence may be instructive in relation to sociogenic sources of variation between cities more generally. Toronto's orientation to street youth has many features of a social welfare model. Under provincial family and welfare legislation, Ontario youth reach the age of majority at 16. This means that youth of this age living apart from their families can receive welfare support from the province; perhaps more significantly, this legislation allows a framework in which the province, municipalities, and philanthropic organizations can provide shelter for youth living apart from their families, especially through a system of youth hostels or shelters. For example, in Toronto in 1992, there were four hostels exclusively for youth aged 16 to 21. Although hostels have their problems (see Chapter Two), the shelter and other services provided are clearly valued by many street youth. Paul's experiences with a number of Toronto agencies led him to observe that:

> I always either, you know, um, there's always, there's enough hostels here, there's always somewhere to go. I mean, it's not going to be pleasant, none of them are pleasant, but they're there.

The situation is much different in Vancouver. Provincial family and welfare legislation mandates that, under most statutes, a youth in British Columbia is legally a "child" or "infant" until the age of 19. Before 19, unmarried youth living apart from their families in Vancouver can receive public welfare support only in unusual circumstances. More significantly, there is no developed system of hostels, shelters, or safehouses for the short-term housing of street youth and there are fewer places that provide support for them on the street (Baxter, 1991). The potential sociogenic significance of the disparity between the social services of the two cities is captured in the comments of several youth. After being homeless in Toronto, Julia hitch-hiked to Vancouver, eventually moving into a squat in the Granville Street area. She said that she was shocked at the differences between the two cities, adding that:

> It was tough because of the lack of services in Vancouver, like not having safehouses and shelters. I think that does make a difference. And the avail-ability of welfare, and food and job-training programs, and all those things can make a difference. I mean, it's true that people won't use them unless they really want to, but what if they do and they're not there? They should be available. . . . That's what I first noticed when I came out here in '88, there was nothing to help me.

Jordy, who had also lived on the streets in both cities, made a similar comment:

> I liked Vancouver way better than Toronto. But Vancouver doesn't have as many things for youth–services and programs like to get back into school, work, housing. I liked Vancouver better, but there's more opportunities here in Toronto.

A related remark by Alan introduced a further problem with the lack of services in Vancouver: "Vancouver's . . . worse off than any other city be-cause they have no, like, drop-in center really for kids to go hang out at. . . . So, there's no safe haven away from the police." Alan's point is instructive because it suggests that Vancouver may have what is ultimately a law enforce-ment or crime control model for dealing with street youth. When Vancouver street youth are picked up by the police, they cannot be taken to a youth hostel. Rather, they are more likely to face one of several less desirable consequences: They may be returned to their families, who are liable to criminal prosecution if they refuse to accept and promise support for their children; they may be placed in government care and sent to a foster or group home; or they may be jailed. As expected, few of these environments offer successful solutions to problems that cause youth to leave home in the first place.

It would not be surprising to find, therefore, that Vancouver youth are more often on the street than those in Toronto, and more liable to police charges. These are theoretically predictable results of crime control and social welfare models applied to the street youth of the respective cities. These projected patterns are components of our larger theoretical model, which locates movement onto the street, street experiences, and police contacts as key events in the life course trajectories of homeless youth.

Ontogenetic and Sociogenic Origins of Leaving Home and Street Crime

Respondents described conflicts that pervaded their home lives, as we report in Chapters Two and Three, and research consistently identifies family violence as a salient factor leading youth to run from and leave home (Janus et al., 1987). Additional examples of family violence from our research highlight the nature of this problem, which, as we further note, can take a reciprocal form involving parents and children.

As with many street youth, Brenda ran from a violent family. Her reflections on life at home capture both the explosive climate that permeates these families and the strain that this can cause:

> I was tired of going, um, I was tired of walking home and getting in the door and crying and, you know, not knowing if I was going to get killed that night or not, kinda thing . . . I didn't like having to, just, kind of, walk on eggshells twenty-four hours a day. . . . And I was going mental. And it was either me or them. I was either going to kill myself or kill my parents, and my parents aren't worth going to jail for.

In many instances, specific acts of violence provided the motivation for finally leaving home. When asked what things led to his leaving home, Barry succinctly replied: "Um, my dad beat the piss out of me." Ryan's home life bore a strong resemblance to Barry's. Ryan told us that he had not been in contact with his parents for several years and had no interest in reestablishing relations with them:

> Um, I wasn't happy there at all, so I just left. That was when I was about 9. I just remember walking around the streets of Vancouver. . . . I was tired of always gettin' hit and shit like this, so I just said, forget it, I don't need that kind of bullshit, you know. No one needs that kind of shit, you know.

However, family violence involves not only mothers and fathers but also other family members, including youth themselves. Derek's description of an altercation illustrates how parents and children may be involved in reciprocal violence. When asked how the last violent event before leaving his suburban home began, Derek responded:

> I kicked in the door. I think that had a lot to do with it, considering he [the father] was standing behind it. He got injured when he grabbed me and threw me up against the wall. First instinct, you know. You know, like you gotta swing if someone puts you up against the wall. I hit him, and then he like, kicked me in the ribs and threw me out.

This reciprocal violence is not exclusive to males. Asked why she left her inner-city home, Cicely replied:

> My mom put me in a group home. I hate her. Physical fights and all that crap. We'd hit each other. I don't care. I'd get my frustrations out.

Many street youth may also already be headed toward street crime before they leave home. This can be reflected, for example, in their participation in a range of deviant activities, of which drug use is most common. Gord's involvement in deviant and illegal activities began early and reflects the exposure to crime that often characterizes inner-city life:

> I started smoking dope when I was, like, 8, 9 years old, like literally when I was 8 or 9 years old. . . . Just, sittin' around the pool halls, you know, people giving you joints and stuff. . . . My family was always poor. Like my mom was always poor. She was, you know, she was always on welfare. So, my older brother sold dope, did whatever he could to make money to help out and to take care of himself. I used to hang out in a pool hall. . . . And all my brother's friends would get me to hold their dope and stuff, 'cause cops would come in and I'd be playing video games, you know. . . . After that it just, you know, I got to know when I was like 10, 10 years old I knew, you know, how to weigh out grams and knew there was sixteen ounces in a pound and twenty-eight grams in an ounce. So when I needed to make my own money, it just seemed totally natural because I knew so many people that would, just, give me dope and say, "Okay, pay me when you can, right?" . . . It was pretty easy actually. It seemed like the only logical thing to do. I did anything – for awhile. Anything to make money. I didn't care. You know, I didn't care if people were home, you know, crawl in through a window and crawl along the house on my knees and go and unhook the VCR and the TV.

Deviant or criminal behavior may encourage leaving home in several ways. Youth may leave of their own accord as a way of escaping familial controls that limit their involvement in criminal activities; they may also flee to avoid court appearances or conditions of probation; and as the following examples illustrate, these youth may also be evicted by their parents. Tyrone left his suburban Toronto home when he was 15.

INTERVIEWER: Why did you first leave home?

TYRONE: Uh, I was a troublemaker when I was younger, so my parents kicked me out. I was just being an idiot in school – skipping classes, getting suspended for firing fire extinguishers down the hall, taking a teacher's turban off, and all that kind of good stuff.

Lucas was also kicked out of his home. Like Tyrone, Lucas was in considerable trouble at school; however, he was also heavily involved in several illegal activities:

Um, when I first got the boot? Um, let's see . . . skipping out of school too much, getting kicked out of school too much. Um, selling narcotics, fighting with siblings, stealing money from relatives and friends. I seemed to be becoming a little bit of an embarrassment in the neighborhood for my mom. And, so her friends kept going, "Kick him out, kick him out – maybe he'll learn."

Gottfredson and Hirschi's (1990) "general theory of crime" suggests that antisocial behaviors like those of Tyrone and Lucas reflect an individual's "criminality" – that is, their failure to develop self-control. They argue that this deficiency encourages early delinquency and later involvement in more serious crime. Gottfredson and Hirschi (1990) go so far as to suggest that:

[T]he fact that crime is by all odds the major predictor of crime is central to our theory. It tells us that criminality (low self-control) is a unitary phenomenon that absorbs its causes such that it becomes, for all intents and purposes, *the* individual-level cause of crime. As a corollary, it tells us that the search for personality correlates of crime other than self-control is unlikely to bear fruit. . . . And, of course, it tells us that theories based on contrary assumptions are wrong. (p. 232)

Gottfredson and Hirschi's emphasis on stability in criminal behavior from early stages in the life course focuses attention on a variety of background factors that may be ontogenetic causes of youth taking to the streets. Recognizing the importance of these factors, Sampson and Laub (1993) treat problem behaviors that are continuous from early childhood as ontogenetic causes of later involvement in crime. Their point, and ours, is to identify a set of variables that comprehensively takes into account ontogenetic causes of later crime. Our analysis treats youth-initiated violence against parents, as well as prior delinquency, as globally absorbing ontogenetic forces leading many youth to the streets.[1] Since even youth-initiated violence can be provoked, and since much home delinquency is a consequence rather than cause of home problems, our modeling of these variables represents a methodologically liberal test of the influence of ontogenetic sources of crime among street youth.

Our simultaneous purpose in this chapter is to identify and estimate the sociogenic influence that city-based social policies have on the nature and volume of the involvement of street youth in crime. To this end, we must fully take into account the roles that ontogenetic forces might play in locating our sample respondents in Toronto and Vancouver. Apart from the influence of the latter factors, however, we propose that distinct social processes are at work in these cities: In contrast to Vancouver, the social welfare model of Toronto provides youth with greater access to stable and secure shelter and reduces exposure to the risks of being on the streets.

We also conceive criminal opportunities as important sociogenic foreground factors. As Eva's experiences demonstrate, being on the streets involves exposure to considerable crime and violence, including opportunities to make money, especially through theft, drug selling, and prostitution. Eva lived with her sister and mother in a small town in northern British Columbia before moving to the provincial capital of Victoria when she was 13 years old. The first friends she made in her new home were experimenting with soft drugs, and when she was 14, she also tried them. Recalling this period, she said:

> It was fun. I don't know, a lot of it was extremely lonely. Like, the only friend I had was my mom, and I didn't wanna just have it that my only friend is my mom. The people I hung around with were all "partyers," and so I just did what everybody else did.

At 15, Eva's drug use and drinking escalated; conflicts with her mother increased, and she quit school. Shortly afterward, she ran from home and headed to Vancouver. Her comments capture the initial attraction of the street and highlight the possibilities for crime:

> Oh, it was fun for a while – we met some really nice people, lots of partying – but down here [Vancouver's East Side] it was different. I found like, people were more violent, and everybody was into using harder drugs, and everything was just really different, and I ran into things, like I started prostituting

and doing illegal stuff [using and selling heroin and armed robbery] and all kinds of crazy stuff down here.

As Eva noted, street people's support for a variety of offenses constitute an important element of criminal opportunities:

> To me, it [selling drugs, stealing, prostitution] was okay, because the only people I hung around with were people that were involved in some sort of criminal activity; so it was kinda like the normy thing, right? Like to me, it's the people I was with gave me direction to believe that it was okay.

Juan shared this sentiment:

> Well, people out here, since we're all the same age and have been through similar experiences, it's more accepting, you know . . . of things you do. Like, even though they're illegal and stuff, it's more accepting. People don't go, you know, "Oh, well, you're a criminal, we won't associate with you." So, whatever, you know. Someone's talking about breaking into a car, breaking into houses and getting stuff, nobody puts up a big fuss. It's part of the routine. As long as you're not a real goof, or anything, you know, you're accepted.

However, in a converse way, each criminal opportunity may not only open the door to increasing illegal possibilities; it may also close off contacts with conventional peers and adults and heighten the risk of police contacts. Street youth have an especially high risk of conflict with legal authorities, in part because they have limited access to private space and spend much of their time in public places (Stinchcombe, 1963). These public places are often "ecologically contaminated" (Sampson, 1986; Smith, 1986), in the sense of being characterized by crime and a disproportionate police presence. In addition, street youth are often seen by the police as suspicious and in need of surveillance (Anderson, 1990). This increases their vulnerability to police charges and convictions, especially in a city like Vancouver with its crime control approach to youth problems.

The sociogenic sequence of transitional events that we propose therefore leads from exposure to street life, through introduction to criminal opportunities and involvement in street crime, to resulting risks of criminal charges, and finally to sustained role involvements in street crime. Although this causal sequence may be generic, we propose that it can also vary in relation to urban context. Thus, the sequence we outline may help to explain how high rates of street crime are sustained and intensified in cities that adopt crime control models, such as Vancouver, and alternatively mitigated in cities that adopt social welfare models, such as Toronto.

As noted earlier, however, convincingly establishing the viability of the sociogenic influences requires a serious consideration of issues raised in the ontogenetic models introduced earlier. This strategy may also help to specify where sociogenic forces apply more and less prominently. We suggest that sociogenic forces probably are more salient causes of nonviolent street crimes such as theft, using or selling drugs, and prostitution, whereas ontogenetic factors are more significantly involved in the causation of violent crime.

Street Life and Street Crime

Our qualitative data indicate that the core of the street crime experience to which homeless youth are exposed involves theft, drugs, prostitution, and violence. Summaries of their involvement in crime indicate that many street youth, particularly those with lengthy street careers, move in and out of these activities to sustain and support their existence on the street. For example, after being kicked out of his Montreal home, Pierre initially headed for Toronto. In the ensuing years, he hitchhiked throughout Canada and the United States, living on and off the street, working at several low and unskilled jobs, panhandling, and as the following indicates, taking advantage of a variety of opportunities in the illegal economy:

> Well, I'm far from a drug dealer, but I've probably sold more drugs than I stole. . . . I've never really been involved in prostitution, but um, I did the odd deals for people and made a couple of bucks on the side.

Pierre's experiences closely resemble those described by many youth. As another example, consider Jordy's history of involvement in street crime:

> I was selling a bit of drugs here and there, stealing still, doing some shoplifting – videos and records from stores, clothing, everything basically. Just being a hustler, man, just going out and hustling money wherever which way I could. If I could con some old man on the street for five bucks, I'd do it.

Notwithstanding this diversity, some youth avoided certain activities. For example, approximately 77 percent of youth who were involved in the drug trade had not worked in prostitution; about one-third of those who had stolen things on the street reported no involvement in drug dealing; and more than three-quarters had avoided the sex trade.

In Chapter Two, we noted that violence is an integral part of street life and arises in a variety of contexts. One of the most common occurrences involves the instrumental use of force. The willingness to use violence as a means to an end is captured in Santori's reply to our question of how she coped when she was short of money: "I go sell dope or beat the shit out of someone and take their money, right? It doesn't matter." Comments by Keith and Paul further highlight the use of violence for economic gains. Both youth were involved in street robbery, but their individual experiences draw attention to the different forms that this crime takes. Keith reported that:

> I started rolling people like a few times. Um, we um, three of us would, um, kick them in the face or whatever. Go through their pockets and take whatever was there. Whatever they had.

Paul's approach added a further component involving fraud:

> I've done some fraud stuff with the welfare. Like uh, but this is all gonna be fast, right? You gotta go and beat somebody up in the nighttime and take their ID . . . and the next morning . . . you go and you get a bunch of emergency welfare money on this guy's ID, and cash the check real quick.

As expected, many youth report that they were also the victims of violent street robberies, and as the following accounts illustrate, these were not restricted to thefts of money. Jake frequently sold marijuana on the Yonge Street strip and reported that he had been attacked several times while dealing:

> Yeah, just selling hash. Some people tried to mug me, and I got shot in the leg, you know. . . . And I was like, in a lot of pain. . . . Another time, I got shot in the rear-end. . . . It went straight through. . . . I had a friend pour some Jack Daniel's on it. Boom – right on it.

Brad also spoke about street robberies of drug sellers: "Well, I've seen people get stabbed. I saw one guy get shot in the head, like right in the throat right here [pointing to his neck] . . . and it was over crack."

Violence also emerges as a punishment or a deterrent. Continuing the behavior patterns of her stepfather, mother, and siblings, Jamie related several incidents in which she used violence as a means of disciplining those who behaved in ways she deemed inappropriate. Recalling an attack on a woman who had told other street people that she was "squealing" to the police, Jamie reported: "I took it in my own jurisdiction to beat the living shit out of her. And I beat her up, took her leather coat, and walked away." Several other youth also saw violence as a means of controlling the disreputable behaviors of others. Boomer personified popular images of a skinhead: brush cut, Doc Marten boots, jeans and suspenders, and sporting several blue-ink tattoos. He made it quite clear that force was the best way to discipline others:

> If any of my friends start doing crack, I'll kick the shit out of them. They'd be going off real quick man, you know. I told my friend, Ray, I catch you sniffing glue, I'll kick the fuck out of you, straight up.

Francine shared this perspective and argued that in many cases, violence was an effective and necessary means of stopping street friends from hurting themselves:

> Downtown street life is like, everyone cares for you. They watch out for you, like they tell you what you're doing wrong, by like violence. Any way they can help . . . just to prove that sometimes violence can help a person stop what they're doing . . . like doing crack. They'd beat the living piss out of them, to just like, stop them.

Given the frequency of violence, it is not surprising that youth also used force, or the violence of their friends, to protect themselves and avenge previous assaults. This emphasis on the importance of friends who could protect them and "beat up" others who bothered or threatened them is reflected in one of Vince's comments. Vince left home at 19. He initially stayed with several friends, but his money and his welcome soon ran out. He ended up on the street when he was ejected from a local hostel for arguing with a worker. There he met several youth who shared his interest in the fantasy/role-playing game Dungeons and Dragons, and together they formed a loosely connected street family. According to Vince, his street friends were his prime source of protection:

> Uh, somebody beats you up, you can always talk to them [street friends], and they'll get somebody to beat them up; or if, you know, if somebody's threatening to kill you, they'll speak to them; if they don't listen to speaking, they'll beat them up.

A further component of street violence is its expressive side, when youth use it as a way of dealing with frustrations in their lives. In many cases, this violence was directed at close friends or intimate partners. Victor met Terry at one of the agencies that counsel street youth. Together with several other youth, they formed a street family and eventually started an intimate relationship. They lived together in squats, apartments, and on the street. Reflecting back on this relationship, Victor said:

> It's not that I'm a, I'm a physical person, but I have been physical with her. I had a hard time expressing myself to her, and because I couldn't do that, I'd take my anger out on her, or take it out on the closest thing to me . . . smash a wall, a window, something, somebody.

As illustrated by one of Kathy's experiences, violence might also be more randomly directed:

> I beat this girl, really, really bad. I was on acid. I was just mad at the whole world. I just wanted anybody to beat up, and she was pouring, bleeding, and I was just hitting her with a steel bar and everything, and everybody's saying, "What?" and I'm saying to everybody, "Am I hurting her yet?"

It is clearly the case that, as a group, street youth are more involved in violent events than other youth. As we suggest at the outset of this chapter, ontogenetic forces, reflected in violence against parents and persistence in problem behavior across the life course, may signal a continuity in street youths' involvement in such events. Alternatively, their nonviolent crime may be more strongly influenced by sociogenic forces, such as the kind of city environment in which adolescents are located.

The Summer Panel Study

The analysis involving the foregoing ideas and presented in this chapter uses the panel data collected in the cities of Toronto and Vancouver. Obviously, our use of these data is motivated by our interest in the increased sociogenic variation that results from differences in the ways that these cities have responded to problems involving street youth. The availability of multiwave panel data also is valuable for verifying the temporal basis of the causal sequences explored in this and other chapters.

We collected our Toronto and Vancouver data during the summer of 1992 in three waves of interviews with street youth who were 16 to 24 years of age. The design of this panel study is detailed in the Appendix to this

volume. Overall, we surveyed 482 youth: 330 in Toronto and 152 in Vancouver. Three weeks later, we began our second-wave interviews and relocated 80 percent of the Toronto respondents and 74 percent of the
Vancouver respondents. After another three weeks, we began our third-wave
interviews and were able to locate 52 percent of the Toronto sample and 58
percent of the Vancouver sample. The quantitative analysis presented in this
chapter is limited to the 376 respondents retained for the first two waves of
this study.

Operationalizing a Model of Street Crime in Two Cities

In Table 5.1, we present the variables included in our model and descriptive
statistics separated by city. Over two-thirds of the respondents ($n = 264$)
were interviewed in Toronto and the rest in Vancouver ($n = 112$). City
location is the key sociogenic factor in this analysis.

We collected detailed life history calender information from respondents, going back to age 10 and beginning with questions about when they
first left home. In both cities, respondents first left home about six years
earlier; the mean age of the respondents was slightly more than 19, which
means respondents first ran away from home when they were about 13 years
old. These age and period at-risk distributions are similar across cities in
spite of gender differences: about 70 percent of the Toronto sample is male,
compared to about 56 percent of the Vancouver sample. We include the
measure of "year left home" in our analysis to control for the period of time
that youth were at risk.

A key set of variables in our model measures violence in the respondents'
families of origin. We began with our own single item asking respondents:
"While living at home, were you ever struck so hard by a parent/stepparent/
guardian that it caused a bruise or bleeding?" However, we noted earlier
that family violence does not flow only from parents toward children. For
example, Zack grew up in a Vancouver suburb and noted that he had
relatively few major problems with his parents until his early teens. At that
age, his father started using force in responding to Zack's admittedly disobe-
dient and delinquent behavior involving drug and alcohol use. When we
asked how he reacted to these quarrels, he replied:

> Me, I'd just lose it. Most of the times when we argued, I was either high or
> drunk or something. And so . . . I'd say, "Screw this, it ain't getting us
> anywhere." So I ran after him and hit him or something like that. . . . We used
> to get into these big arguments, and then, you know, then I toughened up

Table 5.1. Concepts, Indicators, and Descriptive Statistics for Toronto and Vancouver (N=376)

Concepts	Indicators	Toronto X	Toronto SD	Vancouver X	Vancouver SD
City	City Where Interviewed[a]	—	—	—	—
Year Left Home	First Time Left Home from Life History Calendar	86.871	3.873	86.134	8.004
Age	At First Interview	19.758	2.776	19.027	4.940
Gender	Interview Report[b]	.705	.457	.562	.498
Physically Abusive Parent	While living at home, were you ever struck so hard by a parent/stepparent/guardian that it caused a bruise or bleeding?[c]	1.140	1.257	1.464	1.244
Physically Abusive Father	Thinking back in your childhood, tell me how often, for the most part, was your father (stepfather, etc.) *the first* to do the following when you had differences?[d] · Threaten to hit or throw something at you · Throw something at you · Slap, kick, bite, or hit you with a fist (excluding spanking) · Hit you with something (excluding strap) · Beat you up	4.973	5.756	4.768	5.327
Physically Abusive Mother	Above items references to mother/stepmother[d]	4.742	5.380	5.563	5.814
Physically Abused Father	Above items references to respondent and father[d]	1.973	3.633	2.705	4.134
Physically Abused Mother	Above items references to respondent and mother[d]	1.201	2.572	2.313	3.763
Sexually Abusive Family Member	· When you were at home, did one of your parents (mother, stepmother, father, stepfather) or other family members ever suggest having sex with you (including touching or attempting to touch you sexually?)[e] · When you were at home, did one of your parents (mother, stepmother, father, stepfather) or other family members ever have or try to have sex with you?[e]	.564	1.667	.857	2.026
Nonviolent Crime at Home	· Stolen clothes from stores, etc. · Stolen food · Taken things worth between $10–$50 from store (excluding food, clothes) · Taken things worth more than $50 from store (excluding clothes) · Sold something you stole · Broken into house, store, school, etc., and taken money or things like stereo equipment · Broken into locked car to get tape deck, radio, etc. · Used credit or banking cards without owner's permission or passed bad check · Smoked marijuana, hash, etc. · Taken acid, pcp, angel dust, etc. · Sold marijuana or hashish · Sold coke, crack, or LSD[f]	11.727	13.827	18.848	6.349

Table 5.1. (cont'd.)

Concepts	Indicators	X	SD	X	SD
Violent Crime at Home	· Beaten someone up so badly they probably needed bandages or doctor[f] · Used a knife or other weapon in a fight[f] · Attacked someone with the idea of seriously hurting or killing them[f]	1.481	3.195	1.830	3.448
Nights on Street	Since leaving home, how often have you spent a night: [g] · In all-night restaurants, donut shops, etc. · Walking around · In abandoned buildings or cars	4.174	3.115	5.509	3.219
Criminal Opportunities	How often do you have a chance to make money illegally on the street?[h]	2.470	1.617	3.107	1.318
Nonviolent Street Crime (Wave 1)	See Delinquency at Home (Delinquency Scale Values)	24.496	20.866	44.652	3.051
Violent Street Crime (Wave 1)	See Delinquency at Home (Delinquency Scale Values)	2.689	3.840	4.063	4.440
Street Prostitution (Wave 1)	Since leaving home, about how many times have you had sex for money? (Delinquency Scale Values)	.932	2.319	2.063	3.311
Criminal Charges (Wave 1)	Number of reported times charged with crimes by police	1.530	1.938	2.080	2.379
Nonviolent Street Crime (Wave 2)	Nonviolent Delinquency at Home items for each day of last week[i]	3.042	5.006	7.643	7.902
Violent Street Crime (Wave 2)	Violent Delinquency at Home items for each day of last week[j]	.242	.688	.241	.661
Street Prostitution (Wave 2)	Did you work in the sex trade last week?[k]	.189	1.010	.768	1.940

[a]Toronto = 0 (70.2%), Vancouver = 1(29.8%)
[b]Female = 0, male = 1
[c]No, never = 0, yes, once or twice = 1, yes, sometimes = 2, yes, often = 3, yes, always = 4
[d]Never = 0, rarely = 1, sometimes = 2, often = 3, most of the time = 4 (5 items)
[e]Never = 0, once or twice = 1, a few times = 2, often = 3, alot of the time = 4 (2 items)
[f]0 = 0, 1 = 1, 2 = 2, 3–4 = 3, 5–9 = 4, 10–19 = 5, 20–29 = 6, 30–59 = 7, 60+ = 8 (16 items)
[g]Never = 0, once or twice =1, often = 3, alot of the time = 4 (3 items)
[h]No chance at all = 0, less than a few times a month = 1, few times a month = 2, few times a week = 3, few times a day = 4
[i]No = 0, yes = 1 (7days, 16 items)
[j]No = 0, yes = 1 (7 days, 3 items)
[k]No = 0, yes = 1 (7 days)

and everything like that. I went into kickboxing, stuff like that, and then I started to beat up on my dad and got booted out of the house.

To distinguish and measure violence initiated by the respondents and their parents when they had differences, we use a detailed and specially adapted form of the Conflict Tactics Scale developed by Straus (1979, 1990;

see also Straus et al., 1980). This scale includes multiple measures of physical violence by sons and fathers and daughters and mothers.[2] The items asked the street youth – first in relation to themselves, and then in relation to each of their parents – to respond to the following probe about who acted first and how often did what to whom: "Parents and children use many different ways to settle their problems. Thinking back to your childhood, tell me how often, for the most part, you were *the first* to do the following when you and your [specified parent] had differences [emphasis in survey interview]?" The respondents were then asked about threats to hit or throw something; throwing something; slapping, kicking, biting, or hitting with a fist; hitting with something; and beatings.[3] The reports indicate that approximately 60 percent of street youth left families in which a parent had used violence: 55 percent indicated that their mothers or fathers had slapped them, 37 percent said that they had been hit, and 25 percent reported being beaten. For each item, the proportion of youth who used force against a parent was significantly smaller: Approximately 28 percent slapped a parent, 15 percent hit one, and 8 percent said that they had beaten their father or mother.[4]

A further two-item scale of sexual abuse within the family asked whether a family member suggested, attempted, or had sex with the respondent. We did not think it ethically or practically possible to ask in greater detail about the form these acts took or to inquire as to the family member responsible. Prior work indicates that sexual abuse overwhelmingly is perpetrated in families by stepfathers and fathers (Badgley, 1984; Browne and Finkelhor, 1986; Finkelhor, 1993, 1994a,b). Overall, 16 percent of respondents indicated that they had been sexually abused. Comparing abuse across the sample, all measures of violence and sexual abuse are higher in Vancouver than in Toronto, except for physical abuse by fathers.

We use three different time frames to measure involvement in youth crime: before leaving home, since leaving home until the first-wave interview, and for the week preceding the second-wave interview. Thirteen nonviolent and three violent acts and acts of prostitution are scaled separately for the simulated three waves. The nonviolent items include theft and larceny and using and selling drugs, whereas the violent acts refer to three behaviors that reflect the use of excessive if not brutal force: beating someone up so badly that they probably needed bandages or a doctor, using a knife or other weapon in a fight, and attacking someone with the idea of seriously hurting or killing them. While at home, Vancouver youth reported more violent and especially nonviolent crime than Toronto youth.

Perhaps the key intervening variable in our model measures nights spent on the street. This variable reflects the influence of the nomadic search for shelter that we describe in Chapter Two, and constitutes a foreground class condition of the kind discussed in Chapter Four. Our respondents most often reported spending their nights in three distinct ways: walking around the city, in all-night restaurants and donut shops, and in abandoned cars or buildings. The following three accounts capture these common ways of spending nights on the street. The first describes Mary's initial introduction to the streets:

So I was on the streets trying to figure out where the hell I am supposed to go. First I had some guys talking to me. I just kept walking with my head down. Just kept walking. Then another guy said, "Oh, you'd make a lot of money," and this and that. I just said, "Thanks guy, bye." And I walked and walked and walked. Then I sat on . . . a bench right there by one of the bus stops. Sat on the bench, I just sat there like this, and I fell asleep like this for about half an hour. Looked at my watch . . . got up, started walking again. . . . Oh, my, God. . . . Going straight up the hill, and I was going "Oh no." So I was just walking around, and walking and walking and walking, and um . . . I don't know, I decided . . . I just go, "What the hell am I doing up here? There's nothing up here." And I guess in my mind, back of my mind, I had, uh, wanted to go home, and so, I said, "No, man, I'm not going home. No, no, no." I walked all the way back downtown. I walked all night.

Abandoned buildings and cars are also common places to spend nights. Paul's description of several squats indicates the diversity of this alternative type of shelter, as well as its drawbacks:

Like there used to be a house on George Street there, by the Seaton House [an adult male hostel] there, that was, you know, abandoned and condemned and all this, but somebody had beaten a hole in the basement window and stuff. There, there'd be like, sometimes there'd be like ten or twenty people there, you know. I used to sleep there once in a while. There was also this parking garage up on Bleaker Street. I guess, I guess they were building the building and they finished the parking garage but they ran out of money, 'cause there was nothing above it, right? And somebody sawed some bars off the window or something. There was a bunch of uh, these uh, male pros- titutes and transvestites and that, that were living down there like full time, right? They were all crack addicts and that, and some of them were pretty crazy and stuff. Pretty weird. 'Cause you go in there, and it's like pitch, pitch black. There's no windows. Obviously it's all underground so, and there's no electricity, right? . . . There's a lot of really bizarre stuff that goes on in these places. A lot of people don't know. I'm just as happy they don't know. I wish I didn't know.

While it is tempting to think of these nights on the street as transitory and socially disorganized misadventures, they are often more than that. Lisa was part of a group living on the streets. Her experiences reflect a longer-term and more organized way of spending nights on the street that involves taking advantage of commercial settings:

We stayed out at a store called Le Monde. There was a big, they had a big indent before their door, like up on the step there was a big place where the three of us used to sleep. First we just had our coats, and we stayed together during the day. . . . This girl Tracy, she could steal, she could steal anything. They'd just come out, walking out casually and everything, and have their pockets just filled with stuff. They'd steal shampoo and soap and stuff like that. And like, the doors to the Eaton Center open early because of the subway, and no one was ever in the bathroom down by the food court. So we'd go into the bathroom, and we'd wash our hair, and we'd wash up – like we'd bathe in there. That's what we'd do before anybody came in. We'd do that just so we'd be clean for the day, and we'd do our makeup and everything, then we'd go out and put the stuff in the locker and lock it. Just like we didn't live on the streets.

The scale we create captures exposure to the risks that these kinds of settings pose by asking how often respondents spent nights on the street or in squats. Vancouver youth indicated that they spent about one-third more nights on the street than Toronto youth; this difference clearly reflects the absence of shelters and reduced access to support services in Vancouver discussed earlier.

We measure direct exposure to criminal opportunities by asking respondents, "How often do you have a chance to make money illegally on the street?" Similar to their greater exposure to street life, Vancouver youth reported having more criminal opportunities on the street than Toronto youth.

The final links in our model first involve the measurement of street crime since leaving home. We measure first-wave involvement in violent and non-violent crime with items identical to those for illegal activities at home. We measure prostitution by asking, "since leaving home, about how many times have you had sex for money?" Vancouver youth were especially likely to be involved in nonviolent street crime, with average scores nearly double those of Toronto youth, and they report greater involvement in the sex trade. We also include an item that measures the number of times that respondents reported they were charged with crimes by the police since arriving on the street. In Chapter Eight, we elaborate on the role of police sanctions; for now, it is sufficient to note that our model suggests that police charging is an important part of the process of becoming extensively involved in crime, and we expect this process to be more prominent in Vancouver, where respondents were about a third more likely to report being charged.

The second-wave crime measures in our study parallel our earlier items, except that respondents were asked whether they had engaged in the various activities on each of the days of the preceding week. Although little or no difference was found between Toronto and Vancouver involvement in violent street crime, the Vancouver youth more than doubled the Toronto youth in their involvement in nonviolent crime, as well as being more involved in prostitution.

Estimating Models of Street Crime

Since being exposed to the street is such a salient transitional event in the sociogenic part of our model, we begin our analysis in Table 5.2 with the results of regressing nights on the street on the predetermining factors in our model. These variables include year left home, city, age, gender, a combined measure of violent and nonviolent delinquency at home, and various measures of family violence and sexual abuse. This step in our analysis is important because it includes data reduction decisions about the many measures that we have of violence at home.

The first equation estimated in Table 5.2 includes only the single "bruised and bleeding" measure of violence by parents, along with sexual abuse and other predetermining variables. Physically abusive parents has the strongest effect nights on the street, but with this and other variables held constant, younger respondents and those in Vancouver also spent more nights on the street. Both crime at home and year left home have weakly significant effects. Recall that early offending is a globally absorbing measure of ontogenetic differences in self-control in Gottfredson and Hirschi's theory, and year first left home can be regarded in a similar way. Nonetheless, other results of this first equation are consistent with our expectation: Sociogenic differences in abuse by parents and city-

Table 5.2. OLS Regressions of Nights Spent on Street on Abusive Home Experiences and Exogenous Variables

(Eq.)	1			2		
Variable	*b*	SE	ß	*b*	SE	ß
Year Left Home	−.094	.049	−.102*	−.051	.030	−.086*
City (Vancouver = 1)	.837	.352	.122**	.965	.360	.140***
Age	−.162	.081	−.128**	−.160	.083	−.126*
Gender (Male = 1)	.038	.357	.006	.065	.371	.010
Nonviolent Crime at Home	.019	.011	.085*	.021	.011	.097**
Sexually Abusive Parent	.014	.091	.008	.041	.096	.023
Physically Abusive Parent	.574	.126	.300***			
Physically Abusive Father				.062	.030	.112**
Physically Abusive Mother				.052	.031	.091*
Physically Abused Father				.056	.046	.067
Physically Abused Mother				−.031	.062	−.030
Intercept	27.269			27.861		
Adjusted R^2	.130			.102		

* $p \leq .10$
** $p \leq .05$
***$p \leq .01$

specific experiences account for variation in exposure to the street in Toronto and Vancouver.

The second equation in Table 5.2 replaces our single-item measure of parental violence with the multi-item scales that distinguish physical abuse by mothers and fathers and toward mothers and fathers.[5] The maternal and paternal abuse scales have weaker effects but are similar to that for the single-item measure in equation 1. Results presented in Table 5.2 also reveal that effects of youths' abuse of their parents are nonsignificant. These measures of abuse of parents by youth can be regarded as especially reflective of ontogenetic forces, since they indicate problematic behaviors that may originate with the youth involved. Although the violence against parents variables have no significant influence here, we combine them and retain them in our subsequent analysis. Meanwhile, we restrict our consideration of parental abuse to the single-item (i.e., "bruised and bleeding") measure because in this analysis, this single, more parsimonious measure produces comparable but somewhat stronger results than the separate parental violence scales. Regardless of the parental abuse measures used, and in addition to their effects, Table 5.2 also indicates a sizable effect of being in Vancouver. This effect provides support for a sociogenic effect of city on the exposure of youth to the street.

In Table 5.3, we turn to a more general exploration of ontogenetic and sociogenic influences on three kinds of street crime. Our theoretical expectation is that sociogenic influences should be greater for nonviolent street crimes involving theft and drugs, and probably prostitution, whereas ontogenetic influences should be greater for the more violent forms of street crime. The sociogenic influence of greatest interest in our analysis is the city where these youth are interviewed, and youth's abuse of their parents is the most striking example of an ontogenetic influence.

The results presented in Table 5.3 include the bivariate and unmediated causal relationships of city and abuse of parents with the three measures of street crime in the first- and second-wave interviews. The unmediated causal relationships are total causal effects that hold constant exogenous, predetermining effects of year first left home, age, gender, abuse by and of parents, and home measures of nonviolent and violent crime. The results are as theoretically expected: The unmediated sociogenic city effects are by far the largest for nonviolent street crime in the first and second waves, and the ontogenetic abuse of parents coefficients are only significant for violent street crime, again in both the first and second waves. Interestingly, there are also significant sociogenic city effects for street prostitution in the first and second waves, and there is a smaller city effect for violent crime in the first wave. Overall, the results in Table 5.3 reveal that the sociogenic city effects are most prominent in relation to nonviolent street crimes. Nonetheless, the effects of the more ontogenetic abuse of parents on violent street crime are also notable.

A fuller sense of the ways in which the ontogenetic and sociogenic factors in our model affect street crime can be obtained from the path diagrams presented in Figures 5.1 through 5.3. These figures are trimmed models that include only statistically significant ($p \leq .05$) standardized path coefficients larger than .10 in strength. The first of these diagrams is for nonviolent street crime.

As past ontogenetic research and Gottfredson and Hirschi's theory predict, nonviolent crime at home has notable direct effects on involvement in these activities in subsequent waves (see Figure 5.1). However, we do not find a significant effect of youth abusing parents. Moreover, taking the

Table 5.3. Bivariate and Unmediated Causal Relationships of City and Abuse of Parents with Three Types of Street Crime Measured in First- and Second-Wave Interviews [a]

Type of street crime	First wave		Second wave	
	r	ß	r	ß
A. City Coefficients				
Nonviolent Street Crime	.394	.312***	.331	.262***
Street Prostitution	.192	.182***	.192	.196***
Violent Street Crime	.154	.110***	−.001	−.028
B. Abuse of Parents Coefficients				
Nonviolent Street Crime	.121	.010	.144	.061
Street Prostitution	.100	−.004	.069	.023
Violent Street Crime	.175	.142***	.210	.180***

[a] Unmediated relationships are total causal effects that hold constant exogenous, predetermining effects of year first left home, age, gender, abuse by parents, and home measures of nonviolent and violent delinquency.
* $p \leq .10$
** $p \leq .05$
*** $p \leq .01$

stability of crime and its globally absorbing ontogenetic forces into account, there remains substantial evidence of sociogenic influence. The latter is reflected in the theoretically emphasized paths of influence bold-faced in Figure 5.1. These influences are exercised directly and indirectly and can be summarized as follows: They stem from physically abusive parents and city and, as expected, flow through spending nights on the street, criminal opportunities, involvement in nonviolent street crime, and police charges.

A boxed insert in Figure 5.1 decomposes the estimated effects of city on the two waves of nonviolent street crime. The total effects of city are large in the first and second waves. Yet less than a quarter of these effects can be accounted for with predetermining ontogenetic forces that include offending at home. In both waves, the direct effects of city are substantial, and the indirect effects transmitted through the causal chains that we have identified are notable. There is considerable evidence in this model that features of these cities lead to different levels of street youth involvement in nonviolent crime.

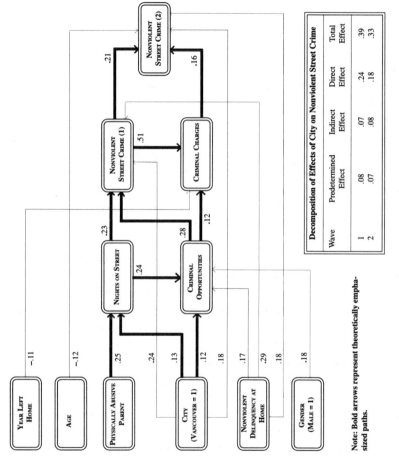

Decomposition of Effects of City on Nonviolent Street Crime

Wave	Predetermined Effect	Indirect Effect	Direct Effect	Total Effect
1	.08	.07	.24	.39
2	.07	.08	.18	.33

Note: Bold arrows represent theoretically emphasized paths.

Figure 5.1 Trimmed model of nonviolent street crime in Toronto and Vancouver (standardized effects, $p < .05$).

A final note should be made about nonviolent offending. When models of nonviolent crime were estimated separately in Toronto and Vancouver, the resulting path coefficients were quite similar across settings, suggesting that the effects of variables like parental abuse and city are additive rather than multiplicative with regard to city. However, there is one notable exception to this pattern involving a significant interaction of city and nonviolent street crime on police charges, with an effect of about .6 in Vancouver and .3 in Toronto. This difference indicates that involvement in nonviolent street crime is significantly more likely to lead to police charges in Vancouver than in Toronto. This is, of course, consistent with the operation of a crime control model in Vancouver.

Figure 5.2 presents a model of violent street crime in Toronto and Vancouver. There are several striking aspects of this model, especially in comparison with Figure 5.1. First, the ontogenetic effects of youth abusing parents are reflected in the direct effects of this variable on violent street crime in both the first and second waves. Second, there is a further strong and direct effect of violent offending at home on violent street crime in the first wave, and through violent street crime in the first wave on the same kind of violence in the second wave. Third, there is no direct sociogenic city effect. These findings underscore the force of ontogenetic factors in the exploration of this particular (violent) kind of street crime. Meanwhile, in contrast to nonviolent street crimes, the effects of spending nights on the street and criminal opportunities – key sociogenic influences in our model – are notably lower in the first wave for violent crime. Nonetheless, and notwithstanding controls for ontogenetic influences, these sociogenic paths of influence are apparent in this model of violent street crime.

A final model of street prostitution in Toronto and Vancouver is presented in Figure 5.3. Since prostitution at home was rarely, if ever, reported by our respondents, we include a measure that combines the violent and nonviolent crime at home scales; however, its effects are not substantial. As might be expected, street prostitution has more in common with nonviolent rather than violent street crime: Effects of physical abuse, city, nights on the street, and criminal opportunities again reflect the significant role of sociogenic factors. The key difference in this model involves the effects of sexual abuse at home on spending nights on the street and on first-wave street prostitution.

The Streets of Toronto and Vancouver

Criminological research has not made great progress in recent years in understanding the roles of ontogenetic and sociogenic causes of crime.

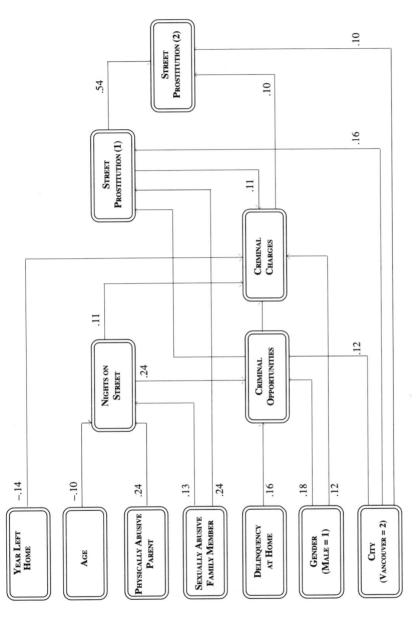

Figure 5.3 Trimmed model of street prostitution in Toronto and Vancouver (standardized effects, p < .05).

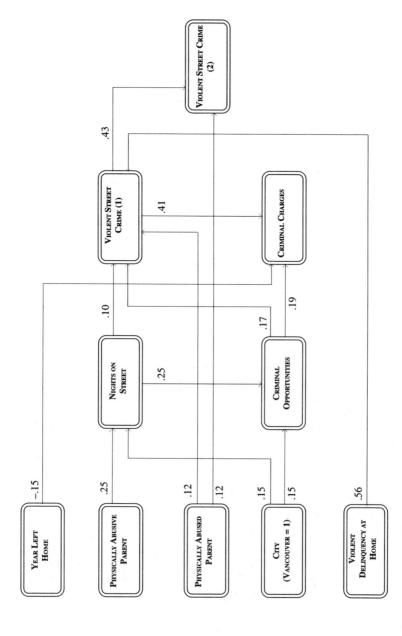

Figure 5.2 Trimmed model of violent street crime in Toronto and Vancouver (standardized effects, p < .05).

Indeed, these sources of crime are seldom considered simultaneously in crime research; when they are, little attention is given to the relative effects of ontogenetic and sociogenic factors for specific kinds of crimes. In the absence of informed scholarship, concerned citizens and policy analysts struggle with individual and social attributions of criminal responsibility and related decisions about intervention. A purpose of the analysis presented in this chapter is to examine the relative roles of ontogenetic and sociogenic variables in the causation of different kinds of crime among Toronto and Vancouver street youth; these adolescents experience considerable variation in individual and social factors associated with crime.

Our findings underline the likelihood that some crimes committed by street youth have ontogenetic origins. In particular, we found that violent street crimes display continuity over the life course, as evidenced both by the recurrence of these behaviors while at home and on the street and by their anticipation in youth-initiated violence against parents. There also is little variation across the cities of Toronto and Vancouver in the occurrence of violent crime, which is consistent with the salience of ontogeny in the causation of these events.

However, sociogenic forces are more prominent among the more common, nonviolent crimes. This is reflected most clearly in the strong effect of being in Vancouver as contrasted with Toronto on involvement in crimes involving theft, drugs, and prostitution. We anticipated that Toronto's social welfare model – providing access to overnight shelters and social services – would diminish involvement in these street crimes, whereas Vancouver's crime control model and absence of assistance would make them more common. A key difference between these city settings involves exposure to criminal opportunities. As a result of spending more time on the street, Vancouver street youth are exposed to more opportunities for offending. This exposure to the street and its criminal opportunities intensifies a process of criminal embeddedness that is explored further in the following chapter. Meanwhile, Vancouver youth are also more likely to be charged by the police for their nonviolent crimes, which is, of course, also consistent with a crime control model. More generally, the direct and indirect effects of taking to the streets in these different cities illustrate the significant roles that sociogenic factors play in the causation of nonviolent crime.

The natural variation observed in this analysis between street experiences in Vancouver and Toronto has no certain generalization to other urban settings. It is difficult to know where these two cities might fit in the range of possibilities presented by Canadian cities, much less those of other countries. Nonetheless, the findings of this analysis at least support the view that urban crime and social policies affect the occurrence of crime, especially nonviolent and sex-related street crime. Although some violent crimes, and even some nonviolent crimes, likely have ontogenetic origins, and although it is important to take ontogenetic factors into account, the role of sociogenic factors looms large. On balance, our results offer considerable support for the view that a social welfare approach to the difficulties of homeless youth can mitigate problems of involvement in street crime.

Criminal Embeddedness
and Criminal Capital

WE PEERED FURTHER into the "black box" of street crime by introducing an indicator of "criminal opportunities" in the previous chapter. As anticipated, this variable had sizable direct effects on all types of criminal activity, as well as intervening between our foreground measure of situational adversity (i.e., nights on the street) and crime. Now we explore how criminal opportunities facilitate the embeddedness of street youth in associations that lead to the acquisition of "criminal capital."

Broadly conceived, criminal opportunities are the situational characteristics necessary for a crime to occur. There are several recent conceptualizations of criminal opportunities, including Hindelang et al.'s (1978) lifestyle opportunity theory, Cohen and Felson's (1979) routine activities approach, and the opportunity perspective of Cornish and Clarke (1986). In general, these approaches define criminal opportunities as meetings of motivated offenders and potential victims in settings unsupervised by agents of social control.

We see a further neglected dimension to criminal opportunities. Aside from the presence of potential victims and the absence of social control agents, an important determinant of a criminal opportunity is the potential offender's definition of a situation as one suited for offending. Not all people define an unlocked vehicle, a lone pedestrian on a dimly lit street, a poorly guarded business, or an empty house as possible sites for offending. These settings only become opportunities when a person's understanding of the social world translates them into potential sites of criminality. We suggested in Chapter Four that adverse circumstances encouraged youth to interpret situations as criminal opportunities; however, other factors also stimulate this process.

Conceiving criminal opportunities as contingent on interpretations re-
calls insights of one of North America's preeminent but recently neglected
criminologists, Edwin Sutherland (see Matsueda, 1988). In the next section,
we summarize aspects of Sutherland's theory and demonstrate how his ideas
not only add to our understanding of criminal opportunities but also
resonate with recent work on the importance of social embeddedness and
capital for explaining social behavior.

Differential Association and Tutelage in Crime

According to Sutherland (1947), most criminal behavior is learned through
associations with people who violate the law. These criminal connections
provide a forum for acquiring techniques as well as motives, drives, rational-
izations, and attitudes that facilitate crime.[1] People adopt criminal definitions when this exposure exceeds contact with noncriminal behaviors and
attitudes, and they are most likely to engage in crime when they encounter
opportunities to translate these definitions into actions. In other words,
differential association provides people with the knowledge, skills, and
definitions that encourage them to interpret situations as potential opportunities for offending. Without these experiences, an unlocked car, for
example, might be as likely to cause concern about the safety of the owner's
property as to invite thoughts about burglary.

Sutherland's (1942/1956) interviews with professional thieves provided
the impetus for his theory. According to Sutherland, careers in this type of
crime follow from "contact with professional thieves, reciprocal confidence
and appreciation, a crisis situation, and tutelage" (Sutherland, 1937, p.
212). In focusing on associations and tutelage, Sutherland emphasizes
learning from mentors who pass on criminal skills; at the same time, he
recognizes the importance of social structure and context by noting the role
of a crisis in stimulating opportunities for tutelage and offending.

Although differential association is the cornerstone of Sutherland's
work, he also highlights the structural determinants of these associations –
specifically, normative conflict and differential social organization. Sutherland (1947) argues that normative conflicts arise in heterogeneous societies
where groups disagree about norms, values, and interests. Differential social
organization translates this conflict into crime by influencing the probability (i.e., through unemployment, living in a high-crime area, or lack of
formal and informal sources of social control) of criminal associations,
behavior patterns, and opportunities. We argue that homelessness and
street life represent important sources of the differential social organization

that Sutherland envisioned as contributing to the emergence of crime. It is noteworthy that Sutherland (1942/1956) recognized the importance of homelessness in his discussion of professional theft, an insight probably related to his early experiences as a researcher during the Great Depression (Sutherland and Locke, 1936).

The result of Sutherland's work is an explanation of crime that generalizes across class boundaries and draws attention to four elements: affiliation with criminals in intimate personal groups, communication with these individuals about deviant attitudes, tutelage in techniques for specific criminal endeavors, and the adoption of definitions that legitimate law violation.[2] In the following section of this chapter, we integrate many of Sutherland's insights with more recent contributions; however, we suggest two important modifications to his ideas.

First, we noted earlier that Sutherland emphasizes the importance of crisis situations in explaining the genesis of professional theft; however, in Chapter Four, we observed that in subsequent works, Sutherland downplayed the role of situational effects, focusing instead on definitions. We suggest that the relationship between situations and definitions is more complex than Sutherland indicates and reflects an ongoing process in which each factor influences the other over time.

Second, Sutherland maintains that although some crimes do not require specific skills, or involve skills that can be learned in noncriminal environments, "most require training" (1947, p. 213; see also 1942/1956 and 1944/1956).[3] We modify this statement, arguing that most crimes do not vary in terms of the skills that they "require" but in terms of the level of skill that untrained and trained people use to commit them. A person with little training or adeptness can open an unlocked door, grab the first thing they see, and later sell it to a friend; they can easily steal an unlocked vehicle with the keys in the ignition; and they can divide the drugs they purchase and peddle some to a friend. However, instruction and proficiency enhance the probability of acquiring more advanced techniques for gaining entry into locked and secure places, for stealing and fencing a sizable quantity of goods, for hot-wiring and stripping a vehicle, and for organizing and supervising a group of drug holders, runners, and dealers.

Criminal Embeddedness and Criminal Capital

Sutherland's emphasis on the link between associations and crime has several parallels to more recent work on embeddedness in social networks. According to Granovetter (1985, p. 487), purposive economic actions, including criminal ones, are embedded within networks of social relations. These actions are influenced by the composition of networks and the acquisition of information from network members. Granovetter's work on "the strength of weak ties" (1973), "getting a job" (1974), and job mobility (1992) supports his thesis that social contacts and the interactions they engender expedite employment entry and advancement by allowing people to share information and to bargain and negotiate with one another. As anticipated, those most embedded have the greatest access to information and usually enjoy greater occupational success.

As with Sutherland, Granovetter (1985, 1992) highlights social structure as facilitating social action, yet he cautions that social structure alone is not determinative. While recognizing that background factors (e.g., class, family, and school experiences) influence economic action, Granovetter maintains that people's embeddedness in foreground structural relations may have more telling effects; a social network exerts its greatest effect when it generates trust, establishes expectations, and reinforces social beliefs and norms.

Coleman (1988, 1990) regards social embeddedness as a valuable form of "social capital." According to Coleman, social capital resembles other types of capital in that it facilitates productive action: It generates obligations, expectations, trustworthiness, information channels, norms, and sanctions, all of which contribute to a person's or a group's capacities to engage in social action. Yet Coleman (1988) also notes that social capital is unique: "Unlike other forms of capital, social capital inheres in the structure of relations between actors and among actors" (p. 598). We submit that this occurs across classes and contexts, and in criminal as well as in more conventional careers.[4]

The process that Sutherland calls *tutelage* forms a bridge between Granovetter's notion of social embeddedness and Coleman's conception of social capital. Embeddedness in relationships with those already proficient in crime is a source of capital, for example, as a channel for the acquisition of information. This flow of information provides access to skills and knowledge about crime in the same way that contacts, associations, or ties in more conventional lines of work supply actors with leads to jobs and other business-related knowledge. Thus, embeddedness in ongoing criminal networks may establish the foundation for the development of a type of human capital (Schultz, 1961; G. Becker, 1964) that we call *criminal capital*. This criminal capital includes knowledge and technical skills that promote criminal activity, as well as beliefs or definitions that legitimize offending.[5]

In general, our approach to criminal opportunities and embeddedness synthesizes the insights of Granovetter, Coleman, and Sutherland and in so doing differs from more dominant explanations. Among the most important of these alternative approaches is Gottfredson and Hirschi's (1990) recent blending of sociological and psychological perspectives that focus on self-control. As noted in the preceding chapter, this theory explains crime as the failure of familial socialization to establish self-control early in the life course. From this perspective, criminal behaviors are crudely impulsive, poorly planned activities that require little learning or skill and reflect inadequate self-control and a general insensitivity to others (see also Wilson and Herrnstein, 1985).

An indifference to others also figures prominently in economic explanations of crime. These approaches treat offending as the result of cost–benefit analyses in which actors weigh the rewards of crime against the projected likelihood or costs of punishment (G. Becker, 1968; Ehrlich, 1973; G. Becker and Landes, 1974; Block and Heineke, 1975; Witte, 1980; Schmidt and Witte, 1984; Sah, 1991). These explanations assume that actors choose criminal activities in the same autonomous fashion that they presumably select more conventional economic behavior. From this perspective, explaining criminal behavior does not require "ad hoc concepts of differential association" (G. Becker, 1968, p. 176) nor a "resort to hypotheses regarding . . . social conditions" (Ehrlich, 1973, p. 521).

Although we accept that crime can be characterized by antisocial lapses in self-control and rational-choice calculations, we maintain that much crime is more notably influenced by the criminal embeddedness and criminal capital that deviant social contacts can engender. By underemphasizing these possibilities, self-control and rational-choice theories encourage a more utilitarian approach to crime rather than the more social perspective suggested here. In our view, many street crimes tend not to be the asocial, unplanned, unskilled activities that recent sociological, psychological, and economic theories imply. Moreover, in emphasizing impersonal and autonomous features of criminal behavior, the foregoing approaches reflect a growing tendency to ignore the idea that, like getting a job, getting into crime is a social phenomenon.

In this chapter, we focus on three street crimes that provide economic returns: drug selling, theft, and prostitution. Separately analyzing these activities is consistent with Sutherland's (1947) approach and allows us to examine the saliency of crime-specific relations and the acquisition of a distinctive set of definitions, skills, and information. However, we are not suggesting that these offenses represent criminal specializations or types of criminal careers. As we note in Chapter Five, there is considerable diversity among offending street youth; some report involvement in several types of crimes, and others are more selective. We distinguish these activities to explore how embeddedness in specific relationships (e.g., with those involved in theft) and exposure to particular criminal resources (e.g., offers to teach break-and-enter skills) enhance involvement in various types of crime.

We do not assume that street crimes necessarily mirror the level of sophistication of professional theft analyzed in Sutherland's work; however, we do suggest that instruction and mastery contribute to these crimes. For example, drug dealing is enhanced by knowing something about how to divide drugs and to "cut" them so that customers will not notice the adulteration. Serious theft involves some proficiency in the operation of specific tools and knowledge about how to choose sites for a break and enter, as well as where and how to sell stolen merchandise. Similarly, prostitution involves knowing where to work, the risks involved with certain activities (e.g., using drugs while with a customer), and how to recognize "bad dates." All of these offenses are facilitated further by organizational and negotiating skills, particularly in working with other offenders and handling potential victims and customers, and an ability to distinguish the latter from undercover police (Jacobs, 1993).

Ethnographic Evidence of Embeddedness

Classic as well as more recent ethnographies provide considerable evidence of the role of embeddedness and criminal capital for particular illegal behaviors. In *The Gang*, Thrasher (1927) notes that associations with gang members (e.g., pp. 252–66, 369–408) and criminally inclined adults (e.g., pp. 149, 154) provide a forum for the observation and transmission of the skills of thievery. More than half a century later, Sullivan (1989) provides a rich description of the communication of skills and values in the social organization of adolescent crime in three inner-city New York neighborhoods. Although Sullivan acknowledges that relatively unskilled youth also offend, he reports (e.g., pp. 140–42) that most thieves attribute their success to the acquisition of skills learned from other, more experienced youth and adults.

Sullivan notes that instruction in drug selling is also common and is often facilitated by associations with dealers and consignments from those already working in the drug trade. Padilla (1992, p. 121) makes comparable observations in his study of a Puerto Rican gang in Chicago. Padilla reports that new recruits often achieve competence in theft by "working together with another gang member who has experience, whose role is that of mentor and leader." After demonstrating expertise in stealing, new members progress to running, dealing, and occasionally distributing drugs. For most youth, this is a "gradual process of learning skills and establishing a network of relationships with significant members of the organization in order to become dealers" (p. 151). Bourgois's (1995, pp. 174–212, 264–67) study of East Harlem crack dealers further details the role of tutelage and associations with offenders in encouraging marginalized youth involvement in crime.

Research on adolescents who sell sex for money yields parallel findings. In a study of male hustlers in Toronto, Visano (1987) describes the apprenticeship, sponsorship, emotional support, and sharing of trade secrets and legitimating devices that are centerpieces of adolescent prostitution. According to Visano, "the requirements of hustling are learned by direct assistance, imitation, and repetition" (p. 130) in which "on-the-job instructions are anchored in friendship associations" (p. 131). Other studies of adolescent male (e.g., Reiss, 1961; Luckenbill, 1985) and female prostitution (see Weisberg, 1985) document similar patterns, although for young women, instruction from a pimp or older hustlers working for a pimp may be more common (Weisberg, 1985).

Although these ethnographies support our thesis that embeddedness in criminal associations is an important source of the criminal capital that enhances entry and advancement into certain crimes, our ability to generalize from these studies is limited by two factors. As we noted in Chapter One, most ethnographies use small samples: Sullivan's research involved thirty-eight youth; Padilla and Bourgois each studied a few dozen drug dealers; and Visano spoke with thirty-three hustlers. Second, the subjects of these studies are usually selected on the basis of their criminal activities or membership in juvenile gangs. These samples provide little variation in crime (i.e., there are few nonparticipants or youth who infrequently offend), making it difficult to test competing explanations of illegal behavior.

Alternatively, our data are well suited to studying criminal embeddedness and capital. Unlike the gang youth studied in most ethnographies, many street youth report little or no involvement in crime (see Chapters Three and Four). Furthermore, compared with adolescents sampled in most high-school surveys, adolescents who live on the street occupy structural locations that capture the differential social organization that Sutherland envisioned: They are economically marginalized; they have more extensive exposure to people involved in crime, particularly the economic crimes of the street; and they encounter little of the social control normally experienced by youth (e.g., parental and teacher supervision). In addition, the adversity of street

life makes homelessness an appropriate context to test Sutherland's view
that an emergency or crisis can place people in a precarious position that
stimulates tutelage in crime.

Talking about Tutelage

Our qualitative data provide several examples of the transference of criminal capital through embeddedness in street relationships. Consider Glen's
account of how he became involved in the drug trade:

> Uhm, I used to hang out downtown a lot where there's always drug dealers,
> right? I just hang out there with them and you know, cause they were, uhm,
> they'd do their work all day and then at night go party somewhere. So I got to
> know them pretty good. Then I started to get to know some of the guys that
> were dealing to the guys who were selling on the streets. So one day a guy just
> finally came up to me and said, uh, "Do you want to work for me?" I said
> "Sure."

As this comment suggests, accessing criminal capital is not always easy;
veteran offenders are often cautious about approaching new recruits. Thus,
establishing connections often requires considerable patience and a substantial time commitment on the part of novices.

Once connections are established, the training of recruits may take
several forms. In some cases, tutors provided insights into general skills that
facilitate offending; in other cases, instruction was more specific and on
occasion involved "on-the-job" training. A comment by Jordy reflects the
first type of exposure and refers to his mentor's instruction on how to
identify undercover police:

> I knew that there were cops dressed in ordinary clothing, but I didn't know
> that they were down there watching us . . . and he like pointed some out to
> me. He said, "Look, look around here and see if you see any cops," and you
> know, he pointed out two to me, and then I picked out another one.

This introduction was followed by a period of practice:

> Right, and there were only three that I'd seen. He goes, "Try and find the
> other three, and when you find the other three, you'll know what it's like to
> look for a cop." And so I sat there, and I watched their actions, like all these
> people, like there was about sixty people that were going up and down, and I
> sort of clued in.

Albert's description of his apprenticeship in theft captures the second type of experience in which tutelage includes training in specific techniques: "As for stealing and stuff like that, he [a street friend] showed me basically how to do it . . . breaking into cars, stealing car stereos, and breaking into houses."

As we noted previously, other tutors go beyond offering information and practice and instead provide on-the-job training during a neophyte's initial criminal experiences. This pattern is evident in Simon's introduction to the sex trade:

I was speaking with someone at [a local bar] who just happened to be a street hustler . . . and he said, "Well, I know where you can make money," and that's how I ended up being a prostitute. . . . I did a double with him the first time, and my first time we ripped him [the customer] off. He was really, really drunk, and he just wanted to see me, see me have sex with this guy. But he was really drunk, and he passed out on us, and right away [my friend] knew exactly what to do. He went through the wallet. He gave me all the money, and he took all the credit cards . . . you know, like I was very naive and I wouldn't think of doing anything with the credit cards.

As with other street youth, Simon eventually learned how to make money through the illegal use of banking and credit cards. According to Martin, the most common technique for using the former was as follows:

Uh, you grab someone's wallet, and I don't know, for some reason in them days, they'd often have this little piece of paper with their PIN number written on it. . . . I seem to get lucky like that. So you know, you just go to the bank. Well, geez, they make it easy, and just . . . [pretend to] deposit all this money into a fake envelope and then withdraw money out, wait another twenty-four hours, then do it again. And then throw the card away.

Several women described their entry into prostitution as involving being "turned out" by "boyfriends," an experience that often involved force. In Sheneika's case, her boyfriend was a man in his mid-20s; a friend of her mother, he and Sheneika had been dating for several months before he sent her to the street:

He says "Well, I'm putting you on the street and you can make money." He threatened to kill me, it was just like out of the movies. And I said, "Okay." Well he took me there. He placed me there, and said, "Stand here!" So I stood there. . . . And I actually made a lot of money.

Shortly afterward, Sheneika left her "boyfriend" and began to work independently. However, she noted that starting to work regularly in the sex trade depended on one's embeddedness in a supportive network:

> No, not anybody can stand out there. It's hard to explain. It's just the politics of the street, I guess. You got to know someone. I knew a lot of people . . . and they were working. So, when I walked down the street, and I knew half these people. They said, "If you want to make money, just stand here." And so there, there was no problem. I was protected . . . and I got taught a lot.

Other youth working in the sex trade also reported that they acquired insights about offending from people on the strip. Robert's and Dylan's experiences reflect the transactional nature of buying and selling sex. When we asked Dylan how he became involved in the sex trade, he replied:

> Actually, I'd found out from a female prostitute. Um, she was standing on the street, and I had seen her a couple of times, and so I got into saying "Hi" and things like that. And she asked me at one point what I was doing for money, and I was telling her "Nothing, I'm not working." . . . So she says "You know there's a way of making money." And that's when she came up with like prostitution. She told me about it, but like I said, "I don't know, men, it's like men, I don't do that." So she told me the area, and I didn't try it right away. I waited maybe, probably five or six months before I did it.

Robert recalled that his entry into prostitution was initiated by men he met while spending his first few nights walking the streets of Toronto searching for shelter:

> Well, I mean, being young, 16, I mean all of a sudden you have these men just hovering over you, and it's like you feel special. They were treating me nice. This isn't something I was used to . . . a lot of them would use me for sex.

As time passed, several "friends" gave Robert money and introduced him to others who were also interested in paying for sex. Looking back on these experiences, Robert concluded that:

> I definitely don't think I would have been prostituting, 'cause I mean, I would never have heard about it. I didn't know men prostituted their bodies. I did not know that. And I found that out from downtown.

The comments of several youth also highlight interconnections of need, embeddedness, and crime; these interconnections are captured in Roy's description of his introduction to prostitution:

> I just survived on what I had when I left home. I had about three hundred bucks, and that lasted me for three months. . . . After that, another guy – I'm not going to say his name – he told me about the "stroll". . . . I went up a couple of times [and] just walked around. . . . I was sort of pressured into it, but wasn't pressured. . . . [My friend said,] "That guy stopped. He wants to talk with you." Well, I don't really want to talk. It took him about fifteen minutes to coax me into going over and talking to the guy, and that's the first trick I ever pulled.

Roy added that others working in the sex trade were his only reliable source of information on where to work, what to say, how to dress, what to do with a date, and most important, what to charge:

> Right, people, when I first went, told me, "This is what we charge," and that's what I've always charged. . . . Uh, someone told me, just basically get in the car – sixty bucks. You know, just, if he wants to do anything, you start at sixty and work your way up. And I've never gone below that, 'cause that's what I was told it was.

Several youth also noted that the information and assistance that tutors provided were not always freely given. In many instances, the latter anticipated a return for their knowledge and time, expecting students to support them and help them offend, or share the profits that these novices accrued from offending on their own. As is evident in Thomas's introduction into prostitution, others expected at least some payment for their expertise:

> I went to [an agency] and, um, talked to a couple of counselors there. They recommended I get into a hostel, um, and as I was leaving, one of the guys there asked me if I was interested in making some money. I said "Sure." And then, he took me down to Boys' Town, and I started working that night. He brought me right down there. All he asked for was $40 for the information.

We refer to one other type of experience to demonstrate further the significance of tutelage; this involved youth who aspired to make money through crime but had no or limited access to criminal capital. We quote at length from Winston, who, lacking a mentor, skills, and information, was unsuccessful in his attempt to enter the drug trade:

[A street friend] he give me something [crack] right, and I'm like, "Okay."
But man, I don't know what the hell to do with it. And I'm there with him, and
after a few hours, selling with him, thinking I'm bad too. . . . And later, man,
I'm there but I didn't know where to go to get more, you know. So, I was like, I
didn't want to go out [to the crack district], 'cause next you're down there
and you're like stupid. People would sell you fake, right? I was scared-up
because you know I have this money; but what if this guy sells me shit, and I
can't go, I can't go up to those guys and say I want my money back. . . . I'm
like scared, and I didn't know how to do it, and I didn't go finally.

Later, after being "fronted" crack again by his friend, Winston had further
problems:

So I'm there and I'm cutting it up and, well, I was stupid so I went to the
park . . . and I met this girl in there, she's going, "Oh, let me show you." And I
had cut it before, and she goes, "You know, no one's going to buy that from
you." So, she's like, she's folding it up for me into small pieces . . . and I'm
looking down, and next thing when I look up, police cars, right? They're
coming up on the grass, man, and I'm like scared to death, you know. Like
holy shit. Bad man . . . and I don't know what to do.

Winston dropped the crack, and his "friend" pushed dirt over it. The police
questioned him but did not arrest him. Nonetheless, Winston's success in
drug dealing did not improve:

So I left, man. And then when I came back in the evening, I went to pick up
the stuff, and it's gone! The girl, she's the only one who knows where it is. . . .
She probably smoked all that stuff in one day, man, you know. Forget it, man.

The foregoing accounts provide evidence of the importance of embeddedness in deviant associations and the acquisition and accumulation of
criminal capital. Without embeddedness and criminal capital, youth are less
able to capitalize on criminal opportunities and to become heavily involved
in street crime. We now integrate these insights into testable models of street
crime.

Modeling Criminal Embeddedness and Capital

The key new variables in the analysis that we present next are measures of
criminal embeddedness and capital (see Table 6.1 for summary statistics).
We measure embeddedness with respondent reports of friendships estab-

lished before leaving home and after arriving on the street. As with our measures of crime, these items refer to associations with individuals involved in specific types of offending. That is, we measure separately the proportion of home and street friends who had stolen something worth more than $5 from a store, sold drugs, or worked in prostitution. As the descriptive statistics in Table 6.1 demonstrate, the youth in this study had fairly extensive contact with offenders prior to leaving home: On average, respondents reported that more than half of their friends had committed a theft and about one-third had sold drugs; however, fewer than one in five of the respondents had friends involved in the sex trade.

Respondents' reports for the period since leaving home reveal that associations with offenders increased once youth arrived on the street. The mean scores indicate that, on average, about 70 percent of street friends had stolen things, close to 60 percent had distributed drugs, and approximately 30 percent had worked in the sex trade.

We measure the criminal capital that accumulates through embeddedness in tutelage relationships with items that tap crime-specific instruction by street people and the definitions that support these crimes. We measure tutelage in theft since leaving home with a scale consisting of four items (first wave alpha = .829; second wave = .767). The first indicator is a general measure that asked how often street people offered to help the respondent steal. Our second measure inquired about the extent to which people said they would provide protection for the respondent if s/he wanted to steal things. Protection, or "keeping six," usually involved working as a lookout for police and home or store owners, as well as providing protection during the sale of stolen goods to others involved in the underground economy. Our third indicator asked how frequently street people offered to buy stolen goods or introduce a fence or other potential purchaser. The fourth and final item explored the regularity of offers of instruction in techniques of breaking and entering, the use of burglary tools, or other theft-related skills. According to the results in Table 6.1, on average, street youth had received each of these offers at least once or twice since leaving home.

We use parallel items to measure tutelage in drug selling (first wave alpha = .836; second wave = .781) and prostitution (first wave alpha = .909; second wave = .917), although we are limited to three items for each of these behaviors. We asked how often street associates offered to help sell drugs or start hooking and how frequently they offered to provide protection. We also inquired about the extent to which street people said they would teach the "tricks" of drug trafficking (e.g., how to divide and "cut" drugs) or show the "ropes" of prostitution (e.g., where to work and how

Table 6.1. Concepts, Indicators, and Descriptive Statistics for Measures of Criminal Embeddedness and Capital (N = 376)

Concepts	First wave			Second wave		
	alpha	X	SD	alpha	X	SD
Criminal Home Networks[a]						
Friends who sold drugs		3.287	2.886			
Friends of friends who stole		5.553	3.224			
Friends in prostitution		1.168	1.806			
Criminal Street Networks[a]						
Friends who sold drugs		5.769	3.093			
Friends who stole		7.088	3.321			
Friends in prostitution		2.926	2.935			
Criminal Capital Definitions[b]						
Should be legal to take drugs		3.173	1.364			
Not always wrong to take						
other's property		2.149	1.213			
Prostitution should be legal		2.726	1.452			
Tutelage in Theft[c]	.829			.767		
Offered to teach		1.125	1.314		.351	.857
Offered to help sell stolen goods		1.750	1.363		.941	1.199
Offered to provide protection		1.253	1.322		.556	1.062
Offered to help steal		1.540	1.338		.729	1.091
Tutelage in Drug Selling[c]	.836			.781		
Offered to teach		1.426	1.437		.508	1.007
Offered to provide protection		1.497	1.482		.777	1.264
Offered to help sell		1.564	1.424		.875	1.177
Tutelage in Prostitution[c]	.909			.917		
Offered to teach		.614	1.082		.210	.724
Offered to provide protection		.561	1.091		.218	.773
Offered to help get started		.702	1.125		.231	.760

[a] 0 = None; 1 = 1 to 10%; 2 = 11% to 20%; ... 10 = 91% to 100%.
[b] 0 = Strongly disagree; 1 = disagree; 2 = uncertain; 3 = agree; 4 = strongly agree.
[c] 0 = Never; 1 = once or twice; 2 = a few times; 3 = often; 4 = alot of the time.

much to charge). Table 6.1 reveals that, on average, offers of assistance in drug selling occurred as regularly as those for theft, whereas those involving prostitution were less frequent.

We measure a further dimension of criminal capital with crime-specific items that capture attitudes or beliefs that justify law violations. These indicators measure the respondent's opinion about whether it was always wrong to take others' property and whether drug use and prostitution should be legalized. The descriptive statistics provided in Table 6.1 indicate that, on average, street youth agreed that drugs should be legal; they were also unconvinced that prostitution should be criminalized, and they were uncertain about the wrongfulness of theft.

To assess the net effects on crime of criminal embeddedness and criminal capital, we also consider several home and street variables introduced in previous chapters. These variables effectively control for background factors emphasized in dominant theories, as well as for street experiences and criminal opportunities, including age, gender, violent father and mother, physical and sexual abuse, violence toward father and mother, school problems, crime at home, city, time on the street, lack of shelter, and illegal opportunities. We also include a measure of family criminality; although family members are not a usual source of criminal tutelage, other researchers have noted a relationship between parental criminality and offending (Loeber and Stouthamer-Loeber, 1986; Sampson and Laub, 1993); moreover, some of our respondents left homes in which crime appears to have been commonplace. As documented in Chapter Two, many respondents referred to parental and sibling illegal drug abuse; several youth also mentioned that members of their family were involved in other illegal activities. Arden reported extensive involvement in theft and drug selling before and after leaving home, and he suggested a connection between his offending and that of other family members:

> Me and my cousin went out together. We did all our crime, because our uncles were into it. My dad bootlegs whiskey, and he sells a lot of beer.

Parental criminality is also reflected in Aaron's account of his involvement in theft:

> TVs, VCRs, cameras, I've stolen bottles of liquor, tapes, telephones, computers, anything. . . . Everybody's looking for something. I sold my parents some of the stuff. My parents' friends will buy stuff. Anybody will buy stuff if the price is right.

We control for family criminality with a dichotomous measure reflecting any immediate family members' arrest on a criminal charge.

We estimate two models for each crime measured at the first-wave interviews. The first models include the various control variables and our measures of embeddedness. In the second equation, we add indicators of tutelage and attitudes favorable to crime. After exploring the effects of these variables, we then introduce information on crime at the second wave. We conclude our analysis with an additional test of logical implications drawn from the theoretical perspective advanced in this chapter.

A Quantitative Test

According to the first equation in Table 6.2, several control variables have sizable effects on drug selling measured during the first wave. Consistent with the findings reported in previous chapters, trafficking on the street increases with involvement in selling drugs prior to leaving home and illegal opportunities on the street. Offending is also greater for youth in Vancouver but declines as time on the street increases. However, even with the introduction of these controls, our results demonstrate sizable and significant effects of both measures of embeddedness – that is, drug trafficking increases with the proportion of drug-dealing friends at home and in the respondents' street networks.

According to the second equation in Table 6.2, both measures of criminal capital – tutelage and deviant definitions – also have sizable and significant effects on drug selling. Moreover, introducing these variables results in a significant increase in the amount of variance explained by the model. Also, both variables reduce substantially all of the effects significant in the first equation. The reduction of the effect of illegal opportunities is particularly important because it suggests that, for street youth, tutelage and definitions are key aspects of the mobilization of illegal opportunities and the process of criminal embeddedness.

Our analysis in Table 6.3 reveals that like drug selling, serious theft is significantly related to theft at home, being in Vancouver, and illegal opportunities. Theft has several more unique correlates: gender, lack of shelter, and an unexpected negative relationship with violence toward one's mother. Serious theft is also related to embeddedness, but only to involvement in theft networks at home. Although connections with street friends who steal has a significant bivariate relationship with street theft, its effect is reduced to nonsignificance by the introduction of deviant home networks.

Table 6.2. OLS Regressions of Criminal Embeddedness, Criminal Capital, and First-Wave Drug Selling

	b	SE	b	SE
Age	−.154	.127	−.090	.122
Gender	.785	.572	.729	.555
Violent Father	.007	.064	.001	.061
Violent Mother	−.019	.069	−.001	.066
Physical Abuse	.307	.254	.295	.243
Violent Toward Father	.019	.098	−.029	.094
Violent Toward Mother	−.135	.129	−.154	.124
Sexual Abuse	−.021	.149	−.009	.142
Family Criminality	.123	.490	−.255	.472
School Problems	.106	.081	.099	.078
Home Friends Sold Drugs	.345***	.095	.263***	.092
Sold Drugs at Home	.371***	.075	.324***	.072
City	2.216***	.567	1.890***	.544
Year Left Home	−.159*	.094	−.149*	.089
Criminal Opportunities	1.023***	.174	.732***	.174
Nights on Street	.137	.089	.026	.087
Street Friends Sold Drugs	.286***	.083	.191**	.082
Drug Use Not Wrong			.575***	.179
Tutelage in Drug Selling			.381***	.074
Intercept	14.712		11.764	
Adjusted R^2	.411		.463	
R^2 change			.052***	

* $p \le .10$
** $p \le .05$
*** $p \le .01$

Following the pattern for drug selling, both tutelage and definitional support for theft are significantly related to stealing on the street. Furthermore, both variables reduce the effects of all the control variables and again markedly diminish the effect of opportunities. Adding these variables also produces a significant improvement in the explained variation in serious theft.

Table 6.3. OLS Regressions of Criminal Embeddedness, Criminal Capital, and First-Wave Serious Theft

	b	SE	b	SE
Age	−.314	.332	−.023	.309
Gender	3.330**	1.463	2.874**	1.355
Violent Father	.009	.163	.003	.151
Violent Mother	−.013	.176	−.051	.164
Physical Abuse	.343	.656	.124	.608
Violent Toward Father	.228	.252	.055	.235
Violent Toward Mother	−.889***	.330	−.792***	.306
Sexual Abuse	−.177	.382	.001	.354
Family Criminality	.017	1.257	−.368	1.164
School Problems	.220	.210	.255	.195
Home Friends Stole	.491**	.212	.317	.200
Stole at Home	.363***	.071	.309***	.066
City	5.352***	1.455	4.411***	1.359
Year Left Home	−.458*	.240	.234	.224
Criminal Opportunities	1.707***	.437	1.197***	.415
Nights on Street	.888***	.233	.475**	.223
Street Friends Stole	.180	.197	.140	.182
Stealing Not Wrong			2.119***	.481
Tutelage in Theft			.954***	.154
Intercept	40.708		11.886	
Adjusted R^2	.346		.442	
R^2 change			.096***	

* $p \le .10$
** $p \le .05$
*** $p \le .01$

The results for prostitution in Table 6.4 resemble those described earlier: Street prostitution is positively related to embeddedness in home and street networks populated with those who work in the sex trade. Prostitution also is associated with access to criminal capital: Both tutelage and definitions are

Table 6.4. OLS Regressions of Criminal Embeddedness, Criminal Capital, and First-Wave Prostitution

	b	SE	b	SE
Age	-.067	.067	-.073	.061
Gender	-.001	.304	.226	.288
Violent Father	.060	.034	.042	.031
Violent Mother	.056	.036	.034	.033
Physical Abuse	-.012	.134	.070	.123
Violent Toward Father	-.039	.052	-.052	.048
Violent Toward Mother	-.047	.068	-.049	.062
Sexual Abuse	.246***	.078	.160**	.072
Family Criminality	.521	.260	.223	.241
School Problems	-.071	.043	-.072*	.040
Home Friends Prostitution	.185**	.077	.105	.071
Home Crime	-.017**	.008	-.013*	.007
City	.717**	.301	.628**	.276
Year Left Home	-.127***	.049	-.121***	.045
Criminal Opportunities	.250***	.091	.150*	.084
Nights on Street	-.100**	.046	-.130***	.043
Street Friends Prostitution	.429***	.046	.326***	.044
Prostitution Not Wrong			.233***	.084
Tutelage in Prostitution			.346***	.044
Intercept	13.147		12.329	
Adjusted R^2	.364		.468	
R^2 change			.104***	

* $p \le .10$
** $p \le .05$
*** $p \le .01$

positively related to involvement in the sex trade. Once again, these variables reduce the effects of exogenous variables, particularly criminal opportunities, and substantially increase the amount of explained variance.

Table 6.5 considers the effects of exposure to tutelage during the

Table 6.5. OLS Regressions of Criminal Embeddedness, Criminal Capital, and Second-Wave Drug Selling, Theft, and Prostitution

	Drug selling		Theft		Prostitution	
	b	SE	b	SE	b	SE
Age	.076	.087	−.026	.110	−.038	.053
Gender	.256	.398	.720	.480	.721**	.251
Violent Father	−.033	.044	−.110**	.053	.048*	.026
Violent Mother	.063	.047	.105*	.058	−.028	.028
Physical Abuse	.236	.174	.123	.215	.024	.106
Violent Toward Father	−.014	.068	.064	.084	−.007	.042
Violent Toward Mother	−.040	.089	−.039	.109	.004	.054
Sexual Abuse	.017	.102	.086	.125	−.057	.062
Family Criminality	−.011	.338	.621	.410	−.010	.206
School Problems	.030	.056	−.002	.069	.016	.034
Home Friends Offend	.013	.067	.007	.071	.186***	.061
Offended at Home	.130**	.053	.017	.024	−.004	.006
City	.065	.397	.060	.488	.480**	.238
Year Left Home	.029	.064	−.114	.079	−.071*	.039
Criminal Opportunities	.100	.127	−.193	.148	−.019	.073
Nights on Street	−.011	.062	−.070	.079	−.068*	.037
Street Friends Offend	−.080	.059	.012	.064	.107***	.041
Crime Not Wrong	.223*	.130	.469***	.174	.120*	.072
Offend on Street W1	.135***	.038	.057***	.019	.277***	.045
Tutelage W1	−.054	.058	.018	.061	.037	.044
Tutelage W2	.285***	.065	.325***	.074	.092	.057
Intercept	−5.225		8.790		6.517	
Adjusted R^2	.194		.191		.361	

* $p \leq .10$
** $p \leq .05$
*** $p \leq .01$

second wave. In each case, our measure of deviant definitions is significantly related to second-wave offending. In addition, in the drug-selling and theft models, second-wave tutelage has sizable and significant positive effects on crime, even after controlling for the antecedent variables previously described and for tutelage and crime at the first wave. The effect of second-wave tutelage on prostitution is also positive but falls just below the .10 level of significance.

To test further the logical implications of our theoretical perspective, we estimated an additional set of models that explore the crime-specific nature of tutelage. That is, we replaced the measures of the specific type of criminal tutelage involved with measures of instruction in other criminal activities (e.g., in the theft model, we replaced tutelage in theft with tutelage in drug selling, and then with tutelage in prostitution). In five of these six models, the effect of tutelage on crime is not significant: The only exception is that tutelage in drug selling is significantly related to theft.

Learning to Do Street Crime

It is a widely perpetrated myth, according to Coleman (1990), that society is simply a set of independent individuals who act to achieve goals that they have somehow acquired autonomously. Coleman traces this myth to two sources: the idea that individuals are the most immediately tangible actors in society, and the extraordinary impact on our thinking of political philosophers of the seventeenth and eighteenth centuries who emphasized self-determination and the rights and responsibilities of individuals. Sociological, as well as psychological and economic, explanations of crime increasingly embrace derivations of these ideas in their portrayals of crime as the product of either rational, utilitarian calculations that capitalize on criminal opportunities or individual failings and resistance to social and self-control. These perspectives see opportunities, or alternatively personal deficiencies, as leading individuals to choose crime selfishly as a source of short-term gains. Advocates of these approaches dismiss as unnecessary the argument that one learns criminal behaviors through associations with and instruction from criminals (e.g., see G. Becker, 1968; Ehrlich, 1973; Kornhauser, 1978; Hirschi and Gottfredson, 1980; Gottfredson and Hirschi, 1990). Furthermore, they maintain that the majority of criminal acts are unsophisticated behaviors that do not require special expertise. In short, they assume that guidance in crime is unnecessary.

Sutherland's work provides an important contrast. From his early study with Harvey Locke (1936), *Twenty Thousand Homeless Men*, Sutherland's work displays a consistent concern with exogenous structural conditions of differential social organization and a focus on contexts that he thought most likely to stimulate the learning processes that lead to crime. The homeless were of recurring concern – for example, reappearing in Sutherland's (1937, pp. 223–24) discussion of the history of theft in *The Professional Thief*.

Nonetheless, Sutherland emphasized that structural conditions such as homelessness do not by themselves cause crime. He made this point in relation to other correlates of crime, including age and gender, noting that the key is to identify and document processes through which such factors operate. According to Sutherland, these processes involve affiliation with deviants, tutelage in and mastery of criminal skills, and exposure to and adoption of definitions favorable to crime. Sutherland's emphasis on tutelage anticipates the attention more broadly given by Granovetter and Coleman to the significance of embeddedness in specialized social networks and to the accumulation of social capital through social contacts and communication.

Our findings are consistent with this more social conception of crime. They suggest that adverse experiences such as life on the street and homelessness lead to an embeddedness in criminal street networks and exposure to mentors or tutors. These individuals transmit skills that constitute forms of criminal capital, thereby facilitating involvement in crime. Instead of being indifferent and impervious to others, youth in our study are receptive to others' abilities to relay information and skills relevant to particular crimes. The effects of these experiences are related to, but also independent of, background variables often treated as measuring predispositions or propensities to crime. Thus, our research suggests that embeddedness in criminal networks and the subsequent acquisition of criminal capital are important aspects of getting into some types of crime, in much the same way that similar processes are involved in getting a job. They are processes through which opportunities are transformed into action.

The theoretical approach that we advocate does not discount the role of background factors that may include a propensity to crime formed early in the life course – for example, in the experiences of the youth in our study while still at home. A reflection of this possibility is that in our models, criminal associations at home have significant and substantial net effects on those on the street. The goal of our theoretical approach is to articulate a more elaborate and comprehensive causal understanding of street crime that links both backgrounds and opportunity with embeddedness and tutelage. We have demonstrated the effects of the latter while systematically and comprehensively taking into account effects of the former.

We suggest that our focus on street youth constitutes a telling test of the effects of social embeddedness in that such youth are customarily assumed to be disorganized and unsophisticated participants in crimes that in turn are thought to involve little skill or learning. Moreover, although our findings contrast with those predicted by recent sociological explanations of crime, they are consistent with a number of classic and contemporary ethnographies of urban youth. Our results highlight oversights associated with the assumption that crime results solely from predetermined characteristics or opportunities; they further remind us that ignoring the effects of life situations can cause us to underestimate seriously the importance of social embeddedness in criminogenic environments.

Street Youth in Street Groups

with Jo-Ann Climenhage

WE FOUND IN THE PREVIOUS CHAPTER that embeddedness in criminal networks heightens the involvement of street youth in crime. Yet tutelage in offending is not the only dimension of street youth associations, nor are these relationships the only available source of companionship for street youth. In this chapter, we extend our analysis of street networks and explore in greater detail the associations formed by homeless youth.

Although street youth spend time alone, their life on the street is often intensely social. Research on homeless or street adults indicates that they minimize relationships with other homeless people or form short-term relationships, regardless of their intentions or the intensity of their feelings (Snow and Anderson, 1993; Fleisher, 1995). Homeless youth share some of these tendencies, but they are more inclined to enter into group relationships. Many respondents spoke about other youth with whom they "hung out," describing how they spent their time with them and the nature of their associations. This aspect of street life is the focus of this chapter.

We explore the characteristics of street groups, the reasons for joining them, and the effects of group membership, particularly in terms of criminal involvement. Classical as well as contemporary ethnographies suggest that many youth groups are, for all intents and purposes, gangs that facilitate and promote involvement in crime. Yet, as we demonstrate later, street youth groups are diverse, offering assistance in meeting basic needs of the street, as well as facilitating involvement in crime. Moreover, several features of street youth groupings suggest that, although they share some of the characteristics commonly attributed to gangs, these street groups also have their own unique characteristics.

Our approach to studying street groups is lexical and relational. That is, we focus on the conceptual language that street youth used to describe these groups and their purposes, and we attempt to establish patterns of relationships between membership in these groups and other attitudes and activities. The street youth we interviewed were sometimes ambivalent about identifying the groups to which they belonged with any exact term. However, the label they most frequently used was "street family." When we explicitly asked about membership in street families, 54 percent of respondents indicated that they had been part of a family since leaving home. This led us to investigate further the features that characterized these street groupings.

Describing Street Families

We asked youth who indicated that they were members of street families to describe how these groups formed, how they were organized, the purposes they served, and how they sometimes dissolved, expecting that answers to such questions would provide insight into the nature and purposes of street families.

The events that reportedly led to the formation of these groups were sometimes simply random and spontaneous occurrences. Justin, a member of a Vancouver street family organized around a downtown games arcade, recalled that he was "just hanging around the block. Hangin' out going to parties. . . . Friends introduce you to other friends. It just goes like that." Phillip reported a similar experience; however, his group coalesced around a different popular street site. He remembered "running into a group of people panning around the 7-Eleven store. . . . In the first hour either they like you or they don't."

Regardless of the site of formation, most street families originated from a shared sense of street life – be it the pleasures and freedom that the street could provide, or the crisis and need that it often fostered. Lisa described the following series of events that led to a rather well organized and durable group:

Yeah, okay, this is what happened. We were at Youth Without Shelter [a hostel], and I was going out with Russell and, um, I don't know. . . . He kissed me, and staff saw, and they're like . . . "No, don't touch each other" type of thing, you know, and he kissed me again, so we got discharged. Me and him got discharged, and then Jason discharged himself, and about ten other people discharged themselves that night, and I don't know where everybody else went, but it was just the five of us that stuck together. And we lived together literally on the streets.

This group remained together for several months, sleeping in storefronts and spending days in the subways, arcades, and malls of downtown Toronto.

Nick told us about another group that formed in Vancouver around protests against the United States' involvement in the Gulf War:

> Well, it first started with the Gulf War Peace Camp. I came down to the Peace Camp during the Gulf War and, uh, after the war ended, a bunch of us, like, we got a place together and it's like, even during the war, it's like, when we were staying on the lawn in front of Robson Square, day in and day out, no way to really make any money other than, like panning and stuff. And, uh, I just made . . . a lot of really close friends and like, family.

Nick's closing sentence reflects the tendency of street youth to use family-based phrases to describe the types of relationships they establish on the street. This pattern is most evident in the terms that street youth use when discussing the various roles they adopt. Brendan spoke of a group that began when several youth met in a park located near one of the main Toronto hostels. Brendan noted that this group was approaching dissolution, but he still played a senior, advisory role:

> I'm now one of the only, of the original twenty of us all in total, and I'm the one, there's maybe three of the twenty left. And I'm a big brother sort of thing. Like everybody still comes to me with their problems. It's like, well, what should I do about this or that, and then I'm like, well, you could do this, this, or that, whatever. . . . It's just to have others to rely on, uh, to help them out when they needed it, and to know that if I needed help, I could get it back.

Justin also introduced conventional family titles when speaking about the group to which he belonged. This group originated around a popular site for panhandling and involved a variety of youth with a considerable range of ages, backgrounds, and street experiences. When asked to describe this group, Justin replied:

> We hang around together, tell each other where the food is, and if you're stuck for a place to sleep, they'll tell you where to go, stuff like that. It's like street brother and street sister.

Other youth went beyond sibling analogies and spoke of their street families as having a parent–child structure. This type of group is typified in Blair's description of the various members of his street family and reflects the extent of street youth's incorporation of conventional family roles into their street families:

> Well, there's this, these two people down there, there's a 13-year-old girl [laughs] and I'm 15, but she's like a mother to me, and her boyfriend's like 23. And he's like a father. Because if I'm ever in trouble, I just gotta go to them, and they'll protect me, help me and what not. Help me out if I'm really sad or lonely; they'll comfort me and stuff.

Vince also described himself as a member of a family in which people fulfilled particular social roles. His account further illustrates street youth's recasting of familial terms to fit the complexities of their living situations. In these groups, family identities are not contingent on age, seniority, or resources but are determined by the emotional and psychological support that individual youth provide:

> We had like our own mother, even though she's two years younger than me . . . and like a grandfather and a grandmother and everything. . . . 'Cause some people act like mothers and some people act like fathers, you know? Someone to talk to when you want to talk. Sometimes money. When somebody got paid, or somebody got money, like basically you could borrow money off them 'cause they know when you get money, you'll give it to them.

In some street groups, family definitions were extended to include specific concerns that arose when living on the street. This pattern was reflected in an all-female group in Vancouver in which pregnancy was an organizing concern. In her description of this group, Karla described the bond that emerged between several teenage mothers who shared similar backgrounds and street experiences:

> Um, well, we're all pretty close, 'cause we all got kids, for one thing, we've all got kids and, um, we're just so much alike. Like our families are so much alike. There's, like, quite a bit of similarity, like, we all either got stepmoms or stepfathers, and we don't like 'em. . . . We go to movies together . . . shoot pool. We go to the beach, go to the beach quite a bit. Go to prenatal classes. I've gone to about four prenatal classes in the last two months now, with three different sisters of mine.

However, not all youth groups invoked family-based terminology. Randall acknowledged that "brother" and "sister" relationships were common in street families, but he defined his own street group as having more of a friendship structure:

> I know people in street families that like they're brothers and sisters, and like they're really, really close knit. You know, someone needs something, well, all of them get together, and it's like they try to figure out how to help him. Me and my friends, it's almost the same way, but we don't go like, "brothers and sisters." We're friends, you know, friends take care of each other, you know, and that's the whole thing. I always, whenever something happens, I throw my entire life on the line.

For some youth, street families appeared to make sense because they offered a kind of role specialization that, apart from traditional family roles, helped to make the various aspects of survival on the street more manageable. Brenda made this point, emphasizing the importance of various people's expertise in meeting street needs:

> You just kinda start hanging out with the same people, and you get together, and you each have your, you know, you each have certain expectations of each person, as to what their reactions are going to be to certain situations and what their roles are. Like as in protecting each other or finding the squat to stay in. . . . And, uh, you know, just, uh, basically that's how I ended up in it. I just started hangin' out with people that were already sort of a group and just – I had a role.

Regardless of the structure or roles that characterized the street groups to which they belonged, most youth emphasized that several basic needs prompted the formation and maintenance of a street family. One primary issue was survival. Reflecting on the cooperation within street families and how it helped to solve problems of food and hunger, Brenda noted that:

> The way poverty on the street works, twenty bucks can go a long way. Like you can feed four people on twenty bucks, or you can feed one. It's just a kinda thing where you have to work together and pool your resources. Like if I find a big bag of buns in the dumpster, it's better to be able to distribute those and not just myself eat buns all week. Somebody else'll find tomatoes, and then we have tomato sandwiches. The food doesn't go bad, and you can just eat it really quick.

Similarly, Darlene observed:

> We were there to support each other. Like the other day I had no money. I just got back from Edmonton. I was like, right, starving, and I asked my sister for money – she came through. She got me something to eat. Last night, I had money and I took her out for something to eat. We all work in good ways.

Kirk also spoke about the ways in which street friends helped him to endure the street, and he focused particularly on the economic resources they shared with him:

> Well, it was the only way to survive. I couldn't get welfare 'cause I was too young. We helped each other get by – for example, we'd go on survival trips. Like, we'd go camping, we'd set up a tent, we'd all chip in for a tent, and then we'd, uh, you know, put it up in the Don Valley or something, you know, under the bridge, and we'd live in a tent . . . in the woods. Kind of go to the street for financial help.

However, financial need, shelter, and hunger were not the only concerns, as respondents frequently discussed safety and protection. As noted in earlier chapters, street life is particularly violent, and the risk of victimization is greatest for youth who spend most of their time on the street. According to Sharon, her street group was "a bunch of friends that stick together. Like they watch each other's back for you. . . . Otherwise, I probably would have gotten beaten up, or whatever."

Protection and safety were particular concerns of female street youth in the sample. Roseanne put the issue quite succinctly: "Well, being female and not incredibly unattractive can be really dangerous on the streets. Just being female and not over two hundred pounds is really dangerous on the streets [laughing] even if you are unattractive."

In addition to these needs related to security and subsistence, youth emphasized that street families provided them with essential psychological and emotional support. Respondents frequently noted that above all else, street families were a source of companionship that helped to mitigate the loneliness and isolation of street life. A comment of Nick's captures this sentiment:

> Well, we lived together. We were always there for each other. It's like you're on the street and you get involved with people down there. Um, you really learn what friendship is. . . . If I need them, they're there for me. And that's what a true friend is, someone that's going to be there for you when you need them.

Vince shared this view, stressing the differences between street youth who were "just friends" and those who were "family":

> A street family is like, basically a group of friends but it's more ... some friends, you know, you can't count on them, but like a street family you can count on. If you get in trouble, they'll be there to help you one way or another.

As a comment by Jamie suggests, some youth involved in street families willingly expressed the psychological needs that street families satisfied:

> Like we cared about each other so much that none of us, like I mean, there would be fifteen of us, and we would all share our blankets if we had to, you know ... and a person would never say, "I hate you." ... Like it was always like, I don't know, like if a person thought you were doing something wrong, they wouldn't say, "Don't do it." They would come up and say, "Look, we're really worried about you."

Jamie continued, suggesting that street families could provide the emotional support that youth expected from their families, but which they did not receive:

> Yeah, yeah, we just wanted family, you know, like we just wanted love. . . . We found what we wanted in each other, you know. Like, well, the parts of the family that we didn't have, we found that in each other, you know what I mean? Like, pieces that were missing from our other families, like our real families, that were missing. We put those into the family that we had that was on the street. . . . I think we kind of, we all knew that we were like, we really needed friends, we all knew that we needed a family. . . . We were shitheads, too, but you know, I mean, we would never fuck each other over. We would never do that, never!

Of course, it is an open question, which we pursue further later, how well street families actually do serve these various needs.

Our interviews point to one other important dimension of street families: impermanence. Membership in most groups changed quickly, often over the course of a few weeks. A comment by Sid reflects the processes that lead to departures from street family situations. Sid became involved in a "punk-based" street family by just hanging out with the group, listening to music, and talking about the street. Once in the group, he "drank a lot, found places to stay, and did lots of drugs." Although Sid noted that it was fun and his street family was helpful, problems began to emerge. He observed that things started to slip into what he called "the normal routine": "You know, the soap opera starts to arise. Back-stabbing. People start to get pissed off at each other."

The comments of several of the youth about a decline in contacts with their street families raises the possibility that there is an aging out of these groups. Carlos reported that friendships were a key element of his life, and he noted that the best part of his life at home was his school friends. Once on the street, he was attracted to a group of youth who hung out at a fast-food restaurant, and he eventually became a part of this street family through a friend. When we asked why he chose this group, Carlos replied:

> I became a part of a street family through the need to have people look out for me in terms of personal safety and emotional support. I got a certain degree of freedom that I didn't get at home.

However, he then added:

> It's not important now to be part of the street family because I have a better sense of who I am. I'm wiser than I was a few years ago. I realize that no matter how lonely I am, I'm not alone.

Finally, a number of the respondents in the sample indicated that they had become impatient with younger members joining their street families. For example, Phillip reported that at the time of the interview he found his street family "not as important as it was heavy." In the past, he had felt that his street family was useful, and that it made him feel "he wasn't just a body on a street, but part of a group," but he had since become "fed up with it all." He had begun to disassociate from the group "because there were too many younger kids coming into it." Nonetheless, he indicated that he "still liked to hang out."

Causes and Consequences of Street Families

Our open-ended field interviews provided qualitative insights into the perceived nature and purposes of street families. We also included a series of closed-ended questions about these groups in the structured part of our interviews. These items introduce a quantitative dimension to our sense of these groupings. We began by asking respondents to assess the importance of the following factors as reasons for affiliations with street groups: a desire

Table 7.1. Matrix of Motivations to Join Friends in Street Groups (N = 376)

	Desire to be Connected	Concerns about Safety	Peer Pressure	X
Desire to be Connected [a]				1.923
Concerns About Safety	.492			2.130
Peer Pressure	.250	.364		1.114
Desire for Shelter, Food, Money	.261	.448	.404	1.657

[a] All items coded as: 0 = Not important at all; 1 = not very important; 2 = somewhat important; 3 = very important.

to be connected to others, concerns about safety, peer pressure to join, and the desire to secure shelter, food, and money.

A summary of the respondents' perceived motivations for joining groups is presented in Table 7.1. The right-hand column of this matrix contains the mean score rankings given to each factor. Street youth rated concerns about safety highest, followed by the desire to be connected to others, and the desire for shelter, food, and money; peer pressure was indicated as the least important factor in joining such groups. The matrix of correlations reported in the left-hand part of Table 7.1 further suggests the centrality of anxieties about safety by indicating that these concerns were strongly correlated with the importance attached to being connected to others and the desire to secure shelter, food, and money. Survival and safety on the street were clearly dominant concerns.

In Table 7.2, we analyze the determinants of reported membership in street families in the second wave of our field interviews. We first estimate an equation that includes the kinds of background and objective characteristics that we considered in earlier chapters. This equation indicates that female street youth were more likely to be members of street families, as were youth in Vancouver and those who lacked shelter. Given the material presented earlier in this chapter and in our chapter comparing Toronto and Vancouver, our expectation was that concerns about safety might help to

Table 7.2. OLS Regression of First-Wave Membership in Street Families

Variables	Model 1		Model 2	
	b	SE	b	SE
Age	−.004	.013	−.007	.012
Gender	−.126**	.056	.078	.054
Violent Father	.001	.004	.001	.004
Violent Mother	.002	.005	.001	.004
Father Drinking	.011	.024	.008	.024
Mother Drinking	.028	.031	.028	.030
Father Drug	.023	.045	.025	.043
Mother Drug	−.021	.035	−.031	.034
Broken Home	−.032	.054	−.045	.052
Home Crime	.003	.002	.003	.001
City	.157***	.056	.121**	.054
Year Left Home	−.009	.010	−.012	.009
Nights on Street	.038***	.008	.035***	.008
Desire to be Connected			.042	.028
Concerns about Safety			.115***	.029
Peer Pressure			.019	.026
Food, Shelter, Money			−.019	.026
Intercept	1.306		1.247	
Adjusted R^2	.128		.196	

* $p \le .10$
** $p \le .05$
*** $p \le .01$

account for the gender and city effects just reported. The second equation in Table 7.2 includes the several motivating factors considered in Table 7.1 and supports this expectation. The effect of city is reduced by about one-fifth, and the effect of gender is reduced below statistical significance. In other words, this analysis confirms that female street youth and youth in Vancouver were more likely to be members of street families because of their concerns about their safety. In addition, nights on the street persists as a further factor leading youth to join street families.

We next explore the effects of membership in street families. Our first step in this investigation examines the potential beneficial effects of street families in terms of improving members' emotional well-being. In each wave of the field interviews, we included a standard set of items used to measure depression. These questions asked youth how often they were happy, how frequently they felt lonely, and how hopeful they were about the future. We assess the impact of street family membership on a summary scale of these feelings in the second wave of our study in Table 7.3. Our analysis includes measures of respondents' feelings at the first wave; including these scores in the initial equation allows us to estimate the extent to which other explanatory factors account for change in these depression scores over time.

Our results indicate that the effect of street family membership is strong and significant but, contrary to our expectation, in the direction of increased depression. Controlling for the various motivations to join street families only reduces this effect slightly in the second equation in Table 7.3. However, controlling for nights on the street, which itself significantly increased depression among these street youth, reduces the effect of street family membership below statistical significance. In sum, although street family membership did not reduce feelings of depression among these youth, it also did not, in and of itself, increase depression in these families. Rather, it was the lack of shelter (i.e., nights on the street) that street families experienced that intensified their feelings of depression across the first two waves of this study. Street families did not solve the emotional problems of the youth that joined them, but neither did they in and of themselves increase these problems.

Although they do not appear to solve the psychological problems of their members, street families may fulfill other needs. The qualitative data introduced earlier in this chapter contained several references to the importance of families in finding food, money, and shelter, as well as a source of companionship. To investigate the validity of these accounts, we explore the effects of first-wave membership in a street family on second-wave involve-

Table 7.3. Decomposition of the Effects of Street Family Membership on Feelings of Depression

Variables	Model 1		Model 2		Model 3	
	b	SE	b	SE	b	SE
Age	.034	.052	.040	.052	.050	.052
Gender	.116	.225	.119	.227	.124	.226
Home Delinquency	−.007	.006	−.005	.006	−.006	.006
City	.011	.231	.028	.232	.090	.232
Year Left Home	.003	.038	.010	.038	.021	.038
Street Family	.483**	.210	.463**	.219	.355	.244
Depression W1	.627***	.037	.628***	.037	.610***	.037
Desire for Shelter			.253**	.109	.250**	.108
Concern about Safety			.021	.127	.030	.127
Desire to be Connected			−.063	.120	−.084	.120
Peer Pressure			−.085	.112	−.076	.112
Nights on Street					.078**	.036
Intercept	5.274		6.267		8.131	
Adjusted R^2	.446		.446		.542	

```
*    p ≤ .10
**   p ≤ .05
***  p ≤ .01
```

ment in activities with other street youth. Specifically, we asked how frequently street youth spent time with other youth doing the following: finding a place to stay for the night, looking for food, hanging out, and panning for money. Given our concerns about street networks as a source of criminal embeddedness, we also inquired about the frequency with which street youth stole and used drugs when they were with other street youth. In these analyses, membership is measured at the first wave, and the dependent variables are measured at the second wave. Additional analyses that use variables all measured at the second wave are consistent with those presented here.

The results presented in Table 7.4 indicate that membership in street families is positively and significantly related to spending time in groups with other street youth searching for food, finding shelter, panhandling for money, and hanging out. In general, these results resonate with the descriptions of street families provided by our respondents and affirm that they are important sources of sustenance and security.

Table 7.4 further indicates that street family membership is unrelated to the frequency with which youth use drugs or steal in *groups* with other street youth. However, there is the further issue of how street family membership may be related to the processes of criminal embeddedness and the acquisition of criminal capital discussed in the previous chapter. The figures in Part A of Table 7.5 indicate the proportion of youth involved in crime, whether with other street youth *or* alone, and the average frequency of offending for two groups: youth who reported that they were members of street families and those who indicated that they had never belonged to such groups.

The results in Table 7.5 demonstrate that for every type of offense, members of street families report more extensive involvement. Correlations between street family membership and offending, in Part B of Table 7.5, further confirm this pattern. Moreover, there are also strong and significant correlations between street family membership and our measures of tutelage in Part B of this table. Finally, the effect of street family membership on offending is reduced to nonsignificance in a series of unpresented multivariate equations for each offense that incorporate measures of street family membership and tutelage in that crime. Overall, these findings suggest that although street family membership does not appear to encourage group offending, it does increase individual involvement in crime through tutelage and the processes of embeddedness and criminal capitalization emphasized in Chapter Six.

Families or Gangs?

A final and inevitable question about street families is whether these groups are, in fact, gangs. Answering this question first requires a definition of gangs as this term is commonly used in the study of adolescent groups. Definitions of gangs abound, dating at least to pioneering efforts of Puffer (1912) and Thrasher (1927) early in this century. As befits a century of attention, definitions have become progressively more formal and detailed. An important recent definition is provided by Ball and Curry (1995):

Table 7.4. OLS Regressions of Street Activity

Variables	Hanging out b	SE	Looking for food b	SE	Looking for shelter b	SE	Panhandling b	SE	Using drugs b	SE	Stealing b	SE
Age	-.061*	.033	-.022	.033	-.072**	.036	-.055*	.033	.010	.036	-.046*	.025
Gender	.175	.151	.361**	.147	.065	.163	.051	.151	.397**	.163	.365**	.111
Violent Father	.004	.017	-.001	.016	-.008	.018	-.013	.016	-.027	.018	-.008	.012
Violent Mother	.003	.018	.029	.018	.019	.019	.001	.018	.033*	.019	.015	.013
Physical Abuse	.003	.066	.068	.065	-.059	.071	-.027	.066	-.022	.072	-.043	.049
Violent Toward Father	-.008	.026	-.032	.025	-.015	.028	.005	.026	.068**	.028	.037*	.019
Violent Toward Mother	-.005	.034	-.023	.033	.003	.036	.039	.033	-.014	.036	-.016	.025
Sexual Abuse	-.057	.039	-.017	.038	-.050	.042	-.005	.039	-.085**	.042	-.015	.029
Family Criminality	-.096	.128	-.172	.125	-.075	.137	-.203	.127	.126	.139	.010	.094
School Problems	.004	.022	-.012	.022	.016	.024	-.021	.022	.048**	.024	.006	.016
Home Crime	.002	.004	-.002	.004	.002	.004	-.002	.004	.014***	.004	.002	.003
City	-.339**	.149	-.108	.145	-.513***	.160	-.262*	.148	-.250	.167	.028	.110
Year Left Home	.042*	.024	-.015	.024	-.052**	.026	.013	.024	.037	.026	-.009	.018
Criminal Opportunities	.005	.045	-.019	.044	-.057	.049	.042	.045	.057	.049	.007	.033
Nights on Street	.073***	.024	.112***	.024	.093***	.027	.095***	.024	.028	.025	.016	.017
Member of Street Family W1	.617***	.152	.401***	.148	.398**	.162	.685***	.151	-.143	.164	-.084	.111
Dependent Variable W1	.240***	.048	.095**	.040	.097**	.045	.192***	.040	.338***	.047	.164***	.028
Intercept	-.807		2.314		6.799		.369		-2.929		2.281	
Adjusted R²	.197		.147		.105		.227		.317		.124	

* p ≤ .10
** p ≤ .05
*** p ≤ .01

Table 7.5. Street Family Membership and Second-Wave Crime

Part A:

	Member of a street family (N = 218)			Nonstreet family member (N = 158)		
	X	SD	%	X	SD	%
Drug Use	5.734	6.462	68	3.652	5.268	53***
Theft	1.688	4.986	34	.709	2.751	18***
Drug Selling	1.505	3.757	27	.880	2.976	16***
Prostitution	.853	2.687	13	.323	1.724	5***
Violence	.463	1.310	23	.335	.942	18***
Street Crime	10.243	12.691	79	5.899	8.929	62***

Part B:

	Street family membership[a]
Drug Use	.170***
Theft	.115**
Drug Selling	.089*
Prostitution	.120**
Violence	.054
Street Crime	.188***
Tutelage in Theft	.228***
Tutelage in Drug Selling	.331***
Tutelage in Prostitution	.225***

* $p \le .10$
** $p \le .05$
*** $p \le .01$
[a]Correlation coefficients.

The gang is a spontaneous, semisecret, interstitial, integrated but mutable social system whose members share common interests and that functions with relatively little regard for legality but regulates interaction among its members and features a leadership structure with processes of organization maintenance and membership services and adaptive mechanisms for dealing with other significant social systems in its environment. (p. 240)

As full a definition as this is, it is not sufficient to define the gang as this term is used in a growing research literature. Moving beyond social system and organizational properties of the gang, Ball and Curry therefore suggest further characterological, correlational, and consequential properties that add supplementary detail to their formal definition. These include indications that the gang

> is traditionally but not exclusively male and territorial and is often associated with lower-class, urban areas. Descriptive consequences including perceived antisocial behavior calling forth negative reactions from significant segments of society . . . add further specification.

Ball and Curry are explicit in emphasizing that this is only a start and that more formal and detailed definitions of the gang should follow.

Clearly, the groups of street youth that we studied have some characteristics that resonate with Ball and Curry's definition. As evident in the accounts introduced earlier in this chapter, street families were spontaneous in the sense of often emerging with little planning. They were also semisecret, or at least subterranean, in the sense of often operating away from and as alternatives to spending time in agency-run hostels, shelters, and social service sites. Furthermore, these groupings were interstitial in the sense of forming alliances that were used to relate to and function between other individuals and groups of youth and adults.

Like gangs, the groups to which street youth belonged were also integrated yet mutable; that is, they often involved close social bonds between members, but they were liable to reformation and elaboration as circumstances required. Also, these groups of street youth pursued common interests and functions that often were even more persistent than those faced by most gangs, in the sense of dealing with day-to-day crises of food, clothing, and shelter.

Groupings of street youth were also similar to gangs in tending to disregard the law, especially in the sense of looking for illegal as well as legal sources of shelter that were constantly at risk of official disruption, usually in the form of police warnings to move on or away from selected locations. Other similarities to gangs include the often identifiable leadership roles played by some individuals in these groupings, and the apparent primary mission of some of these groups to assist instrumentally and psychologically in the survival of peers in the harsh day-to-day environment of the street. All of these social system and organizational properties were found in the street groups that we learned about, much as they are described in the literature on gangs.

Notwithstanding these similarities, however, Toronto and Vancouver street families differ from the groups described in gang studies. Notable characterological, correlational, and consequential features emphasized in the gang literature were not always present in the street groups we encountered. These features – focused around territoriality, gender, class, and criminal involvement – are crucial because they are defining characteristics emphasized in most gang research (see Thrasher, 1927; Cohen, 1955; Miller, 1958; Short and Strodtbeck, 1965; Klein, 1971; Moore, 1991; Campbell, 1984; Hagedorn, 1988; Fagan, 1989; Spergel, 1989; Sullivan, 1989; Anderson, 1990; Huff, 1990; Taylor, 1990; Jankowski, 1991; Padilla, 1992).

For example, street families were not consistently territorial. They would often occupy a particular niche in the urban landscape that they inhabited – for example, selecting a location like the ceremonial flame at the Toronto City Hall during night hours as a place for sleeping – but they would share this space with other groups and individuals and move locations as incentives and circumstances dictated. Perhaps the key distinction in this regard was the tendency of these groups to be adaptive rather than possessive in their association with social space.

The street groups that we encountered were also not characteristically male or male dominated. Indeed, as the qualitative accounts presented earlier in this chapter demonstrate, many of these groups had more female than male members. Although female gangs are receiving increasing attention (e.g., Campbell, 1984), the gang literature focuses more prominently on all-male gangs, or gangs in which females are allowed membership on the basis of their relationship with a male gang member. Yet our respondents' first-wave estimates of the number of females and males in their street groups suggest a different experience. In 26 percent of the street groupings, females outnumbered males (this includes 12 percent that were exclusively female), and in 18 percent, there were equal numbers of both genders. Also, although 40 percent of groups were male dominated, females represented at least one-third of the members in half of these groups (the remaining 16 percent of groups had no females). Males in our research tended to be more individualistic in their behaviors and attitudes, whereas females were more collectively oriented, at least in the sense of identifying with street groups.

A greater diversity in class backgrounds also characterizes the groups in our study. In most ethnographies, gangs are composed of a homogeneous group of youth, most often drawn from the under- or working class (e.g., see Moore, 1991; Hagedorn, 1988; Fagan, 1989; Sullivan, 1989; Anderson, 1990; Jankowski, 1991; Padilla, 1992; however, see Monti, 1994). In contrast, the street groups we encountered included youth from across the class continuum and, as noted in Chapter Three, involved a sizable proportion of youth with middle-class backgrounds; rather than being united by their class of origin, these youth shared the foreground class experiences that characterize life on the street.

But perhaps most importantly, the youth in Toronto and Vancouver who indicated that they were members of street families were no more likely to participate with other street youth in crime. Membership in street families is associated with greater overall levels of participation and more frequent offending for a variety of offenses, but street group members were no more prolific in their involvement in *group* offending than were others on the street who were not connected to such groups. Thus, although embeddedness in street groups provides a setting for gaining criminal capital that can facilitate crime, it appears that this process occurs on an individual, rather than at a group or gang, level.

The foregoing features of the groupings we encountered may explain why the Toronto and Vancouver street youth we studied spoke relatively little about their membership in gangs. Nonetheless, there were some circumstances in which references to gangs did emerge; examining these comments provides further insights into the nature of street families and street gangs. For example, Donna had been involved in one of the larger west-coast ethnic-based gangs both at home and on the street. She remarked that many of her friends had "been in a gang of some sort" and that "I'm one of the lucky ones – I haven't been in trouble with the law, but . . . about two years ago . . . I saw one of my best friends get shot dead."

Lee also spoke about his membership in a less organized gang that originated around the sale of hallucinogenics: "[We were] a bunch of fucking kids hanging around. . . . We made a name for ourselves and started making money."

More often, however, when youth in this research spoke of gangs, it was as a reference point for differentiating the activities and structure of the street groups to which they belonged. Keith made this point in response to an inquiry about a gang that he once belonged to and how it compared to a group that he had described as a street family:

Yeah. It was different from the street family, because it wasn't just a street family. It had a purpose. . . . We had all these rules. . . . If you broke them, then you got beat up by the group.

Tim was also heavily involved in an established, highly organized, ethnic-based gang while he lived at home. He drew a distinction between this gang (and the extent and sophistication of its criminal activity) and the street group with which he was involved currently. He recalled that:

> I was in a gang, and I didn't want to be in a gang anymore. I moved into something that was kind of a gang but not really. . . . When I was in the gang, you'd party, you went out to fight people, maybe more. It was really bad. I just didn't need the hassle anymore.

Other youth further distinguished street families, noting the differences between these groups and neighborhood- or school-based gangs of youth who lived at home, in their communities. Ross made this point when describing the difference between Toronto street groups and gangs:

> The people I hear hitting people, hitting girls, say, "I'm going to punch that girl or guy from Regent Park" – they are not street kids. They have a home. They have a place to live. I hear kids from Danforth Tech saying that. They're living at home . . . they have their own groups, school gangs. I call them gangs because they *are* gangs. They're out there hustling people and bullying people into giving them money and stuff like that.

Ross went on to describe an incident in which a gang from an industrial suburb came downtown with advance warning to challenge street youth who gathered daily around a prominent storefront service agency. The visiting gang encountered a larger than ordinary gathering of street youth from a number of smaller groupings that this respondent claimed posed a sufficient retaliatory threat to discourage a violent confrontation. The climax to this episode reportedly occurred in the food court of the adjacent shopping mall:

> We were sitting down there partying, and they showed up. . . . The guys just saw that there were about 150 street kids sitting around up there, and there was no such thing as different little groups – there was a whole bunch of wandering. People would get up, people would be sitting around one table, look over and say "hi" to the person over there, and go over and talk to that person for a while. We had these table hoppers going all over the place. And everybody's doing it. . . . They [the threatening gang] just sort of turned around and walked out.

The veracity of this account is perhaps less important than the respondent's point that the assembled street groups were coordinated for a defensive rather than an offensive purpose.

Jay made a similar point by describing his street group and its capacity to mount a defense, if threatened:

> It's just like a whole bunch of people, just hanging out, if anything happens, you know. They're all there sort of thing, right? It wasn't really a gang. It wasn't like, I mean a gang is more like somebody, like a group of people that directly go out to do a whole bunch of stuff, you know what I mean, to go rob these people, rob this and rob that, or do this, you know. These guys are just cooling out, just hanging out doing what they're doing. . . . But if somebody came in and started causing trouble, then it would more like turn into a gang.

Street Families in Context

We have used a lexical and relational approach in this chapter to study the groups to which street youth often belong. This approach attends to the language and conceptualization that youth use to describe their groups, and it focuses on the relationships involved in the causation and consequences of street group membership.

Although there may be an inclination to think of these groups as gangs, the youth involved are more likely to conceptualize their participation in familial terms. We conclude that they are essentially correct in this conceptualization. Street groupings share many of the formal and abstract properties of gangs, but they are not characterized by features most often emphasized in the gang research literature: These groups tend not to be distinctively male, class-specific, or territorial, and although group membership provides a forum for criminal tutelage and facilitates involvement in a variety of offenses, it does not increase the frequency of group-related crime.

Instead, street families tend to form around issues of survival and support, and individuals within these groups often assume specialized roles that frequently are identified in family terms, including references to street brothers and sisters, and even street fathers and mothers. Although street family memberships are often transient, they address very real and specific survival needs. Both our qualitative and quantitative data indicated that street youth form family-like groups to provide protection and safety and to pursue joint solutions to the problems of finding shelter, food, and money. These needs and concerns are somewhat greater for females than males, and for street youth in Vancouver than in Toronto. In particular, female street youth and youth in Vancouver are more likely to be members of street families because of their concerns about safety.

As we learned of the motivating role that the safety and survival needs of street youth played in forming street families, we began to expect that these groupings might serve a vital role in protecting and even improving the emotional well-being of street youth. To our surprise, our quantitative measures reveal that members of street families were actually more depressed than other youth in our sample. However, our research suggests that it is the lack of shelter that increases depression among these youth rather than street family membership in and of itself. Street families seem to be an important part of the lives of many street youth, but in the end, these pseudo-family structures appear to offer only limited resources for combating the persistent problems of the street.

CHAPTER EIGHT

Street Crime Amplification

HISTORICALLY, SOCIOLOGICAL CRIMINOLOGY was split between its classical and positivist inclinations. Classical criminologists examined offenders entirely through the lens of legal sanction effects on their behaviors, reflecting a preoccupation with issues of criminal deterrence. In contrast, positivist criminologists considered sanctions only as markers of the offenders they wished to study in their search for nonlegal causes of criminal behavior. So far in this book, we have followed the positivist inclination to focus on background, developmental, and foreground causes of crime that are separate from official, legal responses to these acts. In this chapter, we extend our analysis by incorporating the attention of the classical approach to legal sanctions.

Sociological criminologists recently have begun to bridge the separation between classical and positivist criminologies by investigating links between extralegal causes of criminal behavior and the effects of legal sanctions. This exploration is encouraged by concurrent theoretical developments that spark interest in contexts and sequences of parental and legal sanctions in the life course. Over the course of their lives, street youth often experience both severe parental and legal sanctions. In this chapter, we use recent macro- and microsociological insights into shaming, stigmatization, and sanctioning to construct a dynamic model of criminal behavior that addresses the possibility that legal sanctions may amplify rather than deter trajectories of criminal behavior. This model emphasizes that there can be legal as well as extralegal causes of criminal behavior.

The New Sanction Theories

The deterrence doctrine forms the core of classical criminology. This theory's postulates – that swift, severe, and certain sanctions deter crime – guided criminologists and lawmakers for at least a century after the influential writings of Beccaria (1764/1953) and Bentham (1789/1982). Labeling theorists later seconded the classical concern with sanctions but inverted the direction of expected effects; they argued that sanctions increased subsequent involvements in crime, regardless of offender background (Tannenbaum, 1938; H. Becker, 1963/1973, 1964), and that, with the exceptions of sanctions, the origins of crime were often random (Lemert, 1967).

Labeling hypotheses often have proved as difficult to sustain empirically as earlier deterrence hypotheses (Gove, 1975). The radically opposed expectations of deterrence and labeling theories should have made this outcome predictable, and more recent theories of criminal sanctions have sought to improve on this experience by broadening the explanatory field. For example, Donald Black's (1976) theory of the behavior of law asserts that the family and the state are interconnected systems of social control. Parental sanctioning is social control, even when it includes arbitrary, excessive, or brutal punishment of children, and family violence may sometimes be a form of self-help that substitutes for formal social control, as when abused spouses strike back against their partners' attacks (Black, 1983). Black reasons that variation in family processes of social control often are associated with the nature and timing of legal control. This underlines the point that family contexts can shape or condition the influence of legal sanctions.

Braithwaite (1989) focuses on a different kind of connection between family contexts and criminal sanctions in his proposition that deviance typically elicits one of two responses: positive, reintegrative shaming, or negative stigmatization. Reintegrative shaming is characteristic of benign family settings and certain legal systems such as that of Japan. In these settings, expressions of reacceptance follow disapproval of deviant behavior. According to Braithwaite, reacceptance promotes reintegration and thus reduces recidivism. In contrast, stigmatization is typical of abusive families and criminal sanctions in North America, where the person is punished as much or more than the behavior. In these environments, there is usually little or no provision for reintegration, and the shame of being sanctioned is unabated. Thus, offenders remain socially isolated – a condition that encourages reoffending. The key to Braithwaite's distinction is that reintegrative shaming includes rituals of reacceptance and reabsorption, whereas stigmatization is unremitting and exclusive.[1]

Scheff and Retzinger (Scheff, 1988; Scheff and Retzinger, 1991) add further microlevel detail to our understanding of shame and sanctioning by analyzing their impact on interpersonal bonds. The core of Scheff and Retzinger's theoretical contribution builds on Lewis's (1971) premise that disapproval which leads to unconfronted or unacknowledged shame (i.e., unresolved through reintegration) results in anger. Lewis calls this a *feeling trap*. Scheff (1988) notes that such shame-induced feeling traps have inter- as well as intrapersonal implications:

> When there is a real and/or imagined rejection on one or both sides . . . the deference-emotion system may show a malign form, a *chain reaction* of shame and anger between and within the interactants. This explosion is usually brief, perhaps a few seconds. But it can also take the form of bitter hatred and can last a lifetime. . . . I refer to such explosions as *triple spirals* of shame and anger (one spiral within each party and one between them). (p. 397)

Scheff suggests that this kind of shaming can be especially persistent, observing that *"the unlimited fury of shame/rage in a triple spiral may explain why social influence can be experienced as absolutely compelling"* (p. 397).

Although Scheff and Retzinger do not draw explicit linkages between informal and formal shaming/sanctioning sequences, they do note the direct connection between their formulation and the work by Lewis and Braithwaite:

> Lewis found that unacknowledged (pathological) shame damages the interpersonal bond; Braithwaite found that stigmatizing shame damages the bond between the punisher and the punished. . . . Although Lewis studied discourse at the microlevel and Braithwaite studied punishment at the macrolevel, they reached the same conclusion. We will call it the Lewis–Braithwaite hypothesis: that normal shame and shaming produce social solidarity, whereas pathological shame and shaming produce alienation. (p. 30)

We suggest that the next step is to see a sequential and consequential connection between the experience of unresolved and personally experienced shame and rejection within the family and unmitigated state stigmatization.

Although many family experiences have the potential to foster feelings of the pathological shame that Scheff and Retzinger describe, we suggest that the familial physical and sexual abuse we have considered in earlier chapters are prime sources. Youth who suffer repeated abuse may live in continually escalating shame-rage spirals that are exacerbated by subsequent societal reactions, for example, by legal authorities. Braithwaite anticipates (1989) this possibility:

> Just as the evidence shows that aggression and delinquency are the reaction to excessive use of punishment and power assertion as the control strategy within the family, we might expect rebellion against a demeaning punitiveness on the street to be all the more acute when families have eschewed authoritarianism in favor of authoritativeness. (p. 80)

Scheff and Retzinger (1991, p. 164) make a similar point, noting that parents, teachers, employers, and fellow citizens increasingly recognize large numbers of highly "touchy," angry young people ready to punish any available target for the sins of their past insulters, starting with the shame they felt as children from rejection by caretakers. An implication is that police-imposed sanctions may often be the sequelae that set off spirals or sprees (see also Katz, 1988) of criminal activity by youth previously subjected to brutal and/or arbitrary family punishment.

Lawrence Sherman (1993) similarly emphasizes the explosive and persistent nature of youthful reactions to criminal sanctions and draws on the work of Lewis, Braithwaite, and Scheff and Retzinger in developing what he calls a *defiance theory of the criminal sanction*. Sherman begins by observing that similar criminal sanctions often have opposite or varying effects in different social settings, on different kinds of offenders and offenses, and at different levels of analysis. He suggests that this heterogeneity of outcomes can be explained by closer attention to connections between kinds of offenders and kinds of sanctions. Sherman (1993, p. 450) reasons that "weak theoretical guidance has resulted in a complete absence of variables consistently tested for interaction effects with sanctions" and that "this problem is compounded by the general tendency to report only main effects of sanction tests, without testing for interactions" (see also Hagan and Palloni, 1990).

In a key part of his formulation, Sherman (1993, pp. 458–59) draws on Braithwaite and on Scheff and Retzinger to identify interactions that involve the defiant recidivist reactions of sanctioned criminal offenders. Sherman (1993) reasons that the question of when criminal sanctions lead to defiant responses is addressed by Scheff and Retzinger's sociology of emotions, and that "a great deal of evidence suggests the best name for this proud and angry emotion – and the retaliation it causes against vicarious victims – is defiance" (p. 459). The implication is that when the kind of unresolved personal shame emphasized by Scheff and Retzinger interacts with the unremitting criminal stigma emphasized by Braithwaite, a defiant criminal response is likely to follow. That is, family-based experiences of shame and rejection can interact with state-imposed criminal stigma to provoke what earlier labeling theory referred to as *secondary deviance* (Lemert, 1967) – that is, criminal behavior that follows sanctioning.

Sanction Sequences in the Life Course

Although issues of child abuse were prominent in discussions of delinquency early in this century, and continue to be prominent in the literature on street youth and runaways, Sampson and Laub (1993; see also 1994) lament that today "many sociological explanations of crime ignore the family" (p. 97). They reopen a door to this literature in their discussion of a psychological conflict paradigm that analyzes parental discipline practices and parent–child relations. Drawing in part on Patterson's (1980, 1982) coercion theory and Braithwaite's analysis of stigmatization, Sampson and Laub theorize that erratic, threatening, and harsh or punitive parental discipline and rejection of the child can lead to delinquency; they point further to the exogenous role that parental alcoholism can play in the causation of these problems. Sampson and Laub find substantial empirical support for a parental coercion model in their reanalysis of panel data collected on delinquent and nondelinquent boys in an earlier part of this century in Boston (see Glueck and Glueck, 1950, 1968). This family context model provides a foundation on which to build an analysis of the effects of stressful family experiences on involvement in crime, and Sampson and Laub (1993, pp. 136–37) allude to the further possibility that legal sanctioning may be linked to family contexts in the causation of subsequent criminal involvements.

This possibility is explicitly incorporated in Agnew's (1985, 1992, 1994, 1995) revised general strain theory of crime that we introduced earlier (see Chapters Three and Four). In essence, Agnew (1994) argues that "if you treat people badly, they may get mad and engage in delinquency" (p. 38); these people "are more likely to be born into aversive family environments and so be the recipients of negative behavior for at least the first part of their lives" (p. 17). Agnew (1995) then draws the explicit connection between family context, legal sanctioning, and subsequent behavior:

> The anger/frustration experienced by the individual energizes the person for action, creates a desire for revenge, and lowers inhibitions – including concern for the long-term consequences of one's behavior. As a result, individuals will sometimes engage in delinquent behavior even though such behavior has little prospect for alleviating the negative conditions that stimulated it. Such behavior may even have a high likelihood of negative sanction. This is one reason why the punishment of deviance may sometimes provoke further deviance. (p. 31)

This formulation of a general strain theory anticipated by references to Agnew's work in earlier chapters links together a series of stressful life events in a way that is similarly anticipated in psychological and sociological studies of stress and well-being.

For example, the kind of chain reaction postulated by Scheff and Retzinger and the interrelationship of bad experiences highlighted by Agnew parallels Rutter's (1989) discussion of chains of adversity in the life cycle (see also Caspi and Elder, 1988). Rutter (1989) writes that "the impact of some factor in childhood may lie less in the immediate behavioral change it brings about than in the fact that it sets in motion a chain reaction in which one 'bad' thing leads to another" (p. 27). Rutter further observes that "antisocial behavior . . . will influence later environments through the societal responses it induces – such as custodial or correctional actions that may serve both to 'label' and to strengthen antisocial peer group influences" (p. 42). This chain of adversity can have multiplier effects, as the metaphor of a chain reaction implies.

Peggy Thoits (1983) also points to the multiplicative effects of stressful life events. She observes that

> a person who has experienced one event may react with even more distress to a second . . . ; to the person, life might seem to be spiraling out of control. This would produce . . . [an] interaction between event occurrences; two or more events would result in more distress than would be expected from the simple sum of their singular effects. (p. 69)

Thoits (1983) continues and offers a vulnerability model of interaction in which early stressful events set the foundation for adverse reactions to subsequent events. In this model, "predispositions are remote, enduring physiological and psychological characteristics that . . . enhance . . . the impacts of current life experiences" (p. 80). Thoits notes that this kind of model is not sufficiently developed in the literature on stress.

The cumulation of the work we have reviewed supports our argument that childhood experiences of parental abuse and violence, and the resulting shame spirals these produce, may be predisposing life experiences that interact with later criminal justice sanctions to intensify involvements in crime. This is a model of secondary deviance in which childhood victimization constitutes a family context and a set of informal sanctioning experiences that interact with later formal sanctions imposed by the criminal justice system. Drawing on the theoretical leads of Lewis, Black, Braithwaite, Sherman, Sampson and Laub, and Scheff and Retzinger, we propose that these violent childhood events can initiate sanction sequences that, in interaction with police charges, increase the likelihood of defiantly persistent criminal behavior. This notion of interaction is consistent with the kinds of feeling traps, chain reactions, and resulting crime sprees and spirals depicted in a diverse set of recent formulations. This is a conceptual convergence that deserves empirical testing.

Testing Sanction Sequences

A meaningful exploration of the model of secondary deviance that we propose requires unique data. First, the model is developmental and therefore requires data that locate variation over time. In particular, we require data that allow temporal separation between parental and legal sanctions and primary and secondary deviant acts. A cross-sectional representation of these events would not provide a convincing analysis of this dynamic model.

Second, a meaningful representation of the secondary deviance model requires extensive control for background variables that may cause both crime and sanctioning, so that common causes of the former can be separated from putative effects of the latter. As demonstrated in preceding chapters, these background variables are potentially wide ranging, including (1) differences in age, gender, and life experiences; (2) disadvantaging parental resources and socialization capacities; (3) parent and sibling crime and deviance; and (4) respondents' prior involvements in crime. A model of secondary deviance that does not control for such background differences risks serious misspecification.

Third, the defiance portrayed in our model of secondary deviance implies more serious acts of crime than school-based samples of high school or college students are likely to reveal. Our model infers a level of criminal activity uncommon in random samples of the population and that comes to the attention of, and is frequently sanctioned by, the criminal justice system. A sampling strategy that does not include serious offenders would provide an inadequate representation of this model of secondary deviance.

In sum, a convincing exploration of the proposed secondary deviance model requires panel data that are sensitive to variation in temporal sequence, with extensive measurement of background variation among individuals who are at high risk for serious criminal involvements. These are kinds of data that are of increasing importance in tests of crime theories (e.g., Piliavin et al., 1986), and the Toronto and Vancouver panel study of street youth lends itself to this purpose.

Modeling Street Crime Amplification

As noted earlier, it is important in this analysis to control not only for the background characteristics and experiences considered in earlier chapters but especially for family and early adolescent involvement in deviance. We control for familial criminality with measures introduced in the previous chapter; however, here we separate parent and sibling arrest to control for possible effects of contagion as well as inheritance (Hauser and Mossel, 1985).

In addition to family criminality, we also take into account continuity over time in the criminal behavior of our respondents; thus, we include extensive controls for past offending, as well as police contact. We introduce the detailed retrospective self-report indicators of crime used in earlier chapters, and we include measures of home and first- and second-wave street offending. These items measure sixteen kinds of crime including stealing food and clothing, breaking and entering, simple and aggravated assault, larceny and fraud, drug use and dealing, and since leaving home, having sex for money. We measure police contact with two items based on the number of arrests before leaving home, and since leaving home and prior to the first-wave interview.

The outcome measure for this analysis is criminal activity in the two weeks preceding the second-wave interviews. These data were collected three weeks after the first survey. As we note in Chapter Six, youth reported whether they had engaged in any of sixteen criminal acts on each day (i.e., starting with yesterday, two days ago, etc.) for the immediate preceding week, and then for five days of the week before that (i.e., one day, two days, etc.). At the most, any one activity could be reported to have occurred twelve times in this period. We combine violent and nonviolent acts in a single global measure because Sherman's notion of defiance and related discussions of labeling imply violent as well as nonviolent behaviors. This measure parallels the notion of defiantly persistent crime spirals or sprees that, in discussions of secondary deviance, are reputed to be amplified by the imposition of criminal sanctions. An inventory of all variables included in this chapter is presented in Table 8.1.

We begin our analysis by examining simple bivariate OLS relationships between background characteristics, including our measures of sexual abuse and physical violence and of second-wave offending (see Table 8.2). Later equations include a selection hazard term that corrects for potential bias arising from retention in the second-wave interviews.[2] The most significant correlates of second-wave crime are maternal alcoholism and drug addiction, prior delinquency at home and on the street at time one (during first wave), and being charged on the street at time one. Less significant correlates of second-wave offending include the general measure of physical violence by parents against these youth and the more specific and detailed measure of violence by mothers toward these youth. Gender, parental control and education, being on the street in Vancouver, and being charged while living at home also are less significantly related to second-wave crime.

The next pair of columns in Table 8.2 report results from the OLS regression equation that introduces the physical violence and violent mother measures along with the measures of maternal alcoholism and drug addiction.[3] When the latter measures of chronic chemical dependencies of mothers are included in these equations, they reduce below significance the measured effects of physical and maternal violence.

The structural equation estimated in the final columns of Table 8.2 includes all the background variables in our analysis. Again, none of the abuse or violence measures display significant effects on second-wave crime. Maternal addiction, and to a lesser degree maternal alcoholism, remain significant influences, as do gender, home and street crime, and the effect of being on the street in Vancouver. Meanwhile, with all of these variables held constant, being charged on the street at time one (during first wave) retains its strong and significant influence on second-wave offending. This highly significant effect of being charged at time one on crime at time two (during second wave), despite our controls for a wide array of background variables that include comprehensive measures of prior offending, provides compelling evidence that these sanctions play a notable role in the causation of secondary deviance, or what we have called *street crime amplification*.

Thus far our results provide support for a theory of secondary deviance.

Table 8.1. Concepts, Indicators, and Descriptive Statistics for Analysis of Street Crime Amplification (N = 376)

Concepts	Indicators	X	SD
Sexual Abuse	When you were at home, did one of your parents or other family members ever have or try to have/ suggest having sex with you (including touching or attempting to touch you sexually)?[a] (alpha = .887)	.652	1.784
Physical Violence	While living at home, were you ever struck so hard by a parent/stepparent/guardian that it caused a bruise or bleeding?[b]	1.237	1.261
Violent Toward Father	Threatened to hit or throw something Threw something Slapped, kicked, bit, or hit with fist Hit with something Beat up[c] (alpha = .847)	2.191	3.798
Violent Toward Mother	Above items directed at mother[c] (alpha = .845)	1.532	3.015
Violent Father	Above items directed at respondent[c] (alpha = .891)	4.912	5.626
Violent Mother	Above items directed at respondent[c] (alpha = .896)	4.987	5.518
Maternal Alcoholism	Mother had a drinking problem[d]	.399	.874
Maternal Addiction	Mother had a drug problem[d]	.210	.666
Paternal Alcoholism	Father had a drinking problem[d]	.641	1.074
Paternal Addiction	Father had a drug problem[d]	.144	.562
Father Arrested	Father arrested for criminal offense (Yes = 1)	.301	.459
Brother Arrested	Brother arrested for criminal offense (Yes = 1)	.178	.383
Paternal Education	Level of education achieved[e]	2.803	1.787
Maternal Education	Level of education achieved[e]	3.082	1.693
Family Disruption	One of biological parents absent at age 10 (Yes = 1)	.710	.454
Paternal Unemployment	Father's unemployment experience[f]	1.582	1.078
Maternal Unemployment	Mother's unemployment experience[f]	1.521	.955
Parental Control	Father/mother knew where you were/who you were with when you were out[g] (alpha = .702)	12.439	4.102
Parental Support	Father/mother talked about your thoughts and feelings/did things you wanted to do[g] (alpha = .545)	10.218	3.351

Table 8.1. (cont'd.)

Concepts	Indicators	X	SD
Year Left Home	Year left home	86.652	5.440
Age	Reported years of age	19.540	3.569
Gender	Reported sex (Male = 1)	.662	.474
City	Where interviewed (Vancouver = 1)	.298	.458
Home Crime	Stolen food Stolen clothes Stolen things worth between $10–$50 from store Stolen things worth more than $50 from store Sold something had stolen Broken into a house, store, school, or other building and taken money, or things like stereo equipment Broken into a locked car to get something like a tape deck or radio Beaten someone up so badly they probably needed bandages or a doctor Used a knife or other weapon in a fight Attacked someone with the idea of seriously hurting or killing that person Used or tried to use credit or banking cards without owner's permission or passed bad check Smoked marijuana, hash, etc. Taken acid, pcp, angel dust, etc. Taken coke, crack, etc. Sold marijuana or hashish Sold coke, crack, or LSD[h] (alpha = .835)	15.434	16.686
Street Crime (Wave 1)	Home delinquency items + had sex for money[h] (alpha = .874)	35.471	26.609
Charges While Home	When lived at home, how often charged by the police for a crime[h]	.878	1.548
Charges on Street (Wave 1)	Since leaving home, how often charged by the police for a crime[h]	1.694	2.091
Street Crime (Weeks 1/2, Wave 2)	Street delinquency measures, days acts committed, drug use omitted[i]	1.987/ 3.519	4.032/ 7.049

[a] Never = 0, once or twice = 1, a few times = 2, often = 3, a lot of the time = 4
[b] Never = 0, once or twice = 1, sometimes = 2, often = 3, always = 4
[c] Never = 0, rarely = 1, sometimes = 2, often = 3, most of the time = 4
[d] Not a problem = 0, somewhat of a problem = 1, a serious problem = 2, a very serious problem = 3
[e] Grade school = 1, high school = 2, high school graduation = 3, apprenticeship = 4, college = 5, university = 6
[f] Always employed/housewife/deceased = 1, unemployed once = 2, unemployed several times = 3, unemployed most of the time = 4, unemployed all the time = 5
[g] Never = 1, rarely = 2, sometimes = 3, usually = 4, always = 5
[h] Never = 0, 1 = 1, 2 = 2, 3–4 = 3, 5–9 = 4, 10–19 = 5, 20–29 = 6, 30–59 = 7, 60+ = 8
[i] Number of days specific acts committed.

Table 8.2. Bivariate and Multivariate OLS Coefficients for Main Effects on Second-Wave Street Crime [a]

Independent variables	Bivariate relationships		Multivariate relationships			
	b	SE	b	SE	b	SE
Sexual Abuse	.182	.271			.164	.195
Physical Violence	.853**	.364	.461	.384	−.018	.327
Violent Father	.046	.088			.029	.070
Violent Mother	.175**	.086	.035	.087	.116	.072
Violent Toward Father	.174	.124			.079	.094
Violent Toward Mother	.099	.159			−.121	.127
Maternal Alcoholism	1.706***	.516	.959	.530*	.719*	.411
Maternal Addiction	2.456***	.657	1.660	.692**	1.639***	.539
Paternal Alcoholism	.238	.455			.202	.323
Paternal Addiction	.145	.871			−.915	.583
Father Arrested	1.515	1.066			.175	.759
Brother Arrested	.890	1.264			.783	.862
Paternal Education	−.540**	.266			−.273	.196
Maternal Education	−.414	.284			−.058	.202
Family Disruption	.709	1.078			−.195	.720
Paternal Unemployment	.228	.460			.037	.307
Maternal Unemployment	.582	.514			.421	.341
Parental Control	−.205*	.115			−.014	.085
Parental Support	−.052	.147			.070	.107
Year Left Home	−.053	.090			.038	.060
Age	.009	.139			−.113	.094
Gender	2.158**	1.086			1.795**	.725
City	2.732**	1.095			1.460*	.822
Home Crime	.101***	.026			.050**	.023
Street Crime W1	.103***	.014			.046***	.018
Charges While Home	.525*	.312			−.245	.235
Charged on Street W1	1.083***	.190			.634***	.192
Selection Hazard			12.421**		.574	
Intercept			2.557		−4.459	
Adjusted R^2			.107		.244	

[a] Bivariate coefficients are estimated with the selection hazard included in the OLS equations.
* $p \leq .10$
** $p \leq .05$
***$p \leq .01$

However, our interest is in the further possibility that violence directed against youth by their parents can establish predispositions that interact with criminal sanctioning experiences to cause amplifications in secondary deviance. We move to these multiplicative models in Table 8.3.[4] The first equation in Table 8.3 includes the interaction of the sexual abuse measure and the police charges variable. Although there was no significant main effect of sexual abuse in Table 8.2, Table 8.3 reveals a significant interaction of sexual abuse and police charges on second-wave offending. This effect persists in the presence of all the control variables included in the structural equations estimated in the previous table, including the remaining strong effect of maternal addiction and of home and prior street crime measured in the first wave. Recall that although we do not have measures that link sexual abuse to a specific parent, the research literature is consistent in showing that fathers, stepfathers, and other male family members are overwhelmingly the sources of this abuse.

The second equation estimated in Table 8.3 displays the interaction effect of the bruised and bleeding measure of physical violence with police charges on second-wave offending. This interaction is again significant with all other variables in the equation. This measure of physical mistreatment also does not identify the parental source of maltreatment; however, the items used in the third and fourth equations estimated in Table 8.3 do specify parental sources of abuse, and it is the violent mother measure that significantly interacts with police charges in its effect on second-wave crime. The fifth equation in Table 8.3 includes all three previously significant terms involving sexual and physical violence; of these, the sexual abuse and violent mother interactions with police charges remain significant. This implies that both sexual abuse by fathers and physical violence by mothers interact with criminal sanctioning to amplify involvement in secondary deviance that is above and beyond that predicted by these experiences separately and in addition to prior offending and other background characteristics.

As a final way of confronting the implications of these findings, we reestimated structural equations separately for male and female street youth and for each of the two weeks considered in the second-wave survey. These equations include all the independent variables considered earlier, as well as the sexual abuse and violent mother interactions with police charges on criminal activity in each of the two weeks that preceded the second-wave survey. In total, eight expected interactions were included in this collection of equations. As shown in Table 8.4, four of these inter-

Table 8.3. OLS Interactions of Abuse and Violence with Charges on Street on Combined Second-Wave Street Crime [a]

Independent variables	Eq. 1		Eq. 2		Eq. 3		Eq. 4		Eq. 5	
	b	SE	b	SE	b	SE	b	SE	b	SE
Sexual Abuse x Charges on Street	.281***	.107							.255*	.107
Physical Violence x Charges on Street			.299***	.110					.066	.138
Violent Father x Charges on Street					−.029	.027				
Violent Mother x Charges on Street							.085***	.025	.072**	.031

[a] All equations include selection hazard and all main effects of independent variables in Table 8.2.

* $p \leq .10$
** $p \leq .05$
*** $p \leq .01$

Table 8.4. OLS Interaction Effects of Parental Abuse and Violence and Charges on Street on Street Crime, Decomposed by Gender and Week of Second Wave [a]

Interaction terms	First week		Second week	
	b	SE	*b*	SE
A. Sons (*N* = 249)				
Sexual Abuse x Street Charges	.284***	.095	.283**	.114
Violent Mother x Street Charges	.036***	.015	.048***	.018
B. Daughters (*N* = 127)				
Sexual Abuse x Street Charges	.086**	.037	.045	.064
Violent Mother x Street Charges	.043***	.014	.036	.023

[a] All equations include selection hazard and all main effects of independent variables in Table 8.2.
* $p \leq .10$
** $p \leq .05$
*** $p \leq .01$

actions were significant at the .01 level, two were significant at the .05 level, and a seventh was nearly significant at the .10 level. The weakest and clearly nonsignificant effect was among female street youth in the second week. Notwithstanding the exceptions noted, this analysis suggests that although these interaction effects may be strongest and most consistent among males, there is also support for their influence among female street youth.

A Qualitative Coda

The analysis presented in this chapter thus far has been behavioral, even though the theoretical background to the analysis includes a focus on emotions. In this sense, our analysis has more in common with the work of Braithwaite than with Scheff and Retzinger. The latter explain the tendency to study shaming behaviors more than emotions in terms of the low-visibility aspect of the emotion of shame:

> Although the emotion of shame is disguised in our society to the point of virtual invisibility, shaming behavior is more visible. We are much more aware of behaviors that ridicule, reject, or degrade than we are of their effects – that

is, the states of shame caused by these behaviors – because the shame is usually hidden. (1991, p. 174)

The hidden nature of shame raises problems of falsification for purposes of hypothesis testing that we have avoided through the use of behavioral measures of parental rejection and legal degradation – in our case, self-reports of sexual and physical mistreatment and police charges. As anticipated, our extensive open-ended interviews provide many illustrations of the problems encountered by street youth when they discussed experiences involving emotions of shame. We found that although most youth showed little reluctance in answering specific behavioral questions about parental abuse, crime, and police contact, many were more hesitant in describing their feelings about these experiences. However, as Scheff (1988) suggests, some feelings of shame can be recognized in other forms of expression:

> Overt, undifferentiated shame involves painful feelings that are not identified as shame by the person experiencing them. These feelings are instead referred to by a wide variety of terms that disguise the shame experience: feeling foolish, stupid, ridiculous, inadequate, defective, incompetent, awkward, exposed, vulnerable, insecure, having low self-esteem and so on. (p. 401)

Our interviews provide several examples of these kinds of feelings of foolishness and stupidity mixed with defiance among previously abused youth who described their reactions to being caught and charged by the police. The previously abused youth involved in these illustrations were angry with themselves for being "stupid enough" to get caught by the police, as well as with the obtuseness of the police.

Glen was physically abused by both of his adopted parents. He noted that his disinterest in school and low grades frustrated his teacher parents and often led to violent outbursts, a scenario reflected in the following incident:

> My dad was hitting me in my bedroom, and I tried to run past him to get out of the bedroom, and I pushed him, and he caught me, and he laid me down on my stomach, and he put his knees on my back, grabbed my neck and twisted it, and he said, "If you ever do that again, I'll kill you." And, uh, he was hitting me with a broomstick that night, and I was full of bruises just after that. I'd planned to run away like, numerous times before that, but finally this is it you know. I thought, I'm not going to put up with it anymore, and I just packed stuff and left.

Glen recalled a later street encounter with the police in which he was charged with possession of drugs. He ends his description with the kind of self-deprecating sentiments emphasized by shame theorists:

> Like a couple of times a year, they [the police] just walk through the street and just grab people. . . . I got grabbed. . . . I was walking down the street and there was two large men. . . . I started running, but I would have got away too if I wasn't drunk. 'Cause I hit the other sidewalk, and I kicked it, and I tripped, then, yeah, they jumped on me, and I had, um, an ounce and a half of hash. . . . I mean, it wasn't very smart. I just, I'm so arrogant.

Neither the arrest nor feelings of foolishness and arrogance deterred Glen from continued conflict with the law. He was later charged with disorderly conduct in an encounter that he described in the following way:

> The cops were walking by, and I guess I said something I shouldn't have. And, um, so he came over, and he said, uh, "Do you have a problem?" and I was mouthing off. Then he said, "How old are you?" I said, I told him I was 16, and they said, "What's your name?" and all this, and I made up a fake name, all sorts of stuff. And they said, uh, "You don't look 16," and I said, "Well, I'm 16." Then I realized it was too late, 'cause I got myself. I shouldn't have never said nothing, right? But I got myself in trouble.

Like Glen, Ted also grew up in a violent home, which he left in his midteens. The following passages describe Ted's reactions to the police and his arrests: His first statement captures his feelings of superiority when he was successful at having his first court case dismissed, whereas the latter contains a number of references to his hostility and sense of stupidity for being charged again shortly afterward.

> INTERVIEWER: So why didn't you end up in jail after your first arrest?
> TED: Well . . . because, uh, I'm kind of smart when it comes to dealing drugs, uh . . . uh . . . I was, I was, selling through a motel, and then the motel was in someone else's name. So, they found the drugs in the motel room. I was in the motel room, and they charged me, and I got out on bail. . . . And when it came to court, they had to drop charges, because the motel wasn't under my name, and the drugs weren't in my possession.
> INTERVIEWER: What about the last one? Do you think you'll be able to get off? What happened?
> TED: I'm not gonna walk, I don't think. I'm gonna get, like, I'm gonna get convicted on it, 'cause he found it on me. I was so stupid. I was drunk. It was outside and . . . I was so stupid, I had a bag of weed in my back pocket, and

he asked, the cop asked me for IDs, and I hauled out my IDs, and the big bag of weed fell out on the, on the ground. I said, "Oops." He was like, "Hmmm, what do we have here?" I said, "Oh, that's nothing." I said, "Can I have that back?" He said, "I don't think so." . . . And we sort of had an argument and a fight.

Combined feelings of anger and foolishness are also present in Sheneika's description of two incidents in which she was charged with prostitution. As we noted earlier, Sheneika had been sexually abused by her stepfather and "turned out" by her "boyfriend":

One guy drove up, and this guy looked like a fucking biker from hell. He had like, a long beard, and he was all scruffy, all kinds of tattoos and blah, blah, blah. He said, "Yeah, I want. . . ." I said, "Yeah, whatever." He said, "Yeah, yeah. I'll pay this much." I said, "Yeah, whatever." He says, "You're under arrest." I said, "You're a goof. You're a fucking goof." Oh, I couldn't believe it. I'm still mad about that. And another guy with glasses like this thick. And he looked just so nerdy. He didn't look like he could fucking lift a piece of paper. . . . And then afterwards he takes off the glasses, and he says, "You know, I don't understand why you do this, you're a beautiful girl." And I said, "You're a goof." That's all I could say. I was, I was more mad than anything else, if I ever got arrested I was pissed off, that they want. . . . It was more like, I don't know, I've been hiding and now you've found me. That kind of thing. You know, yeah . . . I got pissed off at myself for not being clever enough to deek [fake my way] out of the way or something.

Renee's comments about her arrest for prostitution also reflect feelings of shame associated with official contact; her account makes the further point that the police are not the only state agents who can inspire or enhance feelings of shame. Renee was "turned out" by a boyfriend that she met on the streets when she was 15; over the next three years, she worked for several pimps before escaping the streets when she became pregnant. When we first asked Renee about difficulties of street prostitution, she replied: "Uh, um, I guess, people that picked you up." After a few seconds, she added:

Na, actually that wasn't even as bad as the police coming and picking you up and taking you to social services and you had to sit and talk to your social worker.

Lisa's description of her arrest on charges of break and enter includes another source of feelings of shame and hostility. Lisa was 16 when she was arrested, and because of her age, the police contacted her mother and requested that she come to the city jail to escort Lisa home:

She's [my mother] like, "Do you realize you're not gonna be able to cross the border, you're not gonna be able to do anything, and your name is gonna be on police files for ever?" And I'm like, "Mom, shut up, I know, okay. I feel stupid enough as it is. You don't have to rub it in."

Encounters with the police did not deter any of the foregoing youth from further involvement in crime and conflict with the law; the opposite was more likely the case.

The common theme in these accounts is that the youth involved feel more stupid than regretful, more angry than guilty. It is this kind of feeling that Scheff and Retzinger argue animates pathological spirals of shame, and it may be this kind of emotion, built on top of earlier and intense feelings of shame and rejection involving parental abuse and violence, that amplify the kinds of defiant spirals or sprees of secondary criminal involvement that we have modeled in this chapter.

Bridging Classical and Positivist Criminology

Classical criminology presumes a uniform world in which all offenders can be deterred by swift and certain sanctions; in contrast, positive criminology assumes that crime can only be understood by examining factors other than legal sanctions. Only recently has sociological criminology begun to integrate its classical and positive antecedents by identifying interactions of kinds of offenders and sanction experiences that might account for variations in trajectories of criminal careers.

Drawing on theoretical contributions of Lemert, Black, Braithwaite, Scheff and Retzinger, Agnew, Sherman, Sampson and Laub, Rutter, and Thoits, we propose that predisposing family contexts of parental abuse and violence interact with police sanctions to amplify involvements in secondary forms of street crime. These interactions identify sanction sequences that increase risks of secondary deviance, resulting more often in defiance of, than deterrence by, law.

The interactions we observe include those between parental mistreatment and criminal sanctions; these are strongest among males but are also apparent among female street youth. Although these interactions involve forms of sexual abuse that overwhelmingly involve fathers and stepfathers, they also include an unanticipated effect of physical violence by mothers. The latter effect may reflect the emphasis in traditional sex roles on the nurturing role of mothers and the consequence that youth are, therefore, more sensitive to feelings of rejection and shame in response to physical violence from mothers. It is also important to note that this maternal violence may be causally linked to violence that mothers experience at the hands of spouses. Furthermore, Simons et al. (1994) note that because women are assigned the more burdensome roles in child care, their parenting is more vulnerable to the influence of external stressors. More generally, our findings suggest that the potential for abuse and its effects in interaction with criminal sanctions is well distributed across the genders.

Some doubts may persist about our findings. The first may involve the retrospective validity of reports about childhood abuse provided during late adolescence and early adulthood. Conflicting and perhaps counterbalancing concerns are raised about such reports. Although it is said that these reports might be inflated by the desire to excuse later disreputable behaviors, it also is suggested that constraints about social desirability might suppress the willingness to report these events. We incorporated multiple measures of parental mistreatment to counter these kinds of problems in our research. Straus (1979, 1990) developed such measures for just this purpose, and they are as reliable in our research as in many prior studies, with alpha reliability coefficients above .8. Beyond this, we believe the strongest claim to validity for our findings lies in their consistency: Across time and gender, we find an array of sexual and physical mistreatment measures leading to a consistent pattern of interaction effects. It seems unlikely that deception would lead to such systematic results.

A second doubt may nonetheless persist that these measures can so neatly separate the flow of violence between children and parents. We again resist this argument by reference to the multiple measurement strategy directed specifically at this problem, and by noting the earlier onset of parental violence reported in Chapter Five. However, it is interesting to entertain the possibilities that the alternative interpretation raises. Suppose that our analysis demonstrates only that aggressive children provoke their parents and later the police into sanctioning their offensive behavior. The problem would nonetheless remain that the imposition of criminal charges is counterproductive: The likelihood of further crime is increased rather than reduced. This interpretation leads as well to the disconcerting conclusion that sanctions vary in their effects across kinds of offenders, and that such sanctions are often counterproductive among those who are most likely to experience them.

Interactions involving sequences of parental and criminal sanctions bear an interesting and more general connection to the study of turning points and trajectories in the life course (e.g., Robins and Rutter, 1990; Elder, 1994). This kind of analysis often involves a search for specific experiences in childhood, adolescence, or early adulthood that can alter the trajectory of life outcomes. Our research suggests circumstances in which these transitions and turning points are more prolonged and contingent. At least one sociologist, George Herbert Mead, would not have been surprised. In the early part of this century, Mead (1918) noted that criminal sanctions can amplify as well as deter crime, and that events in childhood often are connected with those in adolescence and adulthood in shaping longer-term life outcomes (Mead, 1934). Theories of criminal sanctions probably have been slow to acknowledge and incorporate these insights because, as Mead noted, the observation that offenders vary in their reactions to criminal sanctions conflicts with and complicates norms of uniformity that are central to classical principles of punishment. Our findings suggest that the assumption of uniformity that underwrites these principles is dubious. These findings cast further doubt on the premise that criminal sanctioning is an effective means of dealing with many of the problems of street youth.

Leaving the Street

THIS BOOK PAINTS A MOSTLY GRIM PICTURE of the daily lives of urban street youth. While most young people invest the largest part of their daily energies in the relatively benign worlds of school or work, homeless youth spend most of their time less profitably and more dangerously on the street and in parks, social assistance offices, shelters, and abandoned buildings. Together with friends acquired on the street, they spend a large part of their time looking for food, shelter, and money. Some actively seek and find work, but most remain unemployed, spending their time hanging out, panhandling, partying, and foraging in the shadow economy of the street.

Clearly, the outlook for most of these youth is bleak. Most will experience profound difficulties in making the transition from adolescent to adult roles. Recent structural changes in employment opportunities and the increasing domination of the service sector with its poor-paying and unstable jobs make this transition especially problematic for youth with limited human and social capital (Krahn, 1991; Revenga, 1992). Life course research confirms that the problems of troubled youth often anticipate difficulties in adulthood, in terms of crime, work, marriage, and other measures of well-being (e.g., Robins and Rutter, 1990). This body of research suggests the odds are poor that street youth will successfully traverse the important transitions necessary to move successfully from adolescence to normative adulthood.

Starr (1986) suggests that troubled youth often lack four factors that are important in the transition from adolescence to adulthood: (1) family and other relational support; (2) school experiences that enhance human capital and social skills; (3) part-time work that develops habits required in adult employment; and (4) opportunities for rewarding full-time careers. In contrast, the circumstances of homelessness predict that the trajectories of many street youth will be plagued by problems of inadequate support and incomplete education, combined with spells of unemployment, substance abuse, and crime.

However, there are also some breaks in this otherwise cloudy picture. Although life course research reveals a consistency to life trajectories (Caspi, Elder, and Herbener, 1990), it is also the case that some lives are redirected as a result of significant transitional experiences or "turning points" (Elder, 1975, 1985). Trajectories constitute long-term continuities or lines of development, whereas transitions or turning points are single or multiple events that occur over shorter periods of time and involve changes that are more pronounced and abrupt. In this chapter, we shift our focus from transitions and trajectories that result in crime and related problems to examine effects of finding employment as possible transitional events or turning points in the lives of street youth. Specifically, we explore the effect of finding full-time work on involvement in foraging activities associated with homelessness: hanging out; panhandling; searching for food, shelter, and other necessities; and involvement in crime. We propose that work can introduce a favorable source of dissonance into the lives of street youth, a dissonance that can encourage these youth to reduce their embeddedness in street activities. We hypothesize that as homeless youth become increasingly involved in full-time employment, they tend to move away from the street scene and to seek out more conventional pathways to adulthood.

Work and the Transition to Adulthood

In advanced western societies, acquisition of full-time employment is one of the key factors in the transition from adolescence to adulthood. As Mortimer (1996) notes, full-time work reduces and often ends the more dependent, pre-adult student role; it enhances independence from parents and can provide the financial capital necessary for independent living, conjugal relationships, and the support of children. Status-attainment research (Blau and Duncan, 1967; Sewell, Haller, and Portes, 1969; Sewell, Haller, and Ohlendorf, 1970; Hauser, 1971; Duncan, Featherman, and Duncan, 1972) demonstrates that this transition is influenced by several background factors, including paternal education and employment experiences, as well as aspirations and school performance. Subsequent research reveals that a further array of social psychological factors intervene between these background factors and occupational attainment. Mortimer (1996) notes that these include economic inclinations, such as "tastes for employment versus leisure," and the "propensity for work versus unemployment," as well as social-psychological variables such as motivation, mastery, achievement orientation, self-esteem, and self-efficacy. Recent studies of achievement indicate that employment success is further influenced by traditional parental educational and occupational variables, as well as by parent–child communication and closeness (see Mortimer, 1996).

Research on youth work experience reveals additional links to adult achievement. A growing literature demonstrates that employment during high school can enhance adolescents' subsequent work stability and earnings, particularly when employment provides reasonable economic returns, challenging tasks, and opportunities for advancement (Stern and Nakata, 1989; Steel, 1991; also see Bachman and Schulenberg, 1993).

Given the economic imperative of employment, as well as its centrality to adulthood, it is not surprising to find that joblessness is associated with pathological responses, including emotional distress, self-blame, and depression (Kessler, Turner, and House, 1989). Moreover, early and frequent unemployment can entrench these feelings, leading to a withdrawal from the labor market and increased participation in debilitating activities such as substance abuse and other deviant behaviors.

Employment and Crime

In earlier chapters, we report that the majority of street youth experience considerable unemployment. For most youth, the lack of a high-school diploma significantly reduces the likelihood of obtaining work (Rosenbaum, Kariya, Settersten, and Maier, 1990); for street youth, the lack of a permanent address and money for work-related expenses (e.g., transportation and suitable clothing) reduces the odds further, often effectively eliminating them as candidates for jobs. Involvement in street life, particularly street crime, probably further reduces the chances of street youth to find permanent employment. This situation reflects the links observed between unemployment and crime in both macro- and microlevel theory and research. As noted by Farrington, Gallagher, Morley, St. Leger, and West (1986), "there is no shortage of theories which predict that unemployment leads to crime" (p. 335). These explanations include classical delinquency theories with their emphasis on material need (Bonger, 1916), strain (Merton, 1938; Cloward and Ohlin, 1960), and weak social bonds (Hirschi, 1969), as well as rational-choice economic models (G. Becker, 1968; Block and Heineke, 1975; Witte, 1980). More recent explanations include Wilson's (1987) thesis that inner-city joblessness and residential isolation stimulate crime among the "truly disadvantaged."

In addition to the diversity of reasons to expect the link, there is also considerable macrolevel evidence of a relationship between unemployment and offending. For example, in a review of sixty-three studies, Chiricos (1987) concludes that there is a positive and often significant association between aggregate-level unemployment and property crime. Subsequent research reveals that the effect is more pronounced at the intracity level and when unemployment is lagged in time series data to reflect its priority (see Land, Cantor, and Russell, 1995). At the individual level, Farrington, Gallagher, Morley, St. Leger, and West (1986) also report a positive relationship between unemployment and delinquency among their panel study of London boys. Hartnagel and Krahn (1989) reach a similar conclusion in their analysis of data from Edmonton youth: They report that, in this sample, offending was highest among unemployed youth and increased with the length of unemployment.

The consistency of these findings is complicated by the likelihood that the relationship between unemployment and crime is reciprocal. In their studies of Philadelphia youth, Thornberry and Christenson (1984) and Good, Pirog-Good, and Sickles (1986) both document that links between unemployment and crime flow in both directions. Hagan (1993) notes that delinquency typically precedes unemployment in the chronology of the life course, and that early offending may often increase subsequent unemployment because crime encourages contact with other offenders and can embed the involved youth in illegal networks. Entrenchment in these networks increases the probability of future unemployment by increasing the amount of time spent with other offenders and limiting access to connections that facilitate normative activities such as finding work. Unemployment solidifies these deviant associations and increases the likelihood of future offending.

Hagan (1993) finds support for the primacy of crime in his analysis of London youth. He reports that delinquency at ages 16 through 19 has a significant effect on unemployment at ages 21 to 22, with youth unemployment held constant. Similarly, in their investigation of the reciprocal nature of this relationship, Thornberry and Christenson (1984) found that the effect of crime on unemployment was stronger and lasted longer than the more immediate effect of unemployment on crime.

The long-term, work-related consequences of criminality are also apparent in life course research. In their reanalysis of the Gluecks' (1950, 1968) data on male delinquents and nondelinquents, Sampson and Laub (1993) report that, as adults, delinquent youth had weaker occupational commitments, experienced more unemployment, and used social assistance more frequently. Hagan's (1991) analysis of panel data from Toronto-area youth yields parallel results that are also gender and class specific. He reports that male, working-class adolescents who identified with a delinquent subculture (i.e., involving minor property crime and fighting) were, as adults, more likely to work in jobs with low occupational prestige; in contrast, juvenile delinquency made little difference in the occupational lives of girls and more advantaged youth.

Youthful delinquency has further consequences in adulthood. Sampson and Laub (1993) find that youth crime is related to several adult deviant behaviors, including alcohol abuse, crime, and arrests; likewise, Hagan (1991) reports that, compared to nondelinquent youth, those who offend in their adolescence experience more problems with police in the post-teen years. These studies add to an extensive body of research that demonstrates the relative stability of antisocial behavior across the life course. Referring to this research, Sampson and Laub (1993) note that its "replications across time and space yield an impressive generalization that is rare in the social sciences" (p. 11).

The long-term effects of continuity in behavior demonstrated in the foregoing studies combine with our knowledge about street life to suggest that unemployed and criminally involved street youth are unlikely to experience a successful transition to adulthood. Yet life course research reveals that stability is not invariant or universal. The persistence of antisocial behavior across the life course is common only among males from and in disadvantaged backgrounds and settings with serious behavior problems (Hagan, 1991; Sampson and Laub, 1993, p. 13). Consistent with this finding, several of the foregoing studies indicate the possibility of change in behavior, particularly deviant behavior. For example, Sampson and Laub (1993, 1996) find that several events redirected the life trajectories of some young delinquents: joining the military, forming a secure and supportive conjugal relationship, and finding meaningful, stable employment. These experiences were significant turning points and were strongly related to desistance from crime and deviant behavior. Similarly, Hagan's (1991) research suggests that many youth who drift into a delinquent subculture in their adolescence leave this subculture in their early 20s.

The Role of Dissonant Contexts

Several processes may help explain why some experiences can change and create turning points in youthful life trajectories. Rosenberg's (1975) theory of dissonant contexts offers one possibility. According to Rosenberg, social locations act as frames of reference for people. These contexts include one's place in the larger social structure and cultural milieu, as well as the more specific contexts – networks and neighborhoods – that people inhabit. Rosenberg notes further that people often find themselves in conflicting contexts – situations that are not inherently dissonant but which are incompatible because of a person's experiences. For example, Rosenberg suggests that the self-esteem of black youth who enter integrated schools declines only if such youth represent a small fraction of the overall school population. In these cases, the lack of black peers means that the integrative experience is dissonant with these youths' previous schooling. Conversely, youth who enter settings where black and white youth are more equally represented encounter less conflicting social milieus; thus, they experience considerably less dissonance and are less likely to alter their self-images.

In general, Rosenberg's theory suggests that people who experience context dissonance resolve it in one of three ways: (1) by changing their views of themselves; (2) by modifying their perceptions of their environment; or (3) by exiting the dissonant context and increasing their involvement in non- or less-dissonant situations. Those who follow the third path resolve their dissonance by withdrawing from the situation that has the fewest social, psychological, or economic rewards and the greatest costs.

Homelessness is a potentially dissonant context. Street youth are outside most social institutions that conventionally provide young people with emotional and economic rewards, security, and status: the family, stable social networks, school, and work. Yet, for youth from violent or neglectful families, or those alienated from school and peers, homelessness initially may be less dissonant than the living situation they left behind.

Consider the case of Jeremy, who from the age of 7 spent the next five years of his life being shuttled back and forth several times a year between his separated parents. At 12, he responded to a beating from his alcoholic father by striking him with a baseball bat and fleeing. The police later found him on the street and took him to a child-care office; he was then made a ward of the government. Between the ages of 12 and 16, Jeremy estimated that he lived in approximately twenty-five foster and group homes. He fled most of these for the streets but was usually picked up by police and sent to another home. On his sixteenth birthday, he was legally able to leave government care; he described his course of action on that day as follows:

> Soon as I turned 16, you know, they said, "You have a place to go, man?" I said, "It's okay, you know, I like living the way I'm living [on the street]."

[They said,] "No, well, you have to live in this placement." [And I said,] "What are you talking about, I like it. Just leave it be."

Asked why he preferred the street over group homes, Jeremy replied:

I don't know, there's no rules. You know what I mean? Well, there's rules set by law, but we'd break them anyways, right? [It] doesn't matter.

Youth who establish street networks and become embedded in the freedom and hedonism of street life may also experience little conflict. Describing his arrival on the street, Glen noted:

I met a few people. . . . They were my first street family . . . we all crashed in a friend's bachelor apartment. It wasn't very big, but there were seven or eight people, you know, all crashed out on the floor all over the place, I found, um, I found it really exciting, 'cause I could get drunk and stoned – do whatever I wanted. And I didn't have a curfew. I didn't have anyone to answer to.

Indeed, as Glen indicated, some youth become attached to street life and often return to it as an alternative to other types of housing:

So, once I went to a receiving home; I stayed there for a couple of weeks, but I missed street life. Funny as that sounds or whatever, I missed it, you know? I missed not having a curfew, and doing, being able to do what I wanted. So I took off again.

Nonetheless, some street youth tire of street life and begin searching for opportunities to leave; these youth repeatedly stressed that employment is the key factor in exiting the street. Alan was accepted into a job-training program in the spring of 1992 after several years on the street. When we asked about the origins of his interest in the program, he replied:

Like, I've been partying every single day, wondering what I'm going to do next day, whatever, right? What I want is a weekly schedule to try and keep me out of trouble and stuff like that, right? That means, like, having a job, having a nice apartment to live in, right?

Most youth argued that it is all but impossible to withdraw from street life without a stable income. Commenting on the difficulty of leaving the street without the benefits of employment, Robert noted:

I mean, whenever I've lost a job, I've always found myself back there [the street], and it's [street crime] not easy money anymore.

In addition to the economic returns provided by employment, the demands of a job are often inconsistent with a homeless lifestyle. Extended involvement in work requires a commitment to scheduling, a continual delay of gratification, and a responsiveness to the authority and demands of others; these are sharp contrasts to the relatively unconstrained use of time, alcohol, and drugs that characterize street life. Thus, as street youth's employment opportunities increase, they may experience dissonance from their simultaneous locations in the two opposing worlds of work and the street.

The enhancement of human and social capital that accompanies steady employment may introduce further sources of dissonance. Street youth who remain employed for prolonged periods enhance their skills, knowledge, training, and work records. These assets facilitate continued participation in the labor force and foster an appreciation of the costs of inadequate human capital (Rosenbaum et al., 1990). This awareness is reflected in a comment Robert made when he explained how looking for a job had introduced several new concerns in his life: "You know, like going out into the work force, you have to start thinking about training and things."

Concurrently, these youth may gain access to conventional sources of social capital (Coleman, 1988, 1990). Involvement in the labor market increases interactions with others; this may lead to a set of personal ties that establish obligations and connections to the institutional frameworks and settings in which they are located. Co-workers may provide important information about job openings or connections for future employment opportunities (Granovetter, 1974), thereby increasing one's involvement in the work world. This process is captured in Paul's thoughts about the benefits of his recently acquired employment:

I'm due to be laid off in September or October, so, that kind of sucks, but I look at it this way. They're really pleased with my work. . . . So at least now I've got a good reference, right? Wherever I go, I can say, "Well, call this guy. He'll tell you I can work, right? [The boss] he said, if he can, like his brother owns a business and, of course, being a businessman he knows other businessmen, he said he'd try to hook me up with something else.

As the number of work-related associations increase and solidify, they may call further attention to the contradictions between street and nonstreet life, making it harder to reconcile the two worlds. Thus, homeless youth who find and keep jobs may experience increasing dissonance as they try to balance their work associations and friendships with unemployed street youth. Aaron's remarks reflect an awareness of the detrimental effects of hanging out with other street youth:

> When you start getting into this brother/sister, brother/sister stuff, you get, you get too involved, you know, because you have to remember, I mean, you're not going to be with these people for the rest of your life, you know, I mean, if you're smart, if you want to get off the streets, get a job.

A major source of conflict for employed youth is the demands made by other street youth, particularly those that involve activities or problems associated with street life. Commenting on his experiences, Winston discussed financial complications he encountered when he first found a job:

> My first paycheck I got like $215. What did I do with it? Actually I don't even know what I did with it, you know. It's like gone. Well, okay, I bought some clothes, and then I went to this party, right, and like, "You know guys, you know I got a job now, do what I want, I'm working right." And they're like, "Oohhh, you?" and all that, and like, "You owe me $5." Yeh, right! If I don't give them, give them money and cigarettes, then everybody's pissed off, 'cause I'm the only one that's working, right? . . . but it won't happen again.

As a comment by Doug suggests, other problems also arise, particularly when respondents are able to use their income to leave the street or a hostel for an apartment:

> Like as a street, as a street person, you know, you get too involved with your friends on the street. [If you get a job and can] get yourself an apartment, well then your street brothers or sisters expect you to take them in. You know, and if you don't take them in, they get all pissed off, and you can't go downtown to go shopping because they're going to be knocking, knocking teeth.

Doug concluded that, given the demands of street friends, the best approach was to remove oneself completely from street life:

> See, that's the thing, like when you move, like when you move into your own place, you don't just move into the closest place around. Think about what you're doing and say, "Okay, wait a second, this isn't the life I want. Wouldn't it be best to get farther away?"

Similar sentiments are evident in a comment made by Alberto. Alberto grew up in the inner city, where he lived in a small apartment in a large complex of government-subsidized housing. In his midteens, he started using and later selling marijuana before escalating to crack; he therefore had considerable exposure to the street before his mother evicted him when he was 16. When we discussed strategies for leaving the street, he stressed the necessity of decreasing the time spent with other street youth:

> But now I know this place, you know what I am saying? I know the whole street life scene. I know the hangings, and, you know, it's like, fuck, I don't want to know, I don't want to know him or her right now, I don't want nothing to do with them, you know. . . . Once you get your own place, you want to just get on with your life, right?

When asked why it was so important to get away from other street youth, Alberto replied:

> 'Cause you get messed up in the bullshit . . . uhm, more drugs . . . uhm, people, people giving me guilt trips, like "I'm kicked out tonight . . . can I come and crash?" It's like, it's not a flophouse, right? It's like, I'm not opening my own shelter . . . people I've met down here come over, but I don't really want them here.

For these youth, avoiding other street youth is key to initiating a nonhomeless trajectory and decreasing their involvement in substance use, crime, and other activities associated with street life. Reflecting on the steps he took to leave the street, Glen captured the necessity of withdrawing from those still involved in the street:

> I had to get a job. Um, I had to stay away from certain people . . . the same old drug dealers downtown. . . . I knew that was what I had to do, right? I just knew that, I, I made the decision that I didn't want, um, I wanted to stay out of trouble, I didn't want to go to jail, you know?

Testing the Effects of Work

We can also explore the effect of employment on embeddedness in street life in quantitative terms. We capture this relationship with data for each of the three waves of the study. Although the analyses in earlier chapters focus on only the first two waves of data, we use information on three waves to extend our exploration here across the summer months. We use this approach for several reasons: Youth employment is particularly volatile during the spring and summer months when large numbers of college, university, and high-school students enter the job market; also, the number of youth on the street often increases in late spring and early summer. Using data from all three waves should reduce the distortion that these phenomena impose in any one time period. Although advantageous in these ways, using all three waves of data reduces our sample size from 376 to 257. We consider later the implications of this reduction in the sample.

We measure work in this analysis in each of the three waves. We measure work at the first wave as the number of months employed in the six months prior to the first interview and since leaving home. This indicator includes work found through job-training programs, as well as through other means. Employment at the second and third waves refers to the number of days worked in the twelve days preceding each subsequent interview. To allow comparisons between the first-wave monthly measures and the second- and third-wave day-based measures, we divide the raw scores by the total possible number of months or days for each period; that is, we divide first-wave employment scores by six, and second- and third-wave work by twelve.

We use ratio measures of the proportion of time worked rather than the more commonly used dichotomous indicator of simple employment, because we assume that finding work is not so dramatic an event that it instantaneously transforms the lives of homeless youth. Indeed, our qualitative data suggest that these youth often alternate between temporary or short-term work unemployment, and activities more consistent with street life. Our assumption is that work-encouraged dissonance unfolds over time, accumulating with the length and extent of employment. Thus, similar to Rutter (1989), we do not see any single employment event as constituting a turning point in the popular sense of the term; rather, we view employment as part of a chain of events that can redirect a homeless trajectory.

To measure embeddedness in street life, we use items first introduced in Chapter Seven. These measures refer to the frequency of involvement in six foraging activities that characterize homelessness: hanging out, searching for shelter, looking for food, panhandling, using drugs, and stealing. Our indicators ask about these involvements in the context of activities pursued with other friends, providing an enhanced sense of embeddedness in an active street life. As a further test, we also explore how employment affects respondents' involvement in street crime, irrespective of their friends' involvement.

We introduce a number of variables to test the robustness of observed effects of work. These controls include those introduced in earlier chapters – age, gender, city, and time on the street – as well as parental education and employment. We include the parental measures to hold constant the intergenerational effects often found in status-attainment research (Blau and Duncan, 1967; Sewell et al., 1969, 1970; Hauser, 1971; Duncan et al., 1972). Although the latter studies do not focus on marginalized people, homeless youth's employment experiences also may be influenced by parental achievement and employment.

We also include two controls for the effects of human capital: a measure of the respondents' average grades in their last year of school and a scale measure of self-confidence. Our measure of self-confidence is based on two items that ask how strongly the respondents agree or disagree with the following statements: "I can do just about anything I set my mind to" and "I am responsible for my own successes." These statements capture elements of what Clausen (1991) calls "adolescent competence" or self-efficacy – an attribute strongly related to adult employment and more stable careers and marriages. As a final control, we add a measure of work from the preceding wave. The inclusion of the prior-wave measure of work makes the analysis an assessment of change in employment since the previous wave.

Finding Work

Our analysis begins with the descriptive data contained in Table 9.1. Remember that these data refer to only those youth who completed all three waves of the study; however, as we demonstrate later, information on the full sample and on those who completed two waves are comparable to the findings reported here. Consistent with previous research, our data reveal that more than two-thirds of the street youth we interviewed were unable to secure work during the time of the study. Information on job-search strategies reveals that at the time of the second wave, 59 percent of those unemployed reported that they were still searching for work, checking want ads, and visiting agencies and prospective employers. Moreover, 47 percent of those without work indicated that they had applied for at least one job in the two weeks prior to the second interview. However, these applications rarely resulted in employment. Respondents noted that, although they applied for many jobs, their homelessness seriously reduced the likelihood of their being hired. For example, when asked about the difficulties he experienced, Pierre replied:

Table 9.1. Employment and Job-Search Strategies of Street Youth

	Wave 2		Wave 3	
Variables	*N*	*%*	*N*	*%*
Employed (*N* = 257)				
No	187	72.8	181	70.4
Yes	70	27.2	76	29.6
Unemployed and looking for work in newspapers, etc. (*N* = 187, 181)				
No	77	41.2	96	53.0
Yes	110	58.8	85	47.0
Unemployed and applied for jobs (*N* = 187, 181)				
No	104	55.6	112	61.9
Yes	83	44.4	69	38.1

Uhm, just not having an address. If you don't have an address, employers, I mean, they take a look at you and they think, if you're not responsible enough to have an address, then you wouldn't be responsible enough to be working.

Other respondents noted that their lack of experience also substantially reduced their chances of being hired. This was reflected in a remark made by Brenda when we asked her about her search for work:

I don't have the job experience, I mean I do have some minor experience, but I don't have a lot.

The frustration associated with limited work experience is well captured in Dorian's statement:

They tell you, "You don't have enough experience." I say, "Well, how am I supposed to get experience if nobody hires me?" You know, it's a catch-22 situation.

Respondents were also acutely aware of the age discrimination that many youth face when searching for work (Rosenbaum et al., 1990). Nancy expressed the resentment that these young people feel when prospective employers dismiss them as possible job candidates once they realize their age:

> Like, people just look at a 19-year-old and think that you can do basically nothing, that you have no mind, that, I don't know. You just, they don't really treat you with the same amount of respect, they don't look at you the same as if, say, someone who's 30 or 40 came along for a job.

Not surprisingly, many youth respond to this situation by abandoning the search for work. By the time of the third interview, the proportion of unemployed youth still searching for work in the want ads dropped from 59 percent to 44 percent. The proportion who applied for work also fell, from 47 percent to 38 percent.

Nonetheless, some youth were able to find and keep jobs. In the first six months of 1992, 27 percent of the 257 respondents had found a job; at the second wave, the same percentage were working, and by the third wave, 30 percent had obtained employment. As expected, the majority of jobs were low-skill, service kinds of work. Yet a wide range of jobs were involved. In addition to the conventional fast-food, janitorial, and retail work characteristic of youth employment, respondents found jobs as rickshaw pullers, participants in research experiments, crossing guards, chicken catchers, and live-bait procurers. Several respondents successfully found employment in skilled jobs less typical of youth work. They worked as welders, meat cutters, carpenters, mechanics, and in other trades; some found employment in offices working as receptionists, title searchers, and counselors; and a few worked in entertainment as disc jockeys, piano players, models, and dancers.

In Table 9.2, we introduce descriptive statistics for the variables we use in our analysis of the effects of employment. We provide employment and street activity data for the 257 respondents who participated in all three waves of the panel, as well as comparable information for those youth who participated in only one or two waves of the study (reported in parentheses). These figures reveal that, for the most part, the first-wave means and standard deviations for the 257 respondents differ very little from those for the entire sample; a similar pattern occurs at time two (second wave) when comparisons are made between the 376 youth who completed two waves and the 257 who finished all three. These patterns suggest that our analyses are not biased by sample attrition, nor are the 257 youth who were retained for three waves uncharacteristic in their employment and street experiences (see the Appendix for additional details on the effects of attrition).

As we noted earlier, the majority of the youth surveyed were not able to find work; however, as the figures in Table 9.2 demonstrate, employment increased across the summer months. The mean for employment at the first wave was .133, by the second wave this rose to .161, and in the third wave it was .202. The summary statistics for street activities reveal that although the majority of youth had been involved with other homeless youth in street activities, their participation also varied as the summer progressed. First-wave mean scores ranging from 1.934 to 2.568 suggest that respondents and other street friends typically searched for food, panhandled, and committed a theft at least once or twice. Means for searching for shelter, using drugs, and hanging out are between 2.926 and 4.0, indicating that these activities were more common. However, involvement in all activities declined somewhat by the second and third waves, with, by the end of the study, hanging out and using drugs still most frequent, having mean scores larger than 2.

In Table 9.3, we present the results of our regression analysis of street activities. Our findings are consistent with the expectations developed from the qualitative data discussed earlier; that is, employment appears to stimulate a withdrawal from street life. Specifically, our data reveal that first-wave employment is negatively and significantly related to reported participation in all six street activities at the second-wave interview: Youth who were able to find and keep a job the longest reported the lowest subsequent involvement in hanging out, searching for food and shelter, panhandling, using drugs, and stealing with their street friends. Importantly, these effects occur even after the introduction of first-wave measures of each dependent variable and the other control variables described earlier.

We further explore the relationship between employment and street activities in Table 9.4. To simplify our presentation, we combine the individual measures of street activities into an omnibus scale (alpha = .736 for first-wave measures, and .719 for second-wave items). According to the equations estimated in Table 9.4, full-time employment in the months preceding the first wave strongly influences second-wave employment; it also has a sizable effect on third-wave employment, but this is reduced to nonsignificance by the intervening effect of second-wave employment. First-wave involvement in street activities is also negatively related to employment at both times; however, it only has a significant deterrent effect in the third wave. Second-wave street activities also discourage employment, as reported in the third interview.

Table 9.2. Descriptive Statistics for Employment and Street Activity in Three Waves of Panel Study (N = 257)

Variables	Wave 1		Wave 2		Wave 3	
	X	SD	X	SD	X	SD
Employment Activity[a]	.133(.118)[b]	.259(.298)	.161(.171)	.312(.321)	.202	.346
Hanging Out with Street Friends[c]	4.000(3.919)	1.100(1.217)	3.739(3.665)	1.277(1.308)	3.253	1.472
Searching for Food with Street Friends[c]	2.568(2.568)	1.336(1.389)	1.942(1.915)	1.241(1.206)	1.638	1.070
Searching for Shelter with Street Friends[c]	2.926(2.917)	1.343(1.359)	2.218(2.221)	1.262(1.305)	1.619	1.084
Panhandling with Street Friends[c]	2.409(2.361)	1.505(1.516)	1.798(1.707)	1.249(1.204)	1.463	1.031
Theft with Street Friends[c]	1.934(1.863)	1.247(1.216)	1.374(1.364)	.862(.850)	1.241	.693
Using Drugs with Street Friends[c]	3.370(3.303)	1.406(1.445)	2.872(2.771)	1.547(1.530)	2.521	1.569
Involvement in Street Life Scale	17.206(16.932)	5.233(5.571)	13.942(13.654)	4.589(4.846)	12.016	5.508

[a] Proportion of prior six months employed in wave one and proportion of prior twelve days employed in waves two and three.

[b] Scores in parentheses are for full sample of 482 cases in wave one and 376 cases in wave two.

[c] 1 = Never; 2 = once or twice; 3 = a few times; 4 = often; 5 = most of the time.

Table 9.3. OLS Regressions of Second-Wave Street Activity

Variables	Hanging out b	SE	Looking for food b	SE	Looking for shelter b	SE	Panhandling b	SE	Using drugs b	SE	Stealing b	SE	Street scale b	SE
Age	-.074*	.039	-.026	.038	-.049	.040	-.014	.032	-.018	.040	-.078***	.025	-.236*	.138
Gender	.312*	.180	.199	.172	-.060	.188	.005	.150	.446**	.184	.245**	.115	1.154*	.638
Paternal Education	.024	.044	.018	.042	.025	.045	.032	.036	-.115**	.045	.006	.028	-.011	.155
Maternal Education	-.077*	.044	-.025	.043	.012	.046	.004	.036	.004	.045	-.007	.028	-.091	.156
Paternal Unemployment	-.034	.071	-.029	.069	-.104	.073	-.030	.059	-.125*	.073	.012	.046	-.325	.252
Maternal Unemployment	.091	.082	.076	.080	.157*	.085	.083	.068	-.059	.085	-.027	.053	.321	.291
Competence	-.003	.036	.052	.035	.017	.037	.002	.030	-.015	.037	.040*	.023	.103	.126
Grades	-.016	.053	.006	.052	-.038	.056	.030	.044	-.096	.055	-.028	.034	-.107	.192
Home Crime	.002	.005	-.002	.004	.003	.005	.001	.004	.018***	.005	.003	.003	.022	.017
City	-.418**	.175	-.192	.168	-.362**	.179	.030	.143	-.025	.192	-.099	.112	1.052	.623
Year Left Home	.024	.030	-.009	.028	-.034	.030	.001	.024	.064**	.031	-.034	.019	.029	.104
Employment W1	-.566*	.297	-.462*	.267	-.604**	.300	-.432*	.247	-.621**	.307	-.459**	.192	-3.058***	1.060
Dependent Variable W1	.473***	.070	.425***	.055	.258***	.060	.526***	.042	.544***	.064	.278***	.040	.457***	.056
Intercept	.985		1.759		5.103		.482		-3.624		5.111		7.285	
Adjusted R^2	.178		.182		.101		.410		.401		.253		.289	

* $p \leq .10$
** $p \leq .05$
*** $p \leq .01$

Table 9.4. OLS Regressions of Second- and Third-Wave Employment and Street Activity

| | Employment | | | | Street activity | | | |
| | Wave 2 Equation 4.1 | | Wave 3 Equation 4.2 | | Wave 2 Equation 4.3 | | Wave 3 Equation 4.4 | |
Variables	b	SE	b	SE	b	SE	b	SE
Age	-.001	.010	-.009	.010	-.244*	.138	-.257	.155
Gender	.019	.047	.124**	.047	1.160*	.639	.836	.720
Paternal Education	-.002	.011	-.001	.011	-.014	.155	-.163	.173
Maternal Education	.009	.012	.018	.011	-.083	.156	.057	.175
Paternal Unemployment	-.020	.018	.014	.019	-.331	.252	-.447	.283
Maternal Unemployment	.006	.021	-.025	.021	.320	.291	-.338	.327
Competence	.001	.009	.007	.009	.105	.126	.016	.142
Grades	.024*	.014	.010	.014	-.101	.192	.071	.217
Home Crime	.003*	.001	.001	.001	.023	.017	.023	.019
City	-.028	.046	-.017	.046	-1.063*	.623	-2.396***	.703
Year Left Home	-.007	.008	.015*	.008	.021	.105	-.183	.118
Employment W1	.298***	.077	.128	.081	-3.028***	1.051	-.921	1.230
Street Activity W1	-.001	.004	-.008*	.005	.455***	.056	.293	.977
Employment W2			.422***	.064			.065	.071
Street Activity W2			-.014***	.005			.483***	.072
Intercept	.564		-1.156		8.094		27.140	
Adjusted R^2	.068		.238		.288		.305	

* $p \le .10$
** $p \le .05$
*** $p \le .01$

The results involving street activity in equations 4.3 and 4.4 of Table 9.4 are also consistent with our expectations. Involvement in street activities at the first wave increases subsequent involvement, as measured at the second wave; similarly, involvement in these activities during the second wave persists in the form of further involvement during the third wave. Notwithstanding the consistency and size of these relationships, equation 4.3 in Table 9.4 reveals that first-wave employment has a sizable negative effect on involvement in street activities during the second wave, independent of the effect of prior involvement in street activities. Also, first-wave employment discourages street activities in the third wave, but this sizable and significant effect is reduced to nonsignificance by the powerful effect of second-wave street activity.

In a final test, we explored the effects of employment on respondents' involvement in crime regardless of their friends' participation. Using the same omnibus street crime measure introduced in Chapter Five, our analysis is consistent with the results already reported (see Table 9.5). First-wave employment significantly reduces involvement in crime during the two weeks prior to the second-wave interview, and first-wave employment has a sizable negative effect on crime during the third wave that is reduced to nonsignificance only with the introduction of crime at the second interview.

Changing Street Trajectories

A considerable body of past research reveals that, for the most part, consistency and stability characterize life trajectories. This does not bode well for the majority of homeless youth who are often unemployed, embedded in criminal networks, and involved in street activities. Yet some youth do leave the street, and in this chapter, we have demonstrated that employment offers one important avenue of escape. Street youth who occupy an increasing proportion of their time working also spend less time hanging out, panhandling, searching for food and shelter, using drugs, and stealing with other street youth; they also report lower overall involvement in crime. That is, they become less embedded in street crime networks, which may become a source of dissonance in relation to alternative opportunities of newly found legal employment.

Our research adds to other studies' findings that occupational opportunities and interventions introduce important changes in the lives of disadvantaged youth (Sampson and Laub, 1993, 1996). However, as Sampson and Laub (1993) note, "of all the themes emphasized in life course research, the extent of stability and change in behavior and personality attributes over

Table 9.5. OLS Regressions of Second- and Third-Wave Employment and Street Crime

Variables	Crime – Wave 2		Crime – Wave 3		Crime – Wave 3	
	b	SE	b	SE	b	SE
Age	-.132	.303	-.083	.307	-.002	.246
Gender	2.735**	1.386	4.941***	1.408	3.252***	1.136
Paternal Education	-.629**	.340	-.292	.345	.095	.278
Maternal Education	-.189	.343	-.137	.349	-.028	.280
Paternal Unemployment	-.349	.554	-.828	.563	-.601	.452
Maternal Unemployment	-.163	.642	-1.434**	.653	-1.342**	.523
Competence	.015	.278	.027	.282	.016	.226
Grades	-.385	.418	-.460	.424	-.242	.343
Home Crime	.136***	.040	.118***	.041	.034	.033
City	4.666***	1.394	5.541***	1.417	2.574**	1.162
Year Left Home	.090	.232	.126	.237	.074	.190
Employment W1	-5.876***	2.323	-5.665**	2.360	-2.267	1.973
Street Crime W1	.109***	.027	.111***	.028	.043*	.022
Employment W2					.681	1.567
Street Crime W2					.614***	.052
Intercept	3.955		1.541		-1.097	
Adjusted R^2	.309		.317		.563	

* $p \leq .10$
** $p \leq .05$
*** $p \leq .01$

time is probably the most complex" (p. 9). The concepts of social embeddedness and dissonant contexts specify some of the important structures
and processes that influence stability and change; thus, they add to our
understanding of some of the complexity involved in changes from criminal
to more conventional careers.

Although most of the youth we interviewed emphasized their desire to
find work and leave the street, this goal is not universal. Those still new to
the street and those still enamored with street life often indicated a general
disdain for employment and an ambivalence about other activities associated with a more traditional, normative lifestyle. For example, Santori
summarized her plans for the future this way:

> I don't want a job. I never wanna work, ever. I'd like to live on the streets the
> rest of my life. But, I would like a place to live with a shower, and that'd be
> fine. I wouldn't care. If I had that squat, I'd live there forever.

Other youth also spoke about the pleasures of the street, and for some, the
lure of crime also increases the attractiveness of the street and is often
simply too much to resist. This point was made clear by Roseanne, when we
asked her about her plans for the future:

> I don't know, I don't have a really heavy-duty outlook on work. I mean, if it's
> something that I like to do, it's okay. You know, it's really cool. But, if it's
> something that I'm just doing so that I can get the money for it, I don't like it.
> I mean, I'd rather just sit out on the street and sell a lot of drugs. . . . You just
> have to sit around and make money and don't have to put up with people's
> bullshit.

For others, the deleterious effects of hanging out and partying with street
friends made finding work all but impossible. Tim estimated that he had
about six jobs since arriving on the street, including work in lumberyards,
landscaping, and unskilled construction. However, he had been unemployed since the start of the summer:

> I could find a job – once I put my head to doin' something, I can get it done.
> It's just, like, that I have a problem with getting things done, though. Drugs
> and alcohol . . . I always start partying rather than looking for jobs.

As Janet noted, even youth with good intentions can find it difficult to leave
the street:

Downtown drags you down . . . it brings you back down here [to the street], and you come down here for a night, you stay out all night, and you forget about work in the morning. You're too tired to go to work, you frigger it all up with work, you're tired and everything. [You get fired] and it brings you back to a hostel. That's what it does to you.

Meanwhile, the importance of work is perhaps most evident in the comments of youth who found jobs. Reflecting on his decision to give up stealing and selling drugs in favor of work, Martin emphasized the link between crime and unemployment when he cogently noted:

I grew up, I guess. I grew up. . . . [My] days of scamming was over . . . time to get a legit job, time to do what I got to do: make legal money.

For many youth, the attraction of legal money over that earned in crime was enhanced by their desire to avoid incarceration; this attraction was pronounced for respondents who realized that the law no longer considered them "young" or "juvenile" offenders and that if arrested they would be charged and sentenced in adult court. The recognition of one's changing legal status is well represented in a remark made by Nigel, who at the time of the third interview was working in a fast-food restaurant:

When you're a juvenile, you get charged and, uh, you get a little slap on the wrist, whatever, and you might get a couple of weeks in jail, maybe a couple of months, right? But like, when you turn 19, it's a different story. When you're an adult, you can go to jail for, like, five, ten years, seven years, whatever, right? So, I might as well get a job and make some legit money. Knowing that the money's, that you've worked for the money, and the money's coming to you instead of making some money somewhere doing "this or that." So, having a job, working for your money, you know that you have money coming to you in the next paycheck in two weeks or so.

Jordy also attributed his recent enrollment in job-skills training programs to a sudden realization; however, his change in consciousness was related to aging and a recognition of the potential costs of street life:

I had to stop. I thought about the consequences. Like, I turned 20 and I just thought, "Wow, man, I'm 20 years old. Holy shit, I'm just getting too old." I kept thinking of the fact that I heard that one out of every five youth between the ages of 16 and 25 will die by the age of 25, in a lifestyle that we live – out on the streets and stuff – which is a true fact, I believe.

Travis expressed a similar sentiment. When we first interviewed Travis, he had not worked since September 1991. At the time of the third interview, he had successfully completed a job-training program, was doing volunteer work, and had found a part-time job in the retail trade. When we asked how this change began, he replied:

I stopped taking drugs, and that's when I got faced with reality. Bam, right in the face! And I was like, wow! there's a lot more to give my thought to than I thought. I have a lot more resources that I can use to my advantage. I just said that's it. I'm going to put all my resources together and see what I can come up with. I made up my mind, no more fooling around. No more of this street crap. I'm getting my life back together. The first few steps are more psychological stuff. You think it's your fault that you are on the streets. If you don't stop, or if you think it's a party, you're going to stay on the streets. You're going to end up like one of those bums with long beards and the hats on. They get me thinking, some day I could be like that.

Other factors also made work more attractive than crime. As Simon argued, money made through offending usually disappeared more quickly than money he earned while employed:

Fifty dollars that you make out there lasts about as long as five dollars does that you make from a paycheck. . . . With myself I am so ashamed or so mad, and I have really bad feelings about pulling tricks, you know, like I was being used enough sexually in my life, and then I subject myself to it again. So then I need to sedate how I'm feeling, so I usually go and get really drunk. So then 80 percent of that money ends up being drinking money. And, like, you know, you have nothing to do all day and then having fifty bucks, you know, you're looking for a place to spend your money. You're looking for anything to entertain yourself.

Finally, it is important to recall that although we have focused on the importance of employment in redirecting homeless trajectories, the work available to homeless youth usually involves employment in the secondary labor market, particularly jobs in the service sector and other unskilled occupations. Generally, these jobs do not enhance workers' skills, and they are not the basis for establishing a career; nor are they the most desirable occupations for making a livelihood (Rosenbaum et al., 1990). Many youth are aware of the limits of these jobs, but they accept them because they provide a place to begin. Jack's comment reflects this strategy and captures the struggle some youth are prepared to undertake in order to leave the street:

> I kept my job because I needed it, and I was just getting by on it, but yet I kept it. I wasn't treated like a human being, I wasn't paid like a human being, but I stuck with it, just to get that little bit further ahead out of a hostel. It's just one notch out.

Street Criminology Redux

ALTHOUGH RESEARCH REPORTED IN THIS BOOK was conducted in Canada, this work was undertaken against a backdrop of theories of crime developed in Europe and the United States, and of research on the homeless in developing countries of Central and South America as well as in North America and Western Europe. This chapter links the pieces of this international story together and addresses theoretical and research issues associated with the study of youth and crime. One of the most salient of these issues is the range of theoretical orientations we use in studying street youth. Some of these perspectives – for example, strain and control theory – usually are seen as incompatible.

We propose that strain, control, and other prominent theories can be bridged within a social capital theory of crime. Our perspective contributes to a growing body of work that suggests advantages of integrating theories of crime (Johnson, 1979; Elliott et al., 1985; Messner et al., 1989), but our approach is distinct in its use of an overarching concept to unite these diverse explanations. To set the context for our theoretical synthesis, we first place the study of street youth within a highly condensed history of American criminology. This history is driven in significant part by changes in the American and more recently the global economy – a force that also contributes to the problems of street youth in developed and developing countries. It is against this backdrop that social capital theory emerges as a powerful framework that synthesizes attention to socially structured background, developmental, and foreground experiences of street youth.

A Background of Concern

Many of the advances in early twentieth-century European (e.g., Bonger, 1916) and North American (e.g., Thomas, 1923; Thrasher, 1927; Shaw, 1929) criminology reflected combined concerns about poverty and the effects of urbanization and industrialization on adults and families, especially children. This emphasis in crime theory and research remained prominent in the United States through the Great Depression and the pre–World War II period. The bleak economic circumstances of this era had a major impact on the early Chicago school of sociological criminology (e.g., Shaw, 1930; Shaw and McKay, 1931) and on others writing about crime during this period (e.g., Sellin, 1937; see especially Merton, 1995).

The post–World War II period and the early 1960s – the Golden Era in American economic history – brought a new prosperity and rising confidence in the capacity of a growing economy to solve many social and economic problems, including problems of poverty and crime. Few remember today that it was John F. Kennedy who pronounced during this buoyant period that "a rising economic tide could raise all ships." During the New Frontier and Great Society years of the Kennedy and Johnson presidencies, it was possible to imagine optimistically that a successful War on Poverty could be waged, in part with the goal of reducing problems of crime that were growing in America.

Criminological theories also flourished during the postwar boom years. Sutherland's (1947) theory of differential association rose to prominence in the two decades following World War II, and control (e.g., Reckless, 1961) and strain (e.g., Cohen, 1955; Cloward and Ohlin, 1960) explanations that had their origins in the works of Shaw and McKay (Shaw, 1929; Shaw and McKay, 1942) and Merton (1938) developed into comprehensive theoretical statements. In the same period, H. Becker (1963/1973, 1964) and Lemert (1967) extended the ideas of Tannenbaum (1938) and popularized the labeling approach to crime. None of these theoretical developments rejected outright the possibility of a connection between class and crime, or that poverty was a source of crime, but they each provided an alternative emphasis, placing greater attention on various factors that intervene between economic conditions and crime.

As the 1960s came to a close, the economic fortunes of many Americans continued to improve in an economy that was expanding at record rates. Despite this prosperity, property and violent crime continued to escalate, and doubts developed that it was economic adversity that was fueling this rise. American criminologists grew increasingly uncertain about the role

poverty played in the causation of crime and began to hedge their theoretical bets about links between class and crime. This is reflected in Shaw and
McKay's (1942) use of social disorganization theory to account for linkages
between impoverished neighborhoods and heightened crime rates, giving
way to Hirschi's (1969) focus on the weakened social bonds of young people
to families and schools in explaining delinquency. In the same period,
Hirschi's (1969) and Kornhauser's (1978) influential critiques of strain
theory discouraged interest in Merton's (1938) pioneering attempt to explain why impoverished groups experienced disproportionate amounts of
crime.

It is doubtful that these theoretical developments alone could have dra-
matically altered concerns about poverty and class in American criminology.
However, an important shift did occur when these theoretical developments
were combined with a methodological move from street-based field studies
to school-based surveys. This shift – signaled most successfully in Hirschi's
(1969) classic monograph – focused attention on the children of relatively
stable parents who infrequently had employment problems and other economic difficulties associated with seriously disadvantaged class circumstances. The more these relatively successful youth were studied, the less
concerned American criminologists became about links between poverty
and crime. The focus shifted to the more transient problems of conventional adolescents' involvements in minor forms of delinquency.

Yet, as this new and methodologically sophisticated form of school criminology reached its peak in American criminology in the middle and late
1970s, the U.S. economy was moving into a period of more modest and
episodic growth. Slower growth and intermittent recessions diminished
expectations that problems of poverty would abate. A "dual economy"
made up of "split" or "segmented labor markets" became an increasingly
important part of American life, with an intensifying division between a
"core or primary labor market" with better paying and more secure jobs,
and a "periphery or secondary labor market" in which wages and job
security were much reduced (Averitt, 1968; Hodson and Kaufman, 1982;
Revenga, 1992). Crime and violence also increased during this period. The
more persistently self-report methods were employed in efforts that con-
vinced some criminologists that there was no linkage between class and
crime, the more other criminologists looked to the increasingly polarized
social and economic circumstances surrounding them and questioned the
repeated application of this methodology in school settings to reach conclusions about class and crime (e.g., Braithwaite, 1989; Sullivan, 1989; Hagan,
1991).

During this period, American criminology was confronting a situation similar to that found in the sociological study of social stratification in the United States. In a partial reaction against the writings of Daniel Patrick Moynihan (1965) and Oscar Lewis (1966), researchers interested in stratification redirected their attention from race and poverty in the inner city and increasingly focused on the roles of education and status in the process of occupational attainment among samples of people with jobs. As a result, social scientists spent much of the last two decades neglecting the consequences of inner-city life, particularly joblessness, in a society where the problems of poverty and crime were becoming more, rather than less, apparent. Yet, as Wilson (1987) convincingly demonstrates, it was increasingly difficult and short-sighted of social scientists to ignore the presence and significance of a growing urban underclass.

Rediscovering the Street

Today, some of the most serious problems of poverty and crime in North America are found among the homeless. Homelessness is most common among adults, but it increasingly involves youth who flee from their homes or are rejected by their families. Once on the street, these youth face problems of poverty and crime that are neither negligible nor unique. Rather, street youth in North America share several experiences with their homeless counterparts in developing countries, for example, in South and Central America (e.g., see Aptekar, 1988; Campos et al., 1994), as well as in developed ones, such as the nations of western Europe (e.g., see Saunders, 1986; Kennedy, 1987; Mingione and Zajczky, 1992; Martinez, 1992). In some significant ways, the similarity of problems across these nations is as notable as the differences.

This unsettling point is made by Wright et al.'s (1993) recent comparison between street youth in one of the poorest nations in the western hemisphere, Honduras, and the United States. Wright and his colleagues demonstrate that modern social survey techniques can be used in the streets of developing countries, such as Honduras, just as they can in developed countries, and with results that suggest unsettling conclusions. For example, they find that

> Homeless street children suffer the burdens of disorganized and estranged family life – in Honduras *and* the United States. Homeless street children show exceptional levels of physical illness and mental anguish – in Honduras *and* the United States. Homeless street children are often underfed if not

clinically malnourished – in Honduras *and* the United States [Wright, 1991].
Homeless street children abuse drugs, prostitute themselves, scavenge for
sustenance in the garbage, and become involved in crime – in Honduras *and*
the United States. . . . Homelessness and extreme poverty are far more decisive in setting the conditions of life for children than national context or
cultural differences. When we hold the situation of street children in Honduras up to the mirror, we see . . . ourselves. (Wright et al., 1993, p. 90)

The implications of this conclusion are shocking, yet criminologists and
many other social scientists have not been inclined to address the issues
raised by Wright and his colleagues, and they have been slow to focus their
research on street youth.

Our goal in making these points is not to disparage this century's development of several important traditions of criminological theory, nor to
diminish a school-based criminology focused on self-report techniques.
Rather, our aim is to build on the innovations of both while simultaneously
resurrecting an earlier concern with the impact of a changing economic
context on the street life of the surrounding society. We believe that an
important avenue for this project involves the reinvention of a street criminology that focuses on ways in which youth come to the streets and on the
consequences of their being there. This street criminology can take advantage of the several theoretical traditions introduced previously, and of more
recent developments in sociological theory, as well as self-report survey
techniques, to learn more about the lives of youth living on our cities'
streets.

Social Capital Theory

We propose that the several theoretical traditions we use to study street
youth can be integrated within social capital theory (Bourdieu, 1986; Coleman, 1988, 1990; Sampson, 1992; Hagan, 1994, Chap. 3). Social capital
theory assumes that people acquire at birth and accumulate through their
lives unequal shares of capital that incrementally alter and determine their
life chances. It focuses on ways that individuals succeed and fail in socially
organizing their efforts to attain cultural goals; in doing so, this approach
attends to the place of delinquency and crime along with more conventional activities in life course development (Elder, 1985; Hagan and Palloni,
1988; Sampson and Laub, 1993).

Applying the concept of social capital requires that we elaborate our understanding of how capital is obtained. We acquire access to and accumulate

social capital through sociogenic processes that are structurally and culturally shaped, as well as ontogenetic processes that are individually and developmentally determined (Dannefer, 1984). Several kinds of capital are involved, and it is important to understand how social capital develops and evolves in ways that are analogous to more commonplace forms of capital.

The concept of physical capital is perhaps most familiar in referring to tools, machinery, and other productive equipment. This physical capital plays a central role in establishing and maintaining economic relations. However, economists have added to this the further idea of human capital – that is, the abilities, skills, and knowledge acquired by individuals through inheritance, education, and training (Schultz, 1961; G. Becker, 1964). The capital embodied in humans is somewhat less tangible than that embodied in tools or machinery, but both involve the creation of resources or power through a transformative process, so that "just as physical capital is created by making changes in materials so as to form tools and facilitate production, human capital is created by changing persons so as to give them skills and capabilities that make them able to act in new ways" (Coleman, 1990, p. 304). This human capital is most often created through schooling.

The creation of social capital involves analogous processes that are no less real and probably even more important, even though the product is less tangible than human or physical capital. Social capital originates in socially structured relations between individuals, in families and in aggregations of individuals in neighborhoods, churches, schools, and so on. These relations facilitate social action by generating a knowledge and sense of obligations, expectations, trustworthiness, information channels, norms, and sanctions.

Coleman (1990, p. 305) demonstrates this process of social capitalization with a simple triangular figure in which the end points or nodes of the triangle represent the accumulation of the human capital of two parents and a child. Coleman reasons that for the parents to further the accumulation of human capital through the cognitive development of the child, there must be capital in the nodes *and* the links of the diagram. That is, for the human capital of the parents to be passed on most effectively to the child, this transmission will usually occur through social capital represented in the social structure of all the connecting links between both of the parents and the child. Coleman (1988, 1990) refers to this as a form of *social closure* – in this case, of the social network of the family. However, this closure is important in other social groups, such as those that connect parents and children to other parents, neighbors, and teachers in schools, neighborhoods, and communities. Social groups can maximize their contributions to the development of various forms of capital when they have this characteristic of closure.

Because individuals vary in their access to social capital, they must adapt themselves to existing, continuing, and changing accumulations of social capital in the circumstances that they inherit and inhabit. Adaptations to these situations are expressed through various formations of cultural capital. When social capital is abundant in the community and family, these cultural responses often include the amassing of credentials of higher education and involvements in high culture, for example, including participation in the arts. In these community and family settings, social capital is used to endow children successfully with forms of cultural capital that significantly enhance their life chances (see DiMaggio, 1982, 1987; DiMaggio and Mohr, 1985).

However, in less advantaged community and family settings, without such abundant social and cultural capital, parents are less able to bestow or transmit opportunities to their children. Survival itself may be a struggle, and children and families must adapt to the diminished circumstances and opportunities they encounter. So while many parents who are well situated within secure and supportive social networks may be destined or driven by their capital positions and associated inclinations to endow their children with forms of social and cultural capital that make success in school and later life quite likely, the children of less advantageously positioned and less driven and controlling parents may more often drift or be driven into and along less promising paths of social and cultural adaptation and capital formation (Hagan, 1991).

Interestingly, Sampson and Laub (1993, pp. 18–19) point out that social capital often derives from strong social bonds and relations of *social control*, whereas Robert Merton (1995, p. 23) notes that the concept of social capital incorporates an *anomie-connected* emphasis on contingencies in the ways in which opportunities are nurtured. The implication of these observations is that the concept of social capital synthesizes two great traditions in crime research. Merton (1995) suggests the tardiness of such a conceptual development when he notes that "the powerful concept of social capital remained . . . unformulated back in the 1940s, thus providing us with another conceptual example of what has been identified in the sociology of science as a 'postmature scientific discovery'" (p. 23). Although Coleman (1990, pp. 305–6) was cautious in his claims about the potential of social capital theory, we agree with Merton that this conceptualization has an important capacity to synthesize and stimulate our understanding of crime, for example, by combining attention to processes of social control and opportunity.

Social Capital and Street Youth

The street youth we have studied in this book disproportionately come from families with diminished social capital. This is reflected in the finding that these youth are more likely to have left surplus-population families in which the head of household was unemployed, and disrupted families in which one or both biological parents were absent from the home. These limitations are linked in that youth from surplus-population families are in part more likely to be on the street because of difficulties and disruptions in their families.

The limited social capital available to the children of these surplus-population and disrupted families is a reflection of background and developmental factors emphasized in both Hirschi's (1969) version of control theory and Agnew's (1985, 1992) recent formulation of a sociopsychological strain theory. The place of control theory is reflected in the reduced levels of familial control and erratic parenting common among street youth, whereas the importance of strain theory is evident in the increased levels of coercion that characterize the explosive, violent families that these youth often have left. These youth are in turn also less likely to be committed to schoolwork and more likely to be in conflict with teachers, both of which further diminish the likelihood of their acquiring the social and human capital that derives from schooling.

The downward spiral in the capital positions of young people who take to the street is intensified by foreground experiences on the street. These experiences include both the consequences of release from any benefits of family control that they might have experienced and the new sources of strain in the day-to-day problems of finding shelter, food, and work. Apart from a range of other kinds of variables known to cause criminal behavior, we find consistent evidence of relationships between involvement in street crime and lack of food, work, and shelter. However, these findings represent only a first step in developing an understanding of the processes that lead street youth into crime.

Although some youth come to the streets with individual backgrounds and experiences that lead in a rather predictable ontogenetic fashion to persistent involvement in crime, other youth are swept and pushed into criminal involvements by the circumstances they encounter on the street.

These circumstances can be understood as having a sociogenic form that is central to social capital theory. For example, recall that social capital accumulates not only among individuals but also within communities. Our research illustrates the consequences of this community-level variation.

Toronto and Vancouver differ considerably in the access to social capital that they provide for young people on the street. While Toronto could be characterized as having a social welfare orientation, reflected in the provision of overnight shelters and support services to street youth, Vancouver operates more within the confines of a crime control model, providing few resources or support services for youth on the street. Left to find their own means of subsistence, Vancouver youth are more exposed to traumas of the street and opportunities to become involved in crime. While this did not differentiate the involvement of street youth in Toronto and Vancouver in violent crime, a kind of crime that likely has more ontogenetic origins, it notably increased the participation of Vancouver street youth in nonviolent forms of crime involving drugs, theft, and prostitution. The implication is that an absence of social capital in the form of services and support in Vancouver encourages street youth to capitalize on opportunities that they encounter to become involved in theft, prostitution, and the drug trade.

Thus far, social capital theory has provided a useful way to combine a consideration of the pathways by which youth come to the streets with pressures and opportunities that lead these young people to crime once they are on the street. In turn, a further concern of this theoretical framework with the closure of social networks alerts us to a process of embeddedness that we have found useful in understanding street youth's sustained involvement in different kinds of crime. First, however, consider how social embeddedness operates in more conventional circumstances.

In many people's lives, the personal contacts of individuals, friends, and families, and the networks of relations that flow from these contacts, are important sources of social capital used in finding jobs and making job changes (Granovetter, 1974, 1985; Coleman, 1990, p. 302). Youth in advantaged circumstances are more likely than others to have the social capital that derives from being "socially embedded" in employment networks that make finding and changing jobs easier. Put simply, early employment contacts enhance the prospects of getting a desired job and of subsequent upward occupational mobility.

However, connections into the life of the street may be just as likely in a converse way to increase the probability of unemployment and downward life trajectories once youth leave home and take to the street. For example, the criminal involvements of street peers are more likely to integrate young people into the criminal underworld than into referral networks of legal employment. And involvements in street networks are likely to further distance youth from the school and job contacts that are important in developing legitimate pathways into later life opportunities.

This kind of downward trajectory involves a process of criminal embeddedness that in the case of street youth results from exposure to mentors and tutors encountered on the street. These mentors and tutors transmit information and skills that constitute a form of criminal capital. We have found that embeddedness in these crime networks and the subsequent acquisition of criminal capital provide opportunities to become involved in some types of street crime, in addition to and apart from background ontogenetic measures of predispositions or propensities. The closure of mentoring and tutoring networks around these opportunities for involvement in crime can be thought of as a process through which street youth recapitalize their limited life prospects.

Lacking the social capital of conventional families or peers, it is not surprising that street youth often become associated with groups consisting of other similarly situated young people. We have found that although these groups are sometimes confused with gangs, they tend not to be distinctively male, territorial, or criminal, the salient characteristics of groups emphasized in the criminological literature on gangs. The street youth we studied were more likely to think of themselves as being members of street families. These groups coalesced around issues of mutual support and safety, and they addressed real and specific survival needs of street youth. This was especially true for female street youth and for youth in Vancouver, who had gender- and city-specific concerns about safety.

We anticipated that street families might enhance the social capital of their members, especially by improving their sense of emotional well-being. However, this expectation was not borne out in our research, and although street families seem to form an important part of the lives of many street youth, these pseudo-family structures appear to be neither the source of, nor the solution to, persistent emotional as well as survival problems of youth on the street.

We found that the effects of being on the street are compounded further by being officially labeled and known as a criminal. Street youth with backgrounds of parental abuse were particularly sensitive to the stigmatizing effects of police sanctions and had an especially high risk of intensifying their involvement in crime subsequent to their contacts with the police and being officially sanctioned. This may result from a compounding sense of shame and embarrassment that links earlier intense feelings related to parental rejection and abuse with later law enforcement contacts. Recent developments in labeling theory suggest that these highly charged emotional experiences can lead to defiant spirals or sprees of secondary deviance that in turn lead to increased levels of criminal embeddedness, and a further depreciation of social capital that is a product of the stigma of police contact.

Unfortunately, our application of social capital theory in this research is not a likely source of optimism about the life course prospects of street youth. Our use of this theory to highlight limitations imposed by disrupted family backgrounds and the hazards of embeddedness in criminal networks does not suggest a promising future for many young people on the street. However, social capital theory does point to legal employment as at least one important potential avenue of escape from the street (see also Sampson and Laub, 1993, 1996). Furthermore, the notion of embeddedness usefully identifies competing conventional and street domains that may constructively create feelings of dissonance for street youth who simultaneously occupy both settings.

The notion of "dissonance contexts" suggests that youth may experience increasing discomfort about their involvement in street activities and networks as they find and keep jobs, establish off-street networks, and build human capital. Our research is consistent with this hypothesis and suggests that there is a causal sequence that leads from finding legal employment to movement away from the street and to a declining embeddedness in street activities and networks.

Thus, although most of the work that street youth in our research were able to find was in the secondary labor market, these jobs at least offered some hope to these youth that they could find a life apart from the street; as the focus of social capital theory on social embeddedness makes clear, legal employment is a starting point in the process of acquiring social capital that can lead to more promising life outcomes. We found over the course of the summer during which we tracked street youth in Vancouver and Toronto that those youth who were able to find employment were more likely to begin moving away from the street: They spent less time hanging out, panhandling, searching for food and shelter, using drugs, stealing with other youth, or pursuing other kinds of criminal activities. Youth who began to move along this track and away from the street were not enamored with the employment they found, but they nonetheless saw these entry-level jobs as a place to begin transitions to more conventional lives apart from the street.

From the Street

We believe that social capital theory can be a powerful integrative force in understanding crime, bringing together a number of theories that too often have competed for the exclusive attention of criminologists. An important feature of social capital theory is that it allows a broadening and lengthening of explanatory attention to factors that cause crime and delinquency. For example, this theory has the potential to widen our explanatory attention by revitalizing a Mertonian insight, only partially developed in the anomie tradition, that strains and opportunities derive from broadly social as well as more narrowly economic sources.

The narrowness of too many recent applications of Mertonian anomie theory is pinpointed in Travis Hirschi's (1989) observation that

> Strain theory . . . remains alive, in spite of decades of pounding by research and general neglect by those who might make something more of it. It could be said with justification that the apparent failure of strain theory was the major motive behind the integrationist movement. With strain theory gone, those who accepted the idea that crime has its own motives were left with no place to begin. They therefore revived strain theory and placed it to the extreme left of their models, where it appears to remain today. Put another way, integrationists have patronized strain theory, but they have not contributed to its development. It may deserve more attention than it is now getting. (p. 45)

When Hirschi notes that those who have sought to revive strain theory have placed it at the extreme left of their models, he presumably is referring to the place assigned to economic sources of strain, usually in the form of parental socioeconomic status, in these models (e.g., Wiatrowski et al., 1981).

The concept of social capital provides a means of reinvoking Merton's broader purposes. We use this concept to represent causal forces that derive not just from the class position of families of orientation but also from a variety of institutional sources – including work, family, school, neighborhood, and community – that contribute to the explanation of crime and delinquency. These institutions influence the lives of street youth through mechanisms of social bonding and control, shame and stigmatization, and strain and opportunity. Social capital theory can broaden the study of crime by incorporating a wide range of noneconomic as well as economic causes of crime.

Social capital theory further lengthens the explanatory focus of contemporary criminology by encouraging attention to the ways in which social capital accumulates, is conserved, and/or is diminished over the life course. Despite an implicit awareness of the theoretical importance of life course factors in delinquency as well as crime, most of our theories are still somewhat static in focusing on either delinquency or crime, each too often to the exclusion of the other, and thereby confining attention to specific periods of the life span. However, a social capital theory of crime moves beyond this tendency by making the longitudinal development of capital accumulations and their consequences a central concern. Social capital theory further lengthens the study of crime by emphasizing the cumulative significance of critical events and transitions, such as coming into contact with the police or finding a job, in an expanded consideration of life course trajectories.

There remains the question of how the findings reported in this book fit into a larger agenda of criminological research. Our argument is that there is an important place for a reconstituted street criminology that supplements a recently more prominent school-based criminology. For example, there may be important instances where school and street studies can be coordinated, as in Chapters Three and Four of this book. The combination of school and street samples in these chapters indicates that class circumstances both lead to the street through differences in experiences with families of origin and, in turn, channel involvement in crime through the harsh socioeconomic situations encountered on the street after leaving home. Class circumstances can be more fully understood to influence involvement in crime through a combined awareness of these background and foreground processes.

Variation in foreground experiences of street youth especially lend themselves to intensive study, for as we demonstrate, they allow us to examine fundamental and largely unexplored causal processes that lead to and away from crime. We found that many street youth do not become heavily involved in crime, and finding out how and why this is so can significantly advance our theoretical understanding of crime. We believe that a key to this understanding involves research that can bridge our already well-developed knowledge of background causes of crime with a more probing exploration of foreground processes, such as criminal embeddedness and the formation of criminal capital, that in a more proximate way lead to immediate involvements in street crime. Social capital theory provides a useful framework in which to integrate research on background and foreground causes of crime, and the experiences of street youth are a valuable source of data for this work.

Yet we should also exercise caution in generalizing from our research. We should be especially careful not to suggest that the youth we have studied in two Canadian cities necessarily generalize to youth living on the streets in other parts of the world. In fact, there are good reasons to expect differences as well as similarities. For example, some of the most important differences may have to do with ways in which street youth in different settings relate to their families of origin. There are also likely to be important differences in ways in which street youth are treated in different settings.

The street youth we studied in Canada often moved back and forth from their families of origin, or fragments of these families, before taking to the streets for extended periods. In this sense, these youth retained some connections to their families of origin. However, these connections were often fraught with conflict and were usually quite unstable. In contrast, we noted earlier in this book a distinction that is often drawn in research in the developing countries of Central and South America between youth who are in the street and of the street. The former youth live with their families of origin and find their livelihood in the streets. The latter youth make the street their homes. We know little about how this influences the nature and degree of street youth involvement in crime, and therefore whether similar or different theories are required to account for these different orientations to the street.

We also know that the experience of being on the street can be quite different in the developing countries of Central and South America than in North America, at least in the sense of threats to the safety of these young people. In Central and South America, merchants and the police are known to use violence in their attempts to eliminate problems that they associate with the presence of youth on the street (Scheper-Hughes, 1992). There are recurrent stories of organized killings of street youth, sometimes in substantial numbers. In contrast, street youth in North America probably have more to fear from adults and youth who similarly make their lives on the street, or from adults who come to the streets to victimize young people. Again, we know less than we should about the nature and degree of these differences, and of how these differences might vary the theoretical approaches that we should take to understand the experiences of street youth in various settings.

As we move rapidly into the next century, criminology remains a science that is prominently connected into the national settings in which it is undertaken. We have lacked research designs and imperatives that encourage attempts to understand differences as well as similarities in national crime problems. Yet the problems of street youth and crime clearly have international dimensions, and they pose a set of issues that invite international cooperation in achieving knowledge and understanding. The research reported in this volume represents a modest attempt to reach beyond a single research setting by at least including two cities, albeit in the same country, in its design. We found important differences between these settings. However, far more is required if we are to further our understanding of street youth and the crime problems that so often surround these troubled young people.

The Methodology
of Studying Street Youth

with Jo-Ann Climenhage and Patricia Parker

THIS APPENDIX SUMMARIZES OUR EXPERIENCES studying street and school youth. We begin by describing the data collection techniques used in our original cross-sectional study. We then outline our panel study and provide details of the various strategies we used to reduce attrition. In the following section, we assess the consequences of attrition by comparing youth who were retained and lost from the panel. Finally, we discuss the validity and representativeness of our data and the suitability of using inferential statistics to analyze them.

Each of the authors of this Appendix participated in the design of at least one of the studies and was involved in one capacity or another in collecting the various data sets. Nonetheless, individuals assumed primary responsibilities for particular studies: John Hagan and Patricia Parker gathered the data for the Toronto school study and supervised the Toronto panel study; Bill McCarthy collected the data for the cross-sectional Toronto street study and supervised and took an active part in surveying and interviewing Vancouver youth for the panel study; and Jo-Ann Climenhage helped to supervise the Toronto panel survey and interviewed Toronto street respondents. We use plural pronouns in much of this discussion because they best reflect the collective nature of our work and eliminate cumbersome and awkward phrases.

Making a Start: The First Study

Our decision to study street youth arose from several conversations we had in the fall of 1986. In these discussions, we often noted the benefits of survey-oriented quantitative criminology, but we lamented the preoccupation of this approach with students, a group that lacked significant variation on key variables for the study of crime. After considering various alternative populations, we focused on street youth. The few contemporary studies of street youth provided only limited data on crime, but their findings were consistent with our assumption that this is a group that is highly involved in crime. Recognizing the possible contributions from a study that included both street and school youth, we made our first foray into the street scene.

The initial stage of our research involved contacting nine social service agencies that provide shelter, counseling, and other forms of assistance to youth living on the streets in Toronto. These agencies represent a good cross-section of services and presumably of clients (see Table A.1). We assumed that, given their "expert" knowledge of this population, agency workers could provide us with important insights about the most appropriate research strategy (Schatzman and Strauss, 1973; Converse and Presser, 1986). Agency workers advised us that the diverse, unstable nature of the street youth population presents several problems for social science research. They noted that this population fluctuates daily: Some youth leave the street, others become homeless, and many move into and out of different kinds of living situations. Moreover, youth typically migrate between living on the streets, in hostels, group homes, and hotels, and "crashing" with friends or relatives. The absence of a long-term or permanent place of residence or telephone – and the unlikelihood of long-term employment or enrollment in traditional schools – means that conventional survey techniques used to locate respondents are of limited value when studying the homeless.

Further complications arise because many youth leave homes where they are unwanted or they do not feel safe in returning (Brennan et al., 1978; Janus et al., 1987; Kufeldt and Nimmo, 1987). These youth recognize that if their homelessness is discovered, they may be forcibly detained and returned home or placed in government care. Others who participate in illegal activities already face criminal charges or have violated conditions of probation or parole, and they realize that their detection could lead to arrest and detention. Thus, self-preservation dictates that street youth avoid meddlesome, inquiring strangers, particularly older adults, whom they often suspect are undercover police officers, religious zealots, or evangelists.

Given these constraints, we chose a research design that had several

Table A.1. Agencies Used as Data Collection Sites in Cross-Sectional Study of Toronto Street Youth (1987-88)

Agency name	Service provided	Clients
Covenant House	Shelter, counseling	16–21
Inner City	Drop-in, counseling	16–22
Moberly House	Shelter, counseling	12–16
Peggy Ann Walpole House	Shelter, counseling	females
Robertson House	Shelter, counseling	females
Street Outreach Services	Drop-in, counseling	youth working in prostitution
Toronto Community Hostel	Shelter, counseling	nonspecific
YMCA House	Shelter, counseling	18–25, males
Youth Without Shelter	Shelter, counseling	16–21

components. We decided that the best approach for establishing initial connections with street youth was to use a nonthreatening researcher who could easily gain access to the street but who would not be dismissed as a "poser." This person would spend considerable time on the street and in social service agencies making contacts with street youth, "advertising" the study, and becoming a familiar part of the street scene. The researcher would also screen potential respondents and invite those suitable to participate in the study. Respondents would complete a self-report, anonymous questionnaire, in small groups; this instrument would allow us to collect the amount and type of data necessary for our purposes and would provide respondents with considerable confidence that their answers could not be used to identify or trace them.

Bill McCarthy was well suited to this job. His usual appearance, particularly his long hair, earrings, "grunge" style of dress, and youthful demeanor, made it easy for him to blend with others on the street.[1] He had worked with youth in a number of capacities (e.g., recreational advisor, counselor, and teacher) in several settings (e.g., parks, community centers, schools, and prison) and had considerable experience meeting and talking with youth. He was also well acquainted with street life: He left home as an adolescent, and while hitchhiking across Canada, ate, slept, and hung out on the street and in hostels; he had worked in many of the low-paying jobs common among youth, and he had some experience with the crimes that often occupy them. Yet his graduate-student status made it clear that he was not currently of the street, nor was he posing as a street person for surreptitious reasons (e.g., undercover police work, journalism, or religious conversion).

Before entering the field, we undertook several steps to make our initial questionnaire suitable for street youth. We used several readability scales (i.e., the Lorge, the Fry, and the Gunning–Fog Index) to ensure that our questions could be read and understood by an individual with a seventh-grade reading level. We limited the number of questions to twenty-six pages (approximately a half-an-hour's work) to reduce the study's vulnerability to fatigue. We also incorporated several design features that Sudman and Bradburn (1982; also see Bradburn and Sudman, 1979) recommend to discourage response sets, duplicity, telescoping, and forgetfulness. We then solicited feedback on a draft of our questionnaire from "experts" and "cultural insiders" (Converse and Presser, 1986) – agency workers and street youth – and removed questions that they found difficult or inappropriate. For example, we restructured questions about family origin to reflect the various family permutations in which youth lived, and we eventually removed network questions that elicited friends' identities and were considered too invasive. Finally, we pretested our instrument with a second group of street youth and, in response to their concerns, made additional stylistic changes to the questionnaire.

Collecting the Original Toronto Data

We used two strategies to contact potential respondents for our study. At nine social service agencies, we established a fixed day and hour for the survey that we advertised while hanging out in the agency, through agency workers, on posterboards, and by word of mouth. Using nine agencies as data collection sites allowed us to contact youth at various times of day throughout the week; wherever possible, we also changed the day and time of the interview at each agency once or twice during the data collection period (e.g., from Monday 10 A.M. to Wednesday 7 P.M.).

Our second strategy focused on youth who rarely or never use agencies. Following advice from street workers and street youth, we routinely visited several street settings that were popular among homeless youth. These sites included the major downtown malls, a few inner-city parks, several street corners commonly used for panhandling, the streets known to attract youth working in the sex trade, and a number of well-known locations suitable for sleeping (e.g., the ceremonial flame at Toronto's city hall, the bus and train stations, and the heating grates of several large office complexes). In these places, we distinguished street youth from other youth by observation and conversation: We approached youth only if they were panhandling or preparing to sleep in a public place, and we introduced ourselves by asking about general street topics (e.g., places to sleep or obtain food). Once satisfied that a youth was indeed homeless, we invited him/her to participate in the study.[2]

Obviously, there was no guarantee that we would connect with street youth during nonagency and agency visits, so we spent many hours simply "hanging out." We lounged around agencies, sat in the parks, walked through the streets where youth congregated in small groups and panhandled, strolled the various strips where the sex and drug trades operated, sat in the mall, and went to the video arcades. In each setting, we repeatedly encountered street youth eager to talk about their lives; some were interested in taking part in the study, others were willing but did not have enough time to complete a questionnaire and would consider doing one later, and some were uninterested but open to conversation. We ate too much junk food, inhaled too much of the ubiquitous cigarette smoke that characterizes street life (more than 90 percent of the youth surveyed smoked), and spent too much time in settings that depressed us and the youth we spoke with (i.e., the strip, the malls, the cold park benches, and street corners). Yet hanging out was important: It increased the study's visibility and made the researchers' presence almost commonplace.[3]

Administering the Questionnaire

To encourage interest in our research, we provided each street youth, either individually or in a group, with a verbal description of our study. We spoke about the academic, policy, and more practical aims of our research and the need for their "expertise" about street life.[4] Most youth acknowledged the possible contributions of our study and were willing, able, and often eager to share their thoughts. Those who volunteered were then informed about their rights and obligations as respondents. We explained that they had the right to refuse to answer any questions and that they could quit the survey at any time. Also, they had an obligation to either answer questions truthfully or ignore them. We reminded them that, although they would be completing the survey in a quiet area of a park, a less-traveled street corner, or a place separate from the general meeting area in most agencies, they were not to disturb other youth who were also taking part in the study. We emphasized that we did not know their identities, that we would be the only people to see their responses, and that they were not to place any identifying marks on their questionnaires. We then read aloud the consent form, asked if there were questions, and distributed the form to the respondents. Although everyone completed a consent form, most youth did not clearly sign their name but rather provided an indecipherable signature, a set of initials, a moniker, or a pseudonym.

The final step before completing the questionnaire involved testing the respondents' ability to read. We approached each youth individually and asked him/her to read three questions orally. Thirty-three youth who had difficulty with this task were given the choice of dropping out of the survey (one person chose this option) or having the questionnaire read to them. Each respondent received $10 worth of food coupons. Although not a substantial remuneration, the coupons helped to convey the seriousness of the survey and our appreciation of the respondents' efforts; also, the coupons were a form of payment for the work involved.

The success of our research design is reflected in the enthusiasm of the youth we contacted. In a one-year period (spring of 1987 through the spring of 1988), we spoke with 475 street youth; only 57 of these youth decided against participating (12 percent refusal rate), and only 28 provided incomplete or unusable surveys. Overall, we collected data from a sample of 390 street youth (82 percent response rate). Although the data were collected over a lengthy period, we ensured that there were no duplications by having one person collect all of the data.

As the description of our research suggests, we used a purposive or expert choice sampling design to organize our study of street youth (Kalton, 1983). This approach to sampling takes advantage of field experts' knowledge in order to develop a sampling strategy that enhances the sample's representativeness. Purposive designs are well suited to populations for which probabilities of selection for all members are unknowable.

This is clearly the case for the street youth we studied: A population list was unavailable, the population membership was constantly changing, and the population cannot easily be divided into geographical clusters. Some researchers have used probability designs to study the adult homeless (e.g., Rossi, 1989), but the great majority still use variations on purposive designs (see Shlay and Rossi, 1992). The latter are more economical, and as sampling theorists note, probability designs are essentially tools for large-scale surveys (Kish, 1965, p. 16).

The School Survey

We undertook our self-report survey of school youth at approximately the same time that we began studying youth on the street. Using school board contacts that we had established while conducting earlier research (Hagan, Simpson, and Gillis, 1979), we made arrangements to interview students in three metropolitan Toronto schools in the spring of 1987. Each of these schools was located in a different neighborhood and drew the majority of its students from different ethnic and class groups. We randomly distributed survey invitations in ninth- through twelfth-grade classes and used popular music tapes as an inducement. Interested students returned a signed parental permission form that affirmed that the youth was between 13 and 19 years of age.[5] With the help of several research assistants, we surveyed youth in groups of up to 40 students during their lunch period. In total, we collected data from 563 students and had a response rate of 67 percent, a level consistent with that of other self-report studies (e.g., Elliott and Ageton, 1980; Hindelang et al., 1981; Thornberry and Christenson, 1984).

Panel Research and Street Youth: The Second Study

Following our initial success, we applied for and in 1990 received funding for a second study of street youth. Given our finding that corrections for potential sample-selection bias using the combined school and street samples had only small and insignificant effects on our results (see Chapter Four), we decided that rather than replicating our first study, our resources could be better utilized in a comparative, panel study of street youth in two cities. Data from such a study would allow us to isolate better the temporal occurrence of events in the lives of street youth and identify differences in street life across urban settings; also, panel data would provide important information on street youths' life trajectories and events that operate as turning points, encouraging and discouraging involvement in street crime.

Although our second study replicated many features of the design used in the first study, we added several important components: We increased the number of data collection sites, we introduced several different types of data collection instruments (e.g., structured and semistructured interviews), we revised our sampling strategy, and we used teams of researchers to help collect the data. We also allowed for greater age variation than in our first study, raising the cut-off age for participation from 19 to 24. We originally used 19 as an age limit to match more closely the age distribution of school youth; however, 24 was a more reasonable cut-off point given the second study's greater attention to life trajectories, and given our expansion of the boundaries on the period we call youth (see Chapter One).

In 1990, Jo-Ann Climenhage joined the research team. She had recently completed a Masters degree on street youth in Hamilton (Climenhage, 1989), and her age, research, street experience, and previous work with youth made her an excellent choice as a research leader for the Toronto phase of our project. Building on the success of our first study, she recontacted agency workers at the nine social service agencies that we used as data collection sites in 1987. Again, the agency workers were enthusiastic about our project and agreed to allow us to interview their clients. Workers also provided the names of four additional agencies that had either opened since the first study or that we were unaware of in 1987 (see Table A.2). These thirteen organizations included seven hostels that provide residential facilities specifically for youth, two alternative educational programs, one employment program, and three drop-in centers.

In the next stage of our project, we revised our original survey instrument. We updated our self-report questionnaire and added a structured interview, a life history calendar, and a less structured, more open-ended interview. We pretested these instruments with youth we met at agencies and made appropriate refinements to ambiguous or confusing questions.

We also revised our sampling design. Panel studies require relatively short periods of time for collecting the data for each wave. Given this requirement, we decided to use a "saturation" approach to contact youth and establish membership in the panel. Our objective was to saturate the streets and social service agencies with researchers for a two-week period; the researchers would interview or make an appointment to interview every street youth they encountered. We established fixed days and times for the study and used several techniques to advertise these times in the weeks preceding the interviews: Research leaders hung out on the street, talking

Table A.2. Agencies Used as Data Collection Sites in Panel Study of Toronto and Vancouver Street Youth (1992)

Agency name	Service provided	Clients
Toronto		
Covenant House	Shelter, counseling	16–21
Evergreen	Drop-in, counseling	nonspecific
Kensington Youth	Work skills training	nonspecific
Oasis	School, counseling	nonspecific
Stop 86	Shelter, counseling	females
Street Outreach Services	Drop-in, counseling	youth working in prostitution
Street Haven	Shelter, counseling	females
Touchstone	Shelter, counseling	16–20
Turning Point	Shelter, counseling	16–21
West End	School, counseling	nonspecific
YMCA House	Shelter, counseling	18–25, males
Youthlink	Drop-in, counseling	16–22
Youth Without Shelter	Shelter, counseling	16–21
Vancouver		
Aries Project	Counseling, school	Native youth
Adolescent Street Unit	Counseling, welfare	14–19
Brenda Carr	Art workshop, drop-in	16–21
Connections	Drug/alcohol therapy	14–19
Downtown Eastside	Drop-in, counseling	nonspecific
Gordon House	Work skills training	16–21
Street Youth Services	Counseling, drop-in	youth working in prostitution
Study Centre	School	14–19

with youth and alerting them to the study; we placed posterboards in agencies; and social workers informed their clients.

Bill McCarthy followed a similar strategy in Vancouver. He established contacts with seven social service agencies (see Table A.2) and spent time on the streets locating various street sites where we could contact youth who had little or no agency affiliation. None of the Vancouver agencies can legally provide shelter for homeless youth; nonetheless, they offer access to welfare, legal aid, counseling, health services, drug and alcohol rehabilitation, and education and employment opportunities, and they are an avenue to permanent forms of care (e.g, foster care). Also, agencies are important places for youth to hang out. We took advantage of the latter and pretested the data collection instruments with street youth we met at one of the Vancouver agencies.

As noted earlier, we used research teams to collect the first- and second-wave data. Each team consisted of a research leader and several student research assistants (RAs). Given street youth's tendency to distrust older adults initially, we chose several young university students to work as RAs. We selected the RAs on the basis of their previous experience with youth and their knowledge of the street.[6] The interviewers took part in a two-day training session during which we described the research and the unique aspects of studying homeless youth. RAs spent considerable time studying the data collection instruments, participating in various role-playing scenarios, and doing practice interviewing. As the final stage in their training, the RAs were given tours of the various agencies participating in the study.

During the initial phase of data collection, the research leaders spot-checked the interviews to address any difficulties that the RAs were experiencing. At the end of each day, the research leaders and interviewers also met as a group to discuss the interviewing and offer suggestions for the next day's interviews. The research leaders periodically reassessed the RAs throughout the remainder of the study, but as the study progressed, they devoted an increasing amount of time to talking with street youth. Research leaders also assumed responsibility for contacting youth in nonagency settings and encouraging them to participate in the study; given the demands of the study, this was usually done in the evenings and on weekends.

Youth were asked to read and sign an informed consent form; they were then paid $20 for agreeing to participate in the study.[7] Before starting the interview, RAs emphasized the goals of the research and reminded the respondents that all answers were strictly confidential and anonymous. After the interview, respondents completed the self-report section of the survey. During this period, RAs recorded several descriptive details to assist the research leaders in identifying youth for future interviews: They noted unusual scars, distinguishing tattoos, body piercing, eye and hair color, height and weight, and street- or nicknames. In a population where individuals often do not use their birth names, dates of birth combined with these descriptive characteristics were important means of identifying youth for subsequent interviews. We also used this information to ensure that respondents were not interviewed more than once in each wave of the study.

After completing their interview, respondents who had not met a research leader were introduced and spent some time talking with them. The research leader then scheduled the follow-up interview in three weeks' time and gave respondents a card with the name, university affiliation, and contact telephone number on the front, and the time, date, and place of the interview on the back. Respondents were told to call the number on the business card if they had any questions or were unable to keep their interview appointment. We also asked respondents to list places (e.g., shelters and friends' addresses) where we might be able to locate them for subsequent interviews. We also asked for the names of friends, social workers, or relatives whom we could contact for information about their whereabouts. While we expected a portion of youth to decline to provide such information, the great majority willingly complied: Only 4 percent did not provide any specific contacts.

In the second wave, respondents took part in a forty-five-minute interview (twenty-six pages). In this interview, we asked them about their activities and experiences on a day-to-day basis for the two weeks preceding the interview. For example, we asked respondents where they slept on the night before the interview and on each of the previous eleven nights. We used the same question structure to inquire about the search for food and work and about involvement in crime. Respondents were again paid $20 for their efforts, and when they finished their survey, each received another card detailing the date and place of the third interview (for which they would be paid $10) and a phone number to contact the researchers.

The third-wave interview had two components. The first section was a replication of the second-wave interview and inquired about respondents' activities on a daily basis for the twelve days prior to their interviews. The second part involved an open-ended interview administered by the research leaders. For the latter, we created a list of general questions that covered the main topics of our research (e.g., home, school, street, and crime experiences) and which were asked of each respondent. Interviewers also pursued specific topics when individual respondents expressed an interest. Although the open-ended section provided richer, more detailed information, it required considerably more time to implement. On average, these interviews lasted approximately one hour, with the longest interview running almost three hours. Altogether, we collected over 200 hours of interviews. Unfortunately, the length of these interviews reduced the time available for tracking respondents. Although extending the data collection period may have increased our third-wave response rate, limitations of time and money required that we end the data collection phase of this research.

Recontacting Respondents

Conventional wisdom suggests that the homeless are poor candidates for panel research because they are unlikely to keep appointments and are all but impossible to track. However, more than half of our respondents kept the second interview we scheduled for them, affirming that many homeless youth are capable of meeting such demands if they are sufficiently motivated. We were able to contact an additional one-fifth of our respondents with several tracking strategies, so that, overall, 78 percent of first-wave respondents completed a second interview. We were less successful in locating youth for the third-wave interviews, and only 53 percent of respondents completed all three waves; however, the extent of attrition in our sample is not unexpected. In their panel study of homeless adults in Minneapolis, Sosin, Piliavin, and Westerfelt (1990; also see Piliavin et al., 1993) recontacted approximately 57 percent of their respondents, many of whom were no longer homeless.

Previous reports on techniques to track respondents predominantly focus on the general population (e.g., see Clarridge, Sheehy, and Hauser, 1977; Eckland, 1968; Freedman, Thornton, and Camburn, 1980; Thorton, Freedman, and Camburn, 1982); however, the transient and frequently delinquent nature of the homeless population means that many of the conventional methods for locating and recontacting respondents – and thereby minimizing attrition levels – are unsuitable. Alternatively, we used an approach also adopted by Sosin et al. (1990) in their study of homeless adults, blending traditional and more unconventional search methods to locate respondents for subsequent interviews. In particular, we used three resources: contact information provided by respondents, street worker and street youth networks, and the daily presence of the research leaders.

Our first step in recontacting youth involved the creation of a master list of respondents. This list contained the descriptive data on respondents collected by the RAs and the contact information provided by respondents. We called each number at random times in the morning, afternoon, early evening, and again between 8:00 p.m. and 10:00 p.m. If the phone number connected us directly with the youth, arrangements were made to schedule an appointment. If the call was answered by someone else, we explained that this number had been provided by the respondent and requested that a message from us be passed to the respondent. We did not disclose any details of the respondent's participation in our study but simply stated our university affiliation and the desire to notify the youth of a forthcoming interview.

In many instances, respondents were no longer at the address given; nonetheless, contact persons were useful in updating and providing new leads. For example, in one case, we reached a contact person after the respondent missed his second scheduled interview. The contact provided a vague lead on where the youth might presently be employed. The place of employment turned out to be large, and more information was required. We then telephoned the contact person who supplied the name of the youth's immediate boss. From that information, we found the department and room in which the youth was working and were successful in reaching the respondent and scheduling the next interview. Another youth, who we had initially interviewed in a drop-in center, missed his second interview. His contact informed us that the youth was incarcerated in a closed-custody facility. We spoke with the youth there, and after several phone calls to supervisors at the facility, we were granted permission to conduct the interview. Nonetheless, many of the contacts had a limited use: Several youth had only fleeting affiliation with street agencies, and friends' and acquaintances' telephones frequently were disconnected.

Our second source for recontacting youth involved our connections with street agencies and street youth. Street workers, hostel and agency staff, and social workers used their networks to provide leads on the whereabouts of various respondents and in some instances helped to locate youth directly. Even when agency representatives were unaware of the location of particular youth, they passed along word via other adolescents or workers with whom they were in contact. Hostel workers also gave us access to their current resident lists, and we were able to check for missing respondents.

We also "advertised" directly. We posted reminders about forthcoming interview dates in the agencies, and we left individual messages for youth who listed an agency as a contact place. The notices informed individuals that we wished to schedule their next appointment and provided a telephone number where we could be contacted. The telephone number was connected to an answering machine with a prerecorded message outlining the study's interview schedule. Youth were encouraged to leave messages for the researchers indicating when and where we could contact them to schedule an appointment.

A portion of the homeless population we interviewed had limited or no contact with formal social service delivery systems. In these cases, we enlisted the assistance of other homeless youth to provide leads on the whereabouts of respondents we were trying to locate. In one instance, a youth in our study who had kept his second scheduled appointment virtually disappeared for the next month. The researchers exhausted all contacts provided; they had not received a response to repeated message postings, and none of the agency staff leads had produced any results. When we spoke to another youth with whom the missing respondent was friendly, this individual escorted us to a park where we met the respondent and scheduled his next interview.

Our third resource was the research leaders' daily scheduled and informal visits to agencies and nonagency locations. These visits strengthened the research leaders' rapport with respondents and "front-line" agency staff and helped gain the trust necessary to tap into youth and staff networks. Daily visits also allowed the researchers to remind youth of their interview appointments, and it gave youth another avenue through which to locate the researchers to schedule upcoming interviews. This was particularly important for youth who lost their appointment cards. Finally, helpful leads on the whereabouts of respondents were often passed along in the course of casual conversations.

As these examples suggest, flexibility and perseverance in following up new leads and recycling old leads, as well as repeating steps in the tracing operation, were essential in successfully locating and interviewing street youth. Many interviews were the result of several repeated search attempts, often utilizing more than one method. In one case, a respondent who was unable to keep his appointment for the second interview gave us a number where he could be reached. We phoned this number several times but did not receive a response to the messages we left. A notice was then posted for him at the drop-in center where we had initially interviewed him. The youth responded, leaving a message on our answering machine with a new contact number. We left messages at this number and scheduled a second interview on three separate occasions. The youth missed all three appointments. We then phoned again and scheduled an interview for that evening. We made a follow-up call again later in the day to remind him of the appointment, which he kept.

We used the same contacts to schedule this person's third interview. After several appointments were missed, we called to reschedule and were given a new number where we could contact the youth. The number turned out to be a local hospital. After several more calls, we spoke directly to the respondent, who informed us he had been admitted and was expecting to be released in several weeks' time but was more than willing to be interviewed while in the hospital. We then scheduled a date and time during hospital visiting hours; however, when we arrived, we were informed by the hospital staff that the youth had been allowed out on a pass and had not returned. We were thus forced to begin our search again with the initial contacts. After leaving several messages, we were able to speak directly with the youth and re-schedule another appointment, which the youth failed to keep. Another series of calls were made, and after reaching the youth and scheduling him once again, he finally kept the appointment, and the third interview was completed.

In Table A.3, we provide data on the success of the various strategies used to recontact youth in our panel study. These detailed tracking data were collected only for Toronto and refer to the 330 youth who completed first-wave questionnaires in that city. As noted earlier, in Toronto, we were successful in recontacting approximately 80 percent of first-wave respondents for a second interview and 52 percent for a third interview. Data in Table A.3 indicate that a surprising proportion, 63 percent, of our first-wave respondents kept the appointments originally scheduled for them. We located another 17 percent of our first-wave respondents with our alternative location strategies: We found 5 percent with telephone contacts and message postings, 4 percent through information provided by agency workers and other adolescents, and 8 percent as a result of researcher visits to drop-in centers and other nonagency locations.

Data on third-wave contacts further emphasize the importance of our various contact strategies. Only 7 percent of respondents kept scheduled appointments for their third interviews. However, we contacted another 46 percent of our sample using additional techniques: Information gathered from telephone contacts and message postings helped us find 15 percent, agency and street youth informants led us to 6 percent, and researcher visits to drop-in centers and other locations put us in contact with an additional 25 percent.

Attrition

Sources and consequences of attrition are key issues in panel studies, and researchers have given considerable attention to the detrimental effects of panel attrition (e.g., see McAllister, Goe, and Butler, 1973; Clarridge et al.,

Table A.3. Strategies Used to Recontact Toronto Youth for Second and Third Waves of the 1992 Panel Study (N = 330)

	Kept scheduled interview		Telephone contacts and message postings		Agency and street youth information		Researcher visits to agencies and street locations		Not found	
	N	%	N	%	N	%	N	%	N	%
Second Wave	209	63.33	16	4.85	14	4.24	27	8.18	64	19.39
Third Wave	22	6.67	49	14.85	20	6.06	82	24.85	157	47.58

1977; Freedman et al., 1980; McBroom, 1988; Dodds, Furlon, and Croxford, 1989). Although attrition is obviously important, analyses of the effects of attrition are somewhat surprising. In their analysis of data from seven panel studies on youth and crime, Cordray and Polk (1983) find that although panel members retained throughout the studies differed somewhat from the original sample (i.e., the base), these differences had little effect on multivariate outcomes. They conclude that, even when panel attrition is large, analyses using retained respondents provide reliable estimates of population parameters. Several researchers also report few significant differences between "dropouts" and those who are retained (e.g., see McBroom, 1988; Sosin et al., 1990). Indeed, it appears that attrition only introduces serious distortion when it reaches levels of 50 percent or more (e.g., see Green, 1990; Tebes, Snow, and Arthur, 1992).

In Table A.4, we provide information on some effects of attrition in our panel study. Using *t*-tests, we compare the mean differences in variables for youth who we located for both the first and second waves of the panel study (retained) and those who only completed the first wave (dropped out). According to these data, these two groups have significant mean differences on only twelve of sixty-five variables used in the analyses presented in this work. The youth who we were unable to contact physically abused their mothers more frequently, held more liberal attitudes toward using drugs, and were more involved in theft, drug use, and drug selling at home. On the street, these "missing" youth spent more time looking for food and shelter. They were also more likely to join street families and to seek these families because of pressure and a need for shelter. Notwithstanding these differences, the youth who failed to return for a second interview appear remarkably similar to those who we were able to recontact.

Reliability and Validity

The majority of the questions used in our surveys came from earlier studies (e.g., Hirschi, 1969). A fairly extensive body of literature affirms that these items are reliable and valid and that they can be effectively used in self-report studies (see Hindelang et al., 1981; Inciardi et al., 1993). Our use of several design features recommended for survey research in general (Bradburn and Sudman, 1979; Sudman and Bradburn, 1982) and specifically for self-report studies of crime (Inciardi et al., 1993) further reduced the potential for systematic error in our self-report data. It is well established that the most common source of error in self-report data does not involve

Table A.4. *Attrition Analysis Comparing Youth Retained for Two Waves of the 1992 Panel Study with Those Who Dropped Out After the First Wave*

	Retained (376)		Dropped Out (106)		
	X	SD	X	SD	XDf
Age	19.540	3.569	19.406	2.607	-.134
Gender	.662	.474	.736	.443	.084
Violent Father	4.912	5.626	5.604	6.178	.692
Violent Mother	4.987	5.518	4.774	5.578	-.213
Physical Abuse	1.237	1.261	1.311	1.341	.075
Violent Toward Mother	1.532	3.015	2.453	4.012	.921**
Violent Toward Father	2.192	3.798	2.859	3.958	.667
Sexual Abuse	.652	1.784	.764	1.880	.113
Brother Arrested	.178	.383	.123	.330	-.055
Family Crime	.543	.500	.500	.502	-.043
Father Arrested	.301	.459	.340	.476	.039
Father's Unemployment	1.582	1.078	1.415	.904	-.167
Mother's Unemployment	1.521	.955	1.632	1.017	.111
Paternal Alcoholism	.641	1.074	.792	1.144	.152
Maternal Alcoholism	.399	.874	.396	.813	-.003
Paternal Drug Addiction	.144	.562	.245	.659	.102
Maternal Drug Addiction	.210	.666	.236	.750	.084
Father's Education	2.80334	1.787	2.698	1.800	-.105
Mother's Education	3.082	1.693	3.217	1.821	.135
Family Breakdown	.710	.454	.698	.461	.012
Parental Instrumental Control	12.439	4.102	11.934	4.099	-1.045
Parental Relational Control	10.218	3.351	10.066	3.327	-.152
School Strain	9.021	3.140	9.415	3.312	.394
Home Friends Sell Drugs	3.287	2.886	3.538	2.740	.251
Sell Drugs at Home	1.404	3.522	2.076	3.980	.671*
Home Friends Stole	5.553	3.224	5.368	3.281	-.185
Charged at Home	.878	1.548	.972	1.964	.094
Theft at Home	6.330	9.351	8.367	11.530	2.057*
Violence at Home	1.585	3.271	2.142	4.363	.556
Drug Use at Home	6.114	6.000	7.236	6.201	1.121*

social desirability effects nor purposeful duplicity; instead, it arises from problems associated with recall, particularly telescoping and forgetfulness. Relative to studies of adults, the comparatively brief life histories of street youth, especially in terms of offending, presented considerably fewer opportunities for recall error.

We also used several techniques to enhance respondents' ability to remember events and the time they occurred. We clearly demarcated time periods in our inquiries (e.g., we asked about criminal involvement before leaving home the first time, yesterday, and the previous day); we placed questions about similar topics close to one another (e.g., using and selling drugs); in our interviews, we used a life calendar approach to help respondents locate significant experiences (e.g., when they first left home or slept

Table A.4. (cont'd.)

	Retained (376)		Dropped Out (106)		
	X	SD	X	SD	XDf
Crime at Home	15.434	16.686	19.840	20.419	4.406**
Year First Left Home	86.652	5.440	87.085	3.181	.433
City	.298	.458	.377	.487	-.080
Illegal Opportunities	2.777	1.505	2.868	1.421	.091
Street Adversity	7.636	3.148	8.349	3.024	.713**
Street Friends Sell Drugs	5.769	3.093	6.075	3.085	.307
Believe Drug Use Okay	3.173	1.364	3.453	1.381	.280*
Street Crime	35.471	26.609	39.745	28.318	4.274
Street Drug Selling	5.311	5.922	6.066	6.087	.755
Receive Help Selling Drugs	4.487	3.769	4.717	3.617	.230
Street Friends in Prostitution	2.926	2.935	2.943	2.718	.017
Charged on the Street	1.694	2.091	1.802	2.100	.108
Believe Prostitution Okay	2.726	1.452	2.877	1.452	.151
Street Prostitution	1.269	2.699	1.123	2.540	-.146
Receive Help in Prostitution	1.878	3.033	1.717	3.101	-.161
Street Friends Stole	7.088	3.321	7.189	3.321	.101
Violent Crime on Street	3.702	4.846	3.830	5.335	.128
Street Theft	13.045	14.413	15.604	15.942	2.559
Believe Theft not Wrong	2.149	1.213	2.094	1.109	-.055
Receive Help in Theft	5.668	4.339	5.850	4.213	.182
Look for Food with Friends	2.457	1.356	2.962	1.440	.505***
Hang out Friends	3.920	1.206	3.915	1.258	-.005
Steal with Friends	1.856	1.224	1.887	1.190	.030
Do Drugs with Friends	3.263	1.445	3.443	1.441	.180
Panhandle with Friends	2.303	1.487	2.566	1.604	.262
Look for Shelter	2.851	1.372	3.151	1.293	.300**
Street Employment	.116	.246	.102	.240	-.014
Average Grade	3.160	1.476	3.236	1.613	.076
Membership in Street Families	.580	.494	.689	.465	.109**
Depression	7.963	2.705	7.943	2.449	-.019
Safety	2.130	1.010	2.123	1.084	-.007
Pressure	.997	.995	1.274	1.065	.277**
Shelter	1.657	1.059	1.953	.980	.296**
Connections	1.923	.948	2.019	.915	.096
Adolescent Competence	3.553	2.273	3.943	2.940	.390

* $p \le .10$
** $p \le .05$
*** $p \le .01$

on the streets) in a coherent time line; and we referred to significant life events (e.g., birthdays, the start of the school year, holidays) to help establish the timing of these experiences (Inciardi et al., 1993; Fleisher, 1995).

We are also confident of the validity of our open-ended interview data. The events described by our respondents mirror the self-report and structured-interview material that we collected four to eight weeks earlier in our first-wave surveys and with the data collected in our 1986 study. On a much more specific level, this consistency is reflected in the answers of two respondents who were interviewed by McCarthy while living on the street in

1986 and by Climenhage in 1992; these individuals recounted comparable background experiences in both studies.

It is impossible to know if our sample data are "representative" of the homeless youth population. However, the age and gender distributions of our samples closely match those of social service agencies that serve street youth (see McCarthy, 1990). Also, the backgrounds and street experiences reported by our respondents resemble those documented in other research on Canadian street youth (see Janus et al., 1987; Kufeldt and Nimmo, 1987; Weber, 1991). Finally, we replicated some analyses from our 1986 study with data we collected in 1992 and reached the same substantive conclusions (e.g., compare findings provided in Chapter Six with those in McCarthy and Hagan, 1995).

Analysis

We primarily use OLS and logistic regression to analyze our data. We follow convention and use tests of significance to help establish the importance of particular effects. Theoretically, estimates from purposive sampling designs cannot be evaluated using techniques of statistical inference; however, this is also true for most criminological studies because they use samples plagued by substantial nonresponse (e.g., Hirschi, 1969; Hindelang et al., 1981) or data collected with a nonprobability sampling design (e.g., Sampson and Laub, 1993). Rather than rejecting a large body of social science research because of these problems, we assume that it makes more sense to use caution in interpreting findings from nonprobability designs – as well as from probability samples that have nonresponse – and to verify findings further with repeated studies. Following Mohr (1990), we use significance tests to help assess "whether or not a certain relationship or other quantity is worth further thought – whether it might repay additional research effort."

Discussion

Although the transience and instability that characterizes homelessness places extra demands on survey research, the success of several studies of homeless adults (e.g., Rossi, 1989; Sosin et al., 1990; Cohen et al., 1993; Snow and Anderson, 1993) affirms that this population can be accessed and included successfully in survey research. Also, there is evidence that the homeless provide reliable and valid responses in surveys (see Calsyn, Allen, Morse, Smith, and Tempelhoff, 1993). Our studies suggest that these conclusions are also true for homeless youth. In detailing the procedures used in our studies, we contribute to the growing literature on techniques for studying populations not readily available for standard survey attention (see Dodds et al., 1989; Needle, Jou, and Su, 1989; Rumptz, Sullivan, Davidson, and Basta, 1991; Gregory, Lohr, and Gilchrist, 1992; Cohen et al., 1993). Our studies further challenge conventional assumptions regarding the feasibility of studying street youth over time. By adapting conventional data-gathering techniques to account for the peculiarities of the situations of homeless youth, we were able to mitigate problems of high panel attrition. In our study, we were able to retain more than three-quarters of respondents for a second wave of the survey, and we were able to recontact over half for a third wave.

In isolation, the techniques used in our research and by others who also study high-risk populations have limitations; however, when applied collectively, these techniques combine to form a highly effective set of tools for relocating portions of these populations. We hope that the description of our search process will prove useful to others who attempt such work. In documenting the steps to this search operation in detail, we hope to encourage others to revive the scientific study of street youth and other neglected populations and to create their own methods and strategies to accommodate the characteristics of these groups. We believe the development of such techniques and the sharing of resulting knowledge will make it possible to expand substantially the domain of criminological inquiry.

Notes

1. Street and School Criminologies

1. We recognize that the street is not always a site of desperation or destitution. Many youth described pleasurable aspects of life on the street including the availability of drugs and alcohol; freedom from parents, siblings, and schools; and street friends and families. And, a handful of youth had only praise for street life, arguing that they preferred it to any other possibilities. Nonetheless, when asked about their street experiences, the great majority of youth spoke about the hardships they had experienced and talked about their plans for getting off the streets, out of crime, and on with their lives (cf., Fleisher, 1995).

2. Other researchers (e.g., see Inciardi et al., 1993) use the term "street" as an adjective for youth who live at home or on their own but spend considerable time on the street in illegal activities, particularly the drug trade. We use the term to refer to a different population – that is, youth who, after fleeing from or being thrown out of their home, live on the streets, in shelters or hostels, or temporarily with relatives or friends.

3. Hoping to convey the grammatical form and the vocabulary of street youth, we did not edit the street language of the respondents. We deleted redundancies, incoherent passages, and extraneous comments, but we corrected grammar only when passages were incomprehensible. Although we were unable to capture the tone, facial expressions, and body language of individual street youth, we believe that their words capture the essence of their experiences.

4. Some street youth are hopeful about their futures. Many of these young people cling desperately to dreams of living more conventional, successful lives, hoping to go back to school and finish their education, to find stable and rewarding jobs, to start families, and to have homes. Against the odds,

some actually make impressive strides toward achieving these life goals, as we discuss in Chapter Nine.

5. Inciardi et al.'s (1993) study is an important exception. Inciardi and colleagues collected interview and survey data from 611 Miami youth. Although these data provide important information, particularly about the use and sale of crack, the study is of limited use for our purposes: The sample was selected on the basis of major or chronic involvement so there are no nonoffenders, and few of the respondents appear to have been homeless (e.g., 87 percent lived with their families, and only 1 percent lived on their own).

6. The small sample size of most ethnographies is evident in the number of people involved in several of the more recent street studies: Sullivan (1989) studied 38 males, Padilla (1992) spoke with a few dozen gang members, and Bourgois (1995) spent time with approximately two dozen street dealers. Fleisher's (1995) work is somewhat uncharacteristic in that he established contacts with 194 people; it appears that approximately 28 of these were youth on the street.

7. Studies of the adult homeless also suggest that homelessness is conducive to crime. For example, using police arrest records from Austin, Texas, Snow, Baker, and Anderson (1989; also Snow and Anderson, 1993) find a significantly greater arrest rate for homeless males (aged 16 to 68) than for males who were not homeless. They report an arrest rate for property offenses of 179 per 100,000 for homeless males, compared with 130 per 100,000 for men who have homes (also see Fisher, 1988; Gelberg, Linn, and Leake, 1988).

8. This approach is commonly used in research on the adult homeless. For example, Piliavin, Sosin, Westerfelt, and Matsueda (1993) define the following people as homeless: those who are currently on the street or in a shelter and have been there at least one day, or who since having left a permanent place of residence have stayed with friends or relatives for fewer than seven days and have no fixed address.

3. Taking to the Streets

1. There are, of course, other potential sources of the discrepancy between official and self-report findings about the relationship between class and crime: the domain of offense seriousness considered; the accuracy of subjects' reporting and recall; the categorization and counting of offense frequency; and bias in victim and bystander reporting and police processing. Of these factors, variation in the type of offense appears to be the most important (Hindelang, Hirschi, and Weis, 1979).

2. Our causal ordering assumes that child-rearing patterns precede school conflicts and delinquent behavior. Research is consistent with this approach and reveals that the effects of parenting on problems at school and delinquency

are greater than the effects of these problems on parenting (Sampson and Laub, 1993).

3. A response-based strategy inevitably involves a retrospective component that focuses on conditions and processes leading up to the response or outcome studied. Even though the second data set analyzed later in this book adds a prospective component to our research by tracking street youth during a summer period in Toronto and Vancouver, both studies include a retrospective component. Rare and transient populations such as street youth are impossible to identify prospectively and difficult to track for long periods, and this requires that much of our knowledge of them be obtained retrospectively. This is a frequently encountered problem in the epidemiological study of rare diseases, where the trade-off between retrospective and prospective designs is well understood and developed (see Prentice and Pyke, 1979). When delinquency researchers confront similar problems, they need to make comparable accommodations.

4. For example, unless the weighting of school-to-street youth is pushed beyond 25:1, a ratio that would reduce the number of Toronto street youth by about one-third, there are no notable changes in levels of statistical significance.

5. Although 60 percent of the youth in our street sample came from Toronto, the remaining 40 percent came to this city from all over Canada. We initially were concerned that the inclusion of street youth from outside Toronto with school youth from inside Toronto might bias our results. However, in our street sample, being from outside Toronto bears a near-zero relationship with the measure of serious theft used in this analysis.

6. The one published study (Janus et al., 1987) of Toronto street youth reports a sample that is 63 percent male with a mean age of 17.9. These points of comparison suggest that our sample is representative of the street population under study.

7. The school estimate of surplus population families is consistent with a 1988 General Social Survey based on heads of households (see Hagan and McCarthy, 1992, p. 559n).

8. The second study reported in this volume again indicates that about 7 percent of street youth were from families with an unemployed single parent or both parents unemployed at the time that the youth left home, and about 30 percent of these households had experienced parental unemployment problems at some time.

9. Hindelang et al. (1981, p. 216) find that the best predictors of official delinquency are self-reported theft items nearly identical to those we use, combined with running away from home. As noted earlier, our approach separates street life from crime and treats the former as a key intervening variable that leads to criminal involvement.

10. This strategy incorporates weighted maximum likelihood estimates of logit

response functions, with the separate samples weighted in proportion to their representation in the general population. The function estimated is the "response" of being on the street. In this case, the estimate of the odds of being on the street is multiplied by a weighting factor:

$$\frac{K \exp \{x'b\}}{1 + K \exp \{x'b\}}$$

where x' is a vector of values for the factors that are associated with being on the street and b represents the coefficients that correspond with these factors; $K = (H/N) \times (n/h)$; $H =$ the estimated proportion of the adolescent population who are street youth; $N =$ the estimated proportion of adolescent population who are at school; $h =$ the proportion of the sample who are street youth; and $n =$ the proportion of the sample who are at school.

11. These differences also shed light on the inconsistency of previous studies that look for a direct effect of parental violence on juvenile crime (see Hunner and Walker, 1981; Kratcoski, 1982; McCord, 1983; Brown, 1984; Kruttschnitt, Ward, and Sheble, 1987; Doerner, 1987; Widom, 1989; Straus, 1991).

12. The logit estimates of participation are derived from the equation,

$$P(D^{super}) = \frac{\exp \{b_0 + b_1x_1 \ldots + b_nx_n\}}{1 + \exp \{b_0 + b_1x_1 + \ldots + b_nx_n\}}$$

where super indicates the street or school sample; D stands for the occurrence of delinquency; x_1 is an assumed value of the ith explanatory variable; b_1 is the logit coefficient; and the values assumed by x represent conditions associated with different levels of risk described in the text.

13. In order to do this, it is necessary to establish what the characteristics of these dropouts might be. Past studies, the most notable by Elliott and Voss (1974; see also Elliott, 1966; but see Thornberry, Moore, and Christenson, 1985), suggest that the dropout delinquency rate is highest just before leaving school and declines sharply thereafter. This finding presumably characterizes dropouts who do not take to the streets and probably results from the strain of school being removed from members of this group. The implication is that these youth may still have somewhat higher-risk characteristics than school youth, but almost certainly lower-risk characteristics than street youth. Thus, increasing the values of variables to medium-risk levels (i.e., the means of school and street youth's means) in the school equations simulates the possibility of broadening the school sample to incorporate "off-the-street" dropouts. Since off-the-street dropouts constitute a minority of the potential school population and have a declining risk potential according to the findings of Elliott and Voss, our estimation of the consequences of including this group probably errs in an upward direction.

14. The formula for conditional probability pools logit and tobit models for school and street youth in which we set "compositional components" equal and allow "effect coefficients" to vary. As we note further later, the compositional components of these models take into account background differences between the school and street youth, and the effect coefficients represent the influences of street conditions on youth who take to the streets.

15. This formula states that:

$$P(A) = P(A/B) * P(B) + P(A/B') * P(B')$$

where A is the event of being delinquent, B is the event of being on the street, and B' is the event of not being on the street.

16. The probabilities of specified frequency levels of delinquency are estimated from the model,

$$Y^{super} = b_0 + b_1 x_1 + \ldots b_n x_n + e$$

where [super] indicates the street or school sample; Y stands for the specified incidence level of delinquency; x_1 is an assumed value of the ith explanatory variable; b_1 is the tobit coefficient; and e is an error term. The values assumed by x represent conditions associated with the different levels of risk. It is assumed that e is distributed normally, with a mean and variance of zero. The estimates for b_0, b_1, $\ldots$, b_n allow us to determine probabilities associated with different levels of frequency (e.g., more than 10, 20, 30 thefts). The key difference between a tobit and an OLS regression is that in the tobit the zero value is not considered as an actual value but rather as a class of observations in opposition to the positive values. The likelihood function to be maximized is also modified in this respect.

17. Our decomposition combines four terms from the following equation into three components discussed in the text. The equation is:

$$(Y^{str} - Y^{sch}) = (a^{str} - a^{sch}) + X^{sch} (b^{str} - b^{sch}) + b^{sch}$$
$$(X^{str} - X^{sch}) + E(b^{str} - b^{sch}) (X^{str} - X^{sch})$$

where the superscript [str] is for street and [sch] is for school; Y stands for mean delinquency; X is the mean of the ith explanatory variable; a is the regression constant; and b is the partial regression coefficient for the ith explanatory variable. For notational simplicity, the subscript i is suppressed in this equation. Following Jones and Kelley (1984), the first two terms in this equation are grouped to form the coefficients component, the third term is the compositional component, and the fourth term is the interaction component, as discussed in the text.

4. Adversity and Crime on the Street

1. We also examined effects of measures of situational destitution on drug selling and violence. The results of these analyses are comparable to those reported for theft of food.

2. It is possible that our measure introduces bias because it includes the phrase "had to" in the question "Have you had to steal food since leaving home?" We rephrased the question in our second study, asking simply how often the respondent had stolen food before leaving home and after coming to the street. A comparable proportion of youth in both studies indicated that they had stolen food since leaving home (i.e., 46.9 percent in the first study, and 46.1 percent in the second one); moreover, analyses that use data from the second study to replicate those reported in this chapter mirror those reported here.

3. The means and standard deviations for our dependent variables are as follows: theft of food (.726, .895), serious theft (3.000, 2.269), and prostitution (1.326, 2.158).

4. The means and standard deviations for these variables are as follows: hunger (1.405, .951), shelter (2.640, .947), and unemployment (1.038, .753).

5. Means and standard deviations for these additional control variables are as follows: home friends arrested (2.138, 1.540), minor theft at home (2.362, 2.309), serious theft at home (2.582, 2.304), prostitution at home (.077, .617), number of times left home (7.608, 15.770), length of time on the street (10.323, 5.711), and street friends arrested (2.241, 1.546).

6. Although we include up to 24 independent variables in our models, multi-collinearity is not a problem: All models were successfully estimated with the OLS regression tolerance level set at .3, and diagnostics indicate only two cases of a component associated with a high condition index on two variables (i.e., maternal and paternal instrumental control, and home and street friends arrested). Combining the items in question does not alter the effects noted in the text.

7. We also explored possible interaction effects involving gender and measures of situational adversity. None of these effects are significant in models of theft of food or prostitution; however, gender interactions with unemployment and shelter significantly affect serious theft. These suggest that the effects of joblessness and shelter are pronounced among males.

8. Several studies indicate that Heckman's estimator is not problem-free (Stolzenberg and Relles, 1990; Winship and Mare, 1992); however, there are no alternative problem-free estimators. Problems with this estimator appear to be pronounced in small ($N = 50$) rather than large samples like the one we use and are a more important concern when introduction of this estimator substantially alters the estimated coefficients.

9. The inclusion of two additional variables into the probit equation for leaving

home results in some changes. First, although they remain significant, the negative associations between leaving home and age, intact family, and school goals are somewhat reduced, as are the positive relationships between leaving and parental use of force, conflict with teachers, and age. Second, two new variables are responsible for these changes: Sexual abuse and home friends arrested have significant, positive effects on leaving home. Third, although involvement in serious theft at home has a significant bivariate effect on leaving home, its effect is small and nonsignificant in the full equation. Models that replace serious theft at home first with minor theft and then with prostitution produce similar results.

10. An emphasis on the situational variability that characterizes many life experiences is also evident in some recent work including Horney, Osgood, and Marshall's (1995) study of the relationship between offending and short-term variation in school, work, marital relations, and substance abuse.

11. The limited effect of unemployment may in part reflect that street employment often involves low-paying jobs that provide minimal economic returns.

5. The Streets of Two Cities

1. These globally absorbing and ontogenetic forces are more or less equivalent to what is also sometimes called *propensity* or *criminality* in the research literature on crime.

2. The scales developed by Straus have been used in several hundred studies with results that suggest they are both reliable and valid (see Straus, 1979, 1990). As indicated by the reliability scores reported in Table 8.1, these measures also performed well in our study. Regardless of method of extraction or rotation, exploratory factor analyses consistently reduced our data to the four perpetrator-specific factors used in this analysis.

3. An alternative to treating the items in the Conflict Tactics Scale as a single index is to separate more severe forms of violence (i.e., hitting and beating) from those that may be less severe (e.g., slapping). Although parents were reportedly much more likely to have slapped (about two-thirds) than hit or beaten (about one-third and one-fifth, respectively) their children, mothers and fathers were nearly identical in their reported likelihood of doing so. Also, although mothers were slightly more likely to report having threatened violence or thrown something, overall the similarities in reported violent acts were more striking than dissimilarities. There is a Gutman-like hierarchy to the items, moving from threats to beatings, that we decided to treat as a one-dimensional scale.

4. We also collected data on the onset of family violence, asking respondents the age at which they and their parents used force in their conflicts with each other. Regardless of the parent's gender or the type of violence, parental use of force occurred earlier in more than two-thirds of families; as severity

increased, the proportion rose to more than four-fifths (e.g., maternal beatings).

5. Collinearity is not a significant problem in assessing the respective effects of violence by and against fathers and by and against mothers, as the correlations between these measures are all less than .4.

6. Criminal Embeddedness and Criminal Capital

1. Several recent tests of differential association minimize the importance of tutelage, skills, and training; see McCarthy (1996) for a review and critique of this interpretation of Sutherland's work.

2. The theory of differential association has been reformulated several times and has served as a point of origin for other explanations. None of these reformulations has involved a rejection of Sutherland's ideas about tutelage. For example, Glaser's (1956) differential identification and Burgess and Akers's (1966; also see Akers et al., 1979) differential reinforcement theories both recognize the centrality of learning deviant behaviors from accomplished lawbreakers. Assumptions about tutelage are also central to the works of several subcultural theorists, including Cohen (1955, 1966) and particularly Cloward and Ohlin (1960), as well as those from the labeling (e.g., H. Becker, 1963/1973) and interactionist (e.g., Heimer and Matsueda, 1994) traditions. This recognition encourages our attempt to revive theoretical and empirical interest in the ways in which "criminal skills" are acquired.

3. The generalizability of Sutherland's theory is evident in the array of crimes to which he applied it: from shoplifting, theft (1947), and professional theft (1942/1956) to white-collar crime (1949/1983).

4. Sampson and Laub (1993) also make use of Coleman's work on social capital in their study of crime and the life course; in keeping with the social control tradition, they focus on types of social capital that inhibit rather than encourage crime. In the last chapters of this book, we address the importance of both types of capital.

5. In a previous analysis (McCarthy and Hagan, 1995), we include beliefs that support offending as a control variable on the effect of tutelage on offending. In elaborating our position in this chapter, we incorporate both skills and beliefs as important elements of criminal capital.

8. Street Crime Amplification

1. The implication of Braithwaite's theory is that some family contexts and state-instigated programs are able to use their reintegrative capacities to overcome the longer-term effects of criminal stigmatization. This thesis gains support from recent research which finds that middle-class families are better able than families with fewer resources to counteract the effects of criminal

stigmatization on their adolescent children (e.g., Hagan, 1991; Jessor, Donovan, and Costa, 1991).

2. Our correction for selection is based on a selection hazard equation for retention in the second-wave interviews that includes being on the street in the first-wave interview, the number of nights reported since leaving home, staying on the street in nonagency settings, and the city in which the youth was interviewed. Although this selection hazard is significantly related to self-reported crime in reduced form equations estimated later, when additional variables are included in the structural equations, the selection hazard variable becomes nonsignificant. This encourages our view that selection bias is not a serious problem in this analysis.

3. Self-reported crime in the second wave of this research is measured in a count form that could make the use of Poisson estimations preferable to ordinary least squares regression (see Hagan and Palloni, 1990). However, estimation of Poisson models revealed little variation from the OLS regression results. For example, when the last equation in Table 8.3 was reestimated as a Poisson model, the same two interactions emerged as statistically significant, with associated t-values that were also between two and three.

4. To assure that collinearity problems did not distort the estimation of the interaction effects reported in this chapter, the components of each interaction also were centered in relation to their mean values prior to reestimating the multiplicative terms (see Cronbach, 1987). This transformation reduced correlations between the product and component terms, but it did not substantively alter the statistical significance of the interaction effects estimated with untransformed components.

Appendix: The Methodology of Studying Street Youth

1. Using a young data collector may have helped to discourage the underreporting of deviant activities that appears to have occurred in studies of adolescents that use older interviewers [e.g., see Mensch and Kandel's (1988) analysis of underreporting in the National Longitudinal Youth Cohort Study].

2. Talking with youth about street topics was imperative as we encountered many youth who lived in the suburbs but came downtown with their friends and panhandled for the "thrill" it provided or who, in the warm summer months, slept in the park because they were too drunk or stoned to go home or because it was "cool."

3. As the foregoing makes clear, our study is not an ethnography nor a participant-observer study. We did not establish long-term relations with "key informants" who we visited repeatedly over a long period of time. We did not "befriend" the street youth we met. We talked with them and hung out with them for only short periods; we did not buy them things, take them places, or meet their families, nor did we do many of the other things that

ethnographers typically do in establishing long-term relations with the people they study. The street ethnographies we mentioned in our first chapter are clearly valuable and provide many important insights, but ours is a different project. Nonetheless, some ethnographers claim that it is *only* through the establishment of long-term relationships that researchers can develop the rapport necessary to ask about personal issues and ensure the accuracy of respondents' replies. Yet, as Fleisher (1995, p. 67) notes in his ethnography of street life: "It's easy to be mislead by informants' claims, particularly if a researcher has established a close rapport with informants." Ethnographers typically lack the comparative *qualitative and survey* data necessary to assess the validity of an ethnography's presumed superiority. We address the validity of our data in greater detail in the penultimate section of this Appendix; for now, we simply note the absence of any existing empirical basis for dismissing survey research in the homeless population.

4. Our research has several important implications for policies regarding services for street youth, and we have made efforts to share our results. We have prepared reports for the social service agencies that helped us conduct our research, and we have distributed summaries to the media and various municipal and provincial government offices.

5. A handful of older students were living independently of their families and therefore did not require parental permission to complete a survey.

6. Sudman and Bradburn (1974) report that interviewer effects are rarely a significant source of error; nonetheless, we hired RAs from both genders and several ethnic groups (e.g., Aboriginal, Metis, and African-American) to reduce the potential of any systematic error.

7. In our first study, we had insufficient resources to pay respondents, and instead we gave them food coupons. Our second study was financed by a larger federal government grant that provided money to pay respondents. In the first study, we gave respondents their food coupons after they had completed a survey. By the time of the second study, we realized that paying respondents at the start of the survey had several advantages: (1) it increased respondents' confidence that their participation was completely voluntary, because at any point they could end the interview without incurring a financial loss; (2) it gave respondents a greater sense of power and control in the interview; and (3) it resonated with economic transactions in much of the underground economy where payment is given before services or goods are provided (e.g., sex-trade workers and drug dealers reported that they "always try to get the money first").

References

Adams, Gerald, Thomas Gullotta, and Mary Anne Clancy. 1985. "Homeless Adolescents: A Descriptive Study of Similarities and Differences Between Runaways and Throwaways." *Adolescence* 20:715–24.

Adams, Gerald, and Gordon Munro. 1979. "Portrait of the North American Runaways: A Critical Review." *Journal of Youth and Adolescence* 8:359–73.

Agnew, Robert. 1985. "A Revised Strain Theory of Delinquency." *Social Forces* 64:151–67.

——— 1992. "Foundation for a General Strain Theory of Crime and Delinquency." *Criminology* 30:47–87.

——— 1994. "The Contribution of Social-Psychological Strain Theory to the Explanation of Crime and Delinquency." In Freda Adler and William Laufer (Eds.), *Advances in Criminological Theory, Volume 6: The Legacy of Anomie.* New Brunswick, NJ: Transaction.

——— 1995. "Stability and Change in Crime over the Life Course: A Strain Theory Explanation." In Terence Thornberry (Ed.), *Advances in Criminological Theory, Volume 7: Developmental Theories of Crime and Delinquency.* New Brunswick, NJ: Transaction.

Agnew, Robert, and Sandra Huguley. 1989. "Adolescent Violence Toward Parents." *Journal of Marriage and the Family* 51:699–711.

Akers, Ronald, Marvin Krohn, Lonn Lanza-Kaduce, and Marcia Radosevich. 1979. "Social Learning and Deviant Behavior: A Specific Test of a General Theory." *American Sociological Review* 44:636–55.

Alba, Richard. 1987. "Interpreting the Parameters of Log-Linear Models." *Sociological Methods and Research* 16:45–77.

Allan, Emilie, and Darrell Steffensmeier. 1989. "Youth, Underemployment, and Property Crime: Differential Effects of Job Availability and Job Quality on Juvenile and Young Adult Arrest Rates." *American Sociological Review* 54:107–23.

Anderson, Elijah. 1990. *Streetwise: Race, Class and Change in an Urban Community.* Chicago: University of Chicago Press.

Anderson, Nels. 1923. *The Hobo: The Sociology of Homeless Men.* Chicago: University of Chicago Press.

Aptekar, Lewis. 1988. *Street Children of Cali.* Durham, NC: Duke University Press.

Armstrong, Clairette. 1932. *660 Runaway Boys; Why Boys Desert Their Homes.* Boston: R. G. Badger.

⸻ 1937. "A Psychoneurotic Reaction of Delinquent Boys and Girls." *Journal of Abnormal and Social Psychology* 32:329–42.

Artenstein, Jeffrey. 1990. *Runaways – In Their Own Words: Kids Talking about Living on the Street.* New York: Tom Doherty.

Averitt, Robert. 1968. *The Dual Economy.* New York: W. W. Norton.

Bachman, Jerome, and John Schulenberg. 1993. "How Part-Time Work Intensity Relates to Drug Use, Problem Behavior, Time Use, and Satisfaction Among High School Seniors: Are These Consequences or Merely Correlates?" *Developmental Psychology* 29:220–35.

Badgley, Robin. 1984. *Sexual Offences Against Children: Report of the Committee on Sexual Offences Against Children and Youths.* Ottawa: Canadian Government Publishing.

Ball, Richard, and G. David Curry. 1995. "The Logic of Definition in Criminology: Purposes and Methods for Defining 'Gangs'." *Criminology* 33:225–45.

Barker, G., and F. Knaul. 1991. *Exploited Entrepreneurs: Street and Working Children in Developing Countries.* New York: Childhope USA.

Baum, Alice, and Donald Burnes. 1993. *A Nation in Denial: The Truth about Homelessness.* Boulder: Westview Press.

Baxter, Sheila. 1991. *Under the Viaduct: Homeless in Beautiful B.C.* Vancouver: New Star Books.

Beccaria, Cesare. [1764] 1953. *An Essay on Crimes and Punishments.* Stanford: Academic Reprints.

Becker, Gary. 1964. *Human Capital.* New York: National Bureau of Economic Research.

⸻ 1968. "Crime and Punishment: An Economic Approach." *Journal of Political Economy* 76:169–217.

Becker, Gary, and W. Landes. 1974. *Essays in the Economics of Crime and Punishment.* New York: Columbia University Press.

Becker, Howard. [1963] 1973. *Outsiders: Studies in the Sociology of Deviance.* New York: Free Press of Glencoe.

Becker, Howard (Ed.). 1964. *The Other Side: Perspectives on Deviance.* New York: Free Press of Glencoe.

Bentham, Jeremy. [1789] 1982. *Introduction to the Principals of Morals and Legislation.* New York: Methuen.

Berk, Richard. 1983. "An Introduction to Sample Selection Bias in Sociological Data." *American Sociological Review* 48:386–98.

Black, Donald. 1976. *The Behavior of Law*. New York: Academic Press.
1983. "Crime as Social Control." *American Sociological Review* 48:34–45.
Blau, Joel. 1992. *The Visible Poor: Homelessness in the United States*. New York: Oxford University Press.
Blau, Peter, and Otis Dudley Duncan. 1967. *The American Occupational Structure*. New York: Wiley.
Block, M. K., and J. M. Heineke. 1975. "A Labor Theoretic Analysis of the Criminal Choice." *American Economic Review* 65:314–25.
Blumstein, Alfred, Jacqueline Cohen, and David Farrington. 1988a. "Criminal Career Research: Its Value for Criminology." *Criminology* 26:1–35.
1988b. "Longitudinal and Criminal Career Research: Further Clarifications." *Criminology* 26:57–74.
Bonger, Willem. 1916. *Criminality and Economic Conditions*. Boston: Little, Brown.
Bourdieu, Pierre. 1986. "The Forms of Capital." In J. G. Richardson (Ed.), *Handbook of Theory and Research for the Sociology of Education*. New York: Greenwood Press.
Bourgois, Philippe. 1995. *In Search of Respect: Selling Crack in El Barrio*. Cambridge: Cambridge University Press.
Bradburn, Norman, and Seymour Sudman. 1979. *Improving Interview Methods and Questionnaire Design*. San Francisco: Jossey-Bass.
Braithwaite, John. 1981. "The Myth of Social Class and Criminality Reconsidered." *American Sociological Review* 46:36–57.
1989. *Crime, Shame and Reintegration*. Cambridge: Cambridge University Press.
Brantingham, Paul, and Patricia Brantingham. 1984. *Patterns in Crime*. New York: Macmillan Publishing.
Brennan, Tim, David Huizinga, and Delbert Elliott. 1978. *The Social Psychology of Runaways*. Lexington, MA: Lexington Books.
Briar, Scott, and Irving Piliavin. 1965. "Delinquency, Situational Inducements, and Commitment to Conformity." *Social Problems* 13:35–45.
Brown, Stephen. 1984. "Social Class, Child Maltreatment, and Delinquency Behavior." *Criminology* 22:259–78.
Browne, Angela, and David Finkelhor. 1986. "Impact of Child Sexual Abuse: A Review of the Research." *Psychological Bulletin* 99:66–77.
Brownfield, David. 1986. "Social Class and Violent Behavior." *Criminology* 24:421–38.
Burgess, Robert, and Ronald Akers. 1966. "A Differential Association-Reinforcement Theory of Criminal Behavior." *Social Problems* 14:128–47.
Burt, Martha. 1992. *Over the Edge: The Growth of Homelessness in the 1980s*. New York: Russell Sage Foundation.
Cairns, Robert. 1986. "Phenomena Lost: Issues in the Study of Development." J. Valsiner (Ed.), *The Individual Subject and Scientific Psychology*. New York: Plenum.
Calysyn, Robert, Gary Allen, Gary Morse, Ruth Smith, and Betty Tempelhoff.

1993. "Can You Trust Self-Report Data Provided by Homeless Mentally Ill Individuals?" *Evaluation Review* 17:353–66.

Campbell, Anne. 1984. *Girls in the Gang*. New York: Basil Blackwell.

Campos, Regina, Marcela Raffaelli, and Walter Ude. 1994. "Social Networks and Daily Activities of Street Youth in Belo Horizonte, Brazil." *Child Development* 65:319–30.

Carey, E. 1990, August 11. "10,000 Homeless Kids Roam Metro Street." *Toronto Star*, p. A1.

Caspi, Avshalom, and Glen Elder, Jr. 1988. "Emergent Family Patterns: The Intergenerational Construction of Problem Behaviors and Relationships." In R. Hinde and J. Stevenson-Hinde (Eds.), *Relationship Within Families: Mutual Influences*. Oxford: Clarendon Press.

Caspi, Avshalom, Glen Elder, Jr., and E. Herbener. 1990. "Childhood Personality and the Prediction of Life-Course Patterns." In L. Robins and M. Rutter (Eds.), *Straight and Devious Pathways from Childhood to Adulthood*. Cambridge: Cambridge University Press.

Caspi, Avshalom, Terrie Moffitt, Phil Silva, Magda Stouthamer-Loeber, Robert Krueger, and Pamela Schmutte. 1994. "Are Some People Crime Prone? Replications of the Personality–Crime Relationship across Countries, Genders, Races, and Methods." *Criminology* 32:163–95.

Chilton, Roland. 1964. "Continuity in Delinquency Area Research: A Comparison of Studies for Baltimore, Detroit and Indianapolis." *American Sociological Review* 29:71–83.

Chiricos, Theodore. 1987. "Rates of Crime and Unemployment: An Analysis of Aggregate Research Evidence." *Social Problems* 34:187–212.

Clarridge, Brian, Linda Sheehy, and Taissa Hauser. 1977. "Tracing Members of a Panel: A 17-year Follow-up." In K. F. Schuessler (Ed.), *Sociological Methodology*. San Francisco: Jossey-Bass.

Clausen, John. 1991. "Adolescent Competence and the Shaping of the Life Course." *American Journal of Sociology* 96:805–42.

Climenhage, JoAnn. 1989. *Street Kids: An Ethnographic Study of a Deviant Adolescent Subcultural Group*. Unpublished M.A. thesis, McMaster University.

Clinard, Marshall, and Richard Quinney. 1973. *Criminal Behavior Systems: A Typology*. New York: Holt Rinehart & Winston.

Cloward, Richard, and Lloyd Ohlin. 1960. *Delinquency and Opportunity: A Theory of Delinquent Gangs*. New York: Free Press.

Cohen, Albert. 1955. *Delinquent Boys: The Culture of the Gang*. Glencoe, IL: Free Press.

1966. *Deviance and Control*. Englewood Cliffs, NJ: Prentice-Hall.

Cohen, Evan, Carol Mowbray, Deborah Bybee, Susan Yeich, Kurt Ribisl, and Paul Freddolino. 1993. "Tracking and Follow-up Methods for Research on Homelessness." *Evaluation Review* 17:331–52.

Cohen, Lawrence, and Marcus Felson. 1979. "Social Change and Crime Rate Trends: A Routine Activities Approach." *American Sociological Review* 44:588–608.

Coleman, James. 1988. "Social Capital in the Creation of Human Capital." *American Journal of Sociology* 94S:95–120.

——. 1990. *Foundations of Social Theory*. Cambridge: Harvard University Press.

Colvin, Mark, and John Pauly. 1983. "A Critique of Criminology: Toward an Integrated Structural-Marxist Theory of Delinquency Production." *American Journal of Sociology* 89:513–51.

Conger, Rand, and Glen Elder, Jr. 1994. *Families in Troubled Times: Adapting to Change in Rural America*. Hawthorne, NY: Aldine de Gruyter.

Converse, Jean, and Stanley Presser. 1986. *Handcrafting the Standardized Survey Questionnaire*. Beverly Hills: Sage.

Cook, Thomas, and Donald Campbell. 1979. *Quasi-Experimentation: Design and Analysis Issues for Field Settings*. Chicago: Rand McNally.

Cordray, Sheila, and Kenneth Polk. 1983. "The Implication of Respondent Loss in Panel Studies of Deviant Behavior." *Journal of Research in Crime and Delinquency* 20:214–42.

Cornish, Derek, and Ronald Clarke. 1986. *The Reasoning Criminal: Rational Choice Perspectives on Offending*. New York: Springer-Verlag.

Craig, Sandy, and Chris Schwarz. 1984. *Down and Out – Orwell's Paris and London Revisited*. Middlesex: Penguin.

Cronbach, Lee. 1987. "Statistical Tests for Moderator Variables: Flaws in Analysis Recently Proposed." *Psychological Bulletin* 102:414–17.

D'Angelo, Rocco. 1974. *Families of Sand: A Report Concerning the Flight of Adolescents from Their Families*. Columbus: Ohio State University.

Dannefer, Dale. 1984. "Adult Development and Social Theory: A Paradigmatic Reappraisal." *American Sociological Review* 49:100–16.

DiMaggio, Paul. 1982. "Cultural Capital and School Success: The Impact of Status Culture Participation on the Grades of U.S. High School Students." *American Sociological Review* 47:189–201.

——. 1987. "Classification in Art." *American Sociological Review* 52:440–55.

DiMaggio, Paul, and John Mohr. 1985. "Cultural Capital, Educational Attainment, and Marital Selection." *American Journal of Sociology* 90:1231–61.

Dodds, Suzanne, Andy Furlon, and Linda Croxford. 1989. "Quality and Quantity: Tackling Non-Contact Attrition in a Longitudinal Survey." *Sociology* 23:275–84.

Doerner, William. 1987. "Child Maltreatment Seriousness and Juvenile Delinquency." *Youth and Society* 19:197–224.

Duncan, Otis, David Featherman, and Beverly Duncan. 1972. *Socioeconomic Background and Achievement*. New York: Seminar Press.

Durkheim, Emile. [1897] 1951. *Suicide*. Translated by John Spaulding and George Simpson. Glencoe, IL: Free Press.

Eckland, Bruce. 1968. "Retrieving Mobile Cases in Longitudinal Surveys." *Public Opinion Quarterly* 32:51–64.

Edelbrock, Craig. 1980. "Running away from Home: Incidence and Correlates among Children and Youth Referred for Mental Health Services." *Journal of Family Issues* 1:210–28.

Ehrlich, Isaac. 1973. "Participation in Illegitimate Activities: A Theoretical and Empirical Investigation." *Journal of Political Economy* 81:521–65.

Elder, Glen, Jr. 1974. *Children of the Great Depression: Social Change in Life Experience.* Chicago: University of Chicago Press.

———. 1975. "Adolescence in the Life Cycle: An Introduction." In Sigmund Dragastin and Glen Elder, Jr. (Eds.), *Adolescence in the Life Cycle: Psychological Change and Social Context.* New York: Halstead Press.

———. 1985. "Perspectives on the Life Course." In Glen Elder, Jr. (Ed.), *Life Course Dynamics: Trajectories and Transitions, 1968–80.* Ithaca: Cornell University Press.

———. 1994. "Time, Human Agency, and Social Change: Perspectives on the Life Course." *Social Psychology Quarterly* 57:4–15.

Elliott, Delbert. 1966. "Delinquency, School Attendance and Dropout." *Social Problems* 13:307–14.

Elliott, Delbert, and Suzanne Ageton. 1980. "Reconciling Race and Class Differences in Self-Reported and Official Estimates of Delinquency." *American Sociological Review* 45:95–110.

Elliott, Delbert, David Huizinga, and Suzanne Ageton. 1985. *Explaining Delinquency and Drug Use.* Beverly Hills, CA: Sage.

Elliott, Delbert, and Harwin Voss. 1974. *Delinquency and Dropout.* Lexington, MA: Lexington Books.

English, Clifford. 1973. "Leaving Home: A Typology of Runaways." *Trans-Action* 10:22–24.

Fagan, Jeffrey. 1989. "The Social Organization of Drug Use and Drug Dealing Among Urban Gangs." *Criminology* 27:633–69.

Farber, Edward, Cecilia Kinast, W. Douglas McCoard, and Deborah Falkner. 1984. "Violence in Families of Adolescent Runaways." *Child Abuse and Neglect* 8:295–99.

Farnworth, Margaret, and Michael Leiber. 1989. "Strain Theory Revisited: Economic Goals, Educational Means and Delinquency." *American Sociological Review* 54:263–74.

Farnworth, Margaret, Terence Thornberry, Marvin Krohn, and Alan Lizotte. 1994. "Measurement in the Study of Class and Delinquency: Integrating Theory and Research." *Journal of Research in Crime and Delinquency* 31:32–61.

Farrington, David, Bernard Gallagher, Linda Morley, Raymond St. Leger, and Donald J. West. 1986. "Unemployment, School Leaving, and Crime." *British Journal of Criminology* 26:335–56.

Farrington, David, Lloyd Ohlin, and James Wilson. 1986. *Understanding and Controlling Crime: Toward a New Research Strategy.* New York: Springer-Verlag.

Finkelhor, David. 1993. "Epidemiological Factors in the Clinical Identification of Child Sexual Abuse." *Child Abuse and Neglect* 17:67–70.

1994a. "Current Information on the Scope and Nature of Child Sexual Abuse." *Future of Children* 4:31–53.

1994b. "The International Epidemiology of Child Sexual Abuse." *Child Abuse and Neglect* 18:409–17.

Fisher, Pamela. 1988. "Criminal Activity among the Homeless: A Study of Arrests in Baltimore." *Hospital and Community Psychiatry* 39:46–51.

Fleisher, Mark. 1995. *Beggars and Thieves: Lives of Urban Street Criminals.* Madison: University of Wisconsin Press.

Fletcher, Joseph. 1849. "Moral and Educational Statistics of England and Wales." *Journal of the Statistical Society of London* 12:151–76, 189–335.

Foster, Randall. 1962. "Intrapsychic and Environmental Factors in Running away from Home." *American Journal of Orthopsychiatry* 32:486–91.

Freedman, Deborah, Arland Thornton, and Donald Camburn. 1980. "Maintaining Response Rates in Longitudinal Studies." *Sociological Methods and Research* 9:87–98.

Freeman, Richard. 1996. "The Supply of Youths to Crime." In Susan Pozo (Ed.), *Exploring the Underground Economy: Studies of Illegal and Unreported Activity.* Kalamazoo, MI: W. E. Upjohn Institute for Employment Research.

Garbarino, James, James Wilson, and Anne Garbarino. 1986. "The Adolescent Runaway." In James Garbarino, Cynthia Scellenbach, and Janet Sebes (Eds.), *Troubled Youth, Troubled Families.* New York: Aldine de Gruyter.

Gelberg, Lillian, Lawrence Linn, and Barbara Leake. 1988. "Mental Health, Alcohol and Drug Use, and Criminal History among Homeless Adults." *American Journal of Psychiatry* 145:191–6.

Gibbons, Donald. 1971. "Observations on the Study of Crime Causation." *American Journal of Sociology* 77:262–78.

Glaser, Daniel. 1956. "Criminality Theories and Behavioral Images." *American Journal of Sociology* 61:433–44.

Glueck, Sheldon, and Eleanor Glueck. 1950. *Unravelling Juvenile Delinquency.* Cambridge: Harvard University Press.

1968. *Delinquents and Nondelinquents in Perspective.* Cambridge: Harvard University Press.

Gold, Martin, and David Reimer. 1974. Testimony presented on the "Runaway Youth Act" to the Subcommittee on Equal Opportunity of the United States House Committee on Education and Labor. Washington: Government Printing Office.

Goldberg, Jim, and Philip Brookman. 1995. *Raised by Wolves.* New York: Scalo Publishers.

Good, David, Maureen Pirog-Good, and Robin Sickles. 1986. "An Analysis of Youth Crime and Employment Patterns." *Journal of Quantitative Criminology* 2:219–36.

Gottfredson, Michael, and Travis Hirschi. 1990. *A General Theory of Crime*. Stanford: Stanford University Press.

Gove, Walter (Ed.). 1975. *The Labelling of Deviance: Evaluating a Perspective*. New York: Halstead Press.

Granovetter, Mark. 1973. "The Strength of Weak Ties." *American Journal of Sociology* 78:1360–80.

1974. *Getting a Job: A Study of Contacts and Careers*. Cambridge: Harvard University Press.

1985. "Economic Action and Social Structure: The Problem of Embeddedness." *American Journal of Sociology* 91:481–510.

1992. "The Sociological and Economic Approaches to Labor Market Analysis: A Social Structural View." In Mark Granovetter and Richard Swedberg (Eds.), *The Sociology of Economic Life*. Boulder: Westview Press.

Green, Donald. 1990. "Measuring Self-Report Deviance: Cross-Sectional or Panel Data?" *Social Science Research* 19:301–21.

Greenberg, David. 1977. "Delinquency and the Age Structure of Society." *Contemporary Crises* 1:189–223.

1981. *Crime and Capitalism*. Palo Alto: Mayfield.

Gregory, Marilyn, Mary Lohr, and Lewayne Gilchrist. 1992. "Methods for Tracking Pregnant and Parenting Adolescents." *Evaluation Review* 16:69–81.

Gulotta, Thomas. 1978. "Runaway: Reality or Myth?" *Adolescence* 13:543–9.

Gutierres, Sara, and John Reich. 1981. "A Development Perspective on Runaway Behavior: Its Relationship to Child Abuse." *Child Welfare* 60:89–94.

Hagan, John. 1991. "Destiny and Drift: Subcultural Preferences, Status Attainment and the Risks and Rewards of Youth." *American Sociological Review* 56:567–82.

1992. "The Poverty of a Classless Criminology." *Criminology* 30:1–20.

1993. "The Social Embeddedness of Crime and Unemployment." *Criminology* 31:465–91.

1994. *Crime and Disrepute*. Thousand Oaks, CA: Pine Forge Press.

Hagan, John, A. R. Gillis, and John Simpson. 1985. "The Class Structure of Gender and Delinquency: Toward a Power Control Theory of Common Delinquent Behavior." *American Journal of Sociology* 90:1151–78.

1987. "Class in the Household: A Power-Control Theory of Gender and Delinquency." *American Journal of Sociology* 92:788–816.

Hagan, John, and Bill McCarthy. 1992. "Streetlife and Delinquency." *British Journal of Sociology* 43:533–61.

Hagan, John, and Alberto Palloni. 1988. "Crimes as Social Events in the Life Course: Reconceiving a Criminological Controversy." *Criminology* 26:87–100.

Hagan, John, and Alberto Palloni. 1990. "The Social Reproduction of a Criminal Class in Working-Class London, Circa 1950–1980." *American Journal of Sociology* 96:265–99.

Hagan, John, John Simpson, and A. R. Gillis. 1979. "The Sexual Stratification of Social Control: A Gender-Based Perspective on Crime and Delinquency." *British Journal of Sociology* 30:25–38.

——— 1989. "Feminist Scholarship, Relational and Instrumental Control and a Power-Control Theory of Gender and Delinquency." *British Journal of Sociology* 39:301–36.

Hagedorn, John. 1988. *People and Folks: Gangs, Crime and the Underclass in a Rustbelt City.* Chicago: Lake View Press.

Harris, Anthony. 1977. "Sex and Theories of Deviance: Toward a Functional Theory of Deviant Type-Scripts." *American Sociological Review* 42:3–16.

Hartnagel, Timothy, and Harvey Krahn. 1989. "High School Dropouts, Labour Market Success and Criminal Behavior." *Youth and Society* 20:416–44.

Hauser, Robert. 1971. *Socioeconomic Background and Educational Performance.* Washington: Rose Monograph Series.

Hauser, Robert, and Peter Mossel. 1985. "Fraternal Resemblance in Educational Attainment and Occupational Status." *American Journal of Sociology* 91:650–73.

Heimer, Karen, and Ross Matsueda. 1994. "Role-Taking, Role Commitment, and Delinquency: A Theory of Differential Social Control." *American Sociological Review* 59:365–90.

Hildebrand, James. 1963. "Why Runaways Leave Home." *Journal of Criminal Law, Criminology and Police Science* 54:211–16.

——— 1968. "Reasons for Runaways." *Crime and Delinquency* 14:42–48.

Hindelang, Michael. 1979. "Sex Differences in Criminal Activity." *Social Problems* 27:143–56.

Hindelang, Michael, Michael Gottfredson, and James Garofalo. 1978. *Victims of Personal Crime.* Cambridge: Ballinger.

Hindelang, Michael, Travis Hirschi, and Joseph Weis. 1979. "Correlates of Delinquency: The Illusion of Discrepancy Between Self-Report and Official Measures." *American Sociological Review* 44:995–1014.

——— 1981. *Measuring Delinquency.* Beverly Hills: Sage.

Hirschi, Travis. 1969. *Causes of Delinquency.* Berkeley: University of California Press.

——— 1972. "Social Class and Crime." In Gerald Thielbar and Saul Feldman (Eds.), *Issues in Social Inequality.* Boston: Little, Brown.

——— 1989. "Exploring Alternatives to Integrated Theory." In Steven Messner, Marvin Krohn, and Allen Liska (Eds.), *Theoretical Integration in the Study of Deviance and Crime: Problems and Prospects.* Albany: State University of New York at Albany Press.

Hirschi, Travis, and Michael Gottfredson. 1980. "Introduction: The Sutherland

Tradition." In Travis Hirschi and Michael Gottfredson (Eds.), *Understanding Crime-Current Theory and Research*. Beverly Hills: Sage.

Hirschi, Travis, and Hanan Selvin. 1967. *Delinquency Research*. New York: Free Press.

Hodson, Randy, and Robert Kaufman. 1982. "Economic Dualism: A Critical Review." *American Sociological Review* 47:727–39.

Horney, Julie, D. Wayne Osgood, and Ineke Haen Marshall. 1995. "Criminal Careers in the Short-Term: Intra-Individual Variability in Crime and Its Relation to Local Life Circumstances." *American Sociological Review* 60:655–73.

Howell, M. C., E. B. Emmons, and D. A. Frank. 1973. "Reminiscences of Runaway Adolescents." *American Journal of Orthopsychiatry* 43:840–53.

Huff, C. Ronald (Ed.). 1990. *Gangs in America*. Newbury Park, CA: Sage.

Hunner, Robert, and Yvonne Elder Walker (Eds.). 1981. *Exploring the Relationship Between Child Abuse and Delinquency*. Montclair, NJ: Allanheld, Osmun.

Inciardi, James, Ruth Horowitz, and Anne Pottieger. 1993. *Street Kids, Street Drugs, Street Crime: An Examination of Drug Use and Serious Delinquency in Miami*. Belmont, CA: Wadsworth Publishing.

Jacobs, Bruce. 1993. "Undercover Deception Clues: A Case of Restrictive Deterrence." *Criminology* 31:281–99.

Jacobs, Jane. 1961. *The Death and Life of Great American Cities*. New York: Random House.

Jankowski, Martin Sanchez. 1991. *Islands in the Street: Gangs and American Urban Society*. Berkeley: University of California Press.

Janus, Mark-David, Arlene McCormack, Ann Wolbert Burgess, and Carol Hartman. 1987. *Adolescent Runaways: Causes and Consequences*. Lexington, MA: Lexington Press.

Jencks, Christopher. 1994. *The Homeless*. Cambridge: Harvard University Press.

Jenkins, Richard. 1969. "Classification of Behavior Problems of Children." *American Journal of Psychiatry* 125:1032–39.

———. 1971. "The Runaway Reaction." *American Journal of Psychiatry* 128:168–73.

Jensen, Gary, and Kevin Thompson. 1990. "What's Class Got to Do with It? A Further Examination of Power-Control Theory." *American Journal of Sociology* 95:1009–23.

Jessor, Richard, John Donovan, and Frances Costa. 1991. *Beyond Adolescence: Problem Behavior and Young Adult Development*. New York: Cambridge University Press.

Johnson, Richard. 1979. *Juvenile Delinquency and Its Origins: An Integrated Theoretical Approach*. Cambridge: Cambridge University Press.

Jones, F. L. and Jonathan Kelley. 1984. "Decomposing Differences Between Groups: A Cautionary Note on Measuring Discrimination." *Sociological Methods and Research* 12:323–43.

Kalton, Graham. 1983. *Introduction to Survey Sampling*. Beverly Hills: Sage.

Katz, Jack. 1988. *Seductions of Crime: Moral and Sensual Attractions in Doing Evil.* New York: Basic Books.

Kennedy, Stanislaus (Ed.). 1987. *Streetwise: Homelessness among the Young in Ireland and Abroad.* Dublin: Glendale.

Kessler, Ronald, J. Blake Turner, and James House. 1989. "Unemployment, Reemployment, and Emotional Functioning in a Community Sample." *American Sociological Review* 54:648–57.

Kish, Leslie. 1965. *Survey Sampling.* New York: Wiley.

Klein, Malcolm. 1971. *Street Gangs and Street Workers.* Englewood Cliffs, NJ: Prentice-Hall.

Kohn, Melvin. 1977. *Class and Conformity.* Chicago: University of Chicago Press.

Kornhauser, Ruth. 1978. *Social Sources of Delinquency: An Appraisal of Analytic Models.* Chicago: University of Chicago Press.

Krahn, Harvey. 1991. "The School to Work Transitions in Canada: New Risks and Uncertainties." In Walter Heinz (Ed.), *The Life Course and Social Change: Comparative Perspectives.* Weinheim, Germany: Deutscher Studien Verlag.

Kratcoski, Peter. 1982. "Child Abuse and Violence Against the Family." *Child Welfare* 61:435–44.

Kruttschnitt, Candace, David Ward, and Mary Ann Sheble. 1987. "Abuse-Resistant Youth: Some Factors That May Inhibit Violent Criminal Behavior." *Social Forces* 66:501–19.

Kufeldt, Kathleen, and Margaret Nimmo. 1987. "Youth on the Street: Abuse and Neglect in the Eighties." *Child Abuse and Neglect* 11:531–43.

Land, Kenneth, David Cantor, and Stephen Russell. 1995. "Unemployment and Crime Rate Fluctuations in the Post–World War II United States: Statistical Time Series Properties and Alternative Models." In John Hagan and Ruth Peterson (Eds.), *Crime and Inequality.* Stanford: Stanford University Press.

Larzelere, Robert, and Gerald Patterson. 1990. "Parental Management: Mediator of the Effect of Socioeconomic Status on Early Delinquency." *Criminology* 28:301–23.

Lemert, Edwin. 1967. *Human Deviance, Social Problems and Social Control.* Englewood Cliffs, NJ: Prentice-Hall.

Lemon, James. 1984. "Toronto among North American Cities." In Victor Russel (Ed.), *Forging a Consensus: Historical Essays on Toronto.* Toronto: University of Toronto Press.

Levanthal, Theodore. 1963. "Control Problems in Runaway Children." *Archives of General Psychiatry* 9:122–28.

———. 1964. "Inner Control Deficiencies in Runaway Children." *Archives of General Psychiatry* 11:170–76.

Lewis, Helen. 1971. *Shame and Guilt in Neurosis.* New York: International Universities Press.

Lewis, Oscar. 1966. *La Vida: A Puerto Rican Family in the Culture of Poverty: San Juan and New York.* New York: Random House.

Liebertoff, Ken. 1980. "The Runaway Child in America: A Social History." *Journal of Family Issues* 1:151–64.

Liebow, Elliot. 1967. *Tally's Corner.* Boston: Little, Brown.

Liddiard, Mark, and Susan Hutson. 1991. "Homeless Young People and Runaways: Agency Definitions and Processes." *Journal of Social Policy* 20:365–88.

Loeber, Rolf, and Magda Stouthamer-Loeber. 1986. "Family Factors as Correlates and Predictors of Juvenile Conduct Problems and Delinquency." In Michael Tonry and Norval Morris (Eds.), *Crime and Justice,* Volume 7. Chicago: University of Chicago Press.

Luckenbill, David. 1985. "Entering Male Prostitution." *Urban Life* 14:131–53.

Manski, Charles. 1981. "Structural Models for Discrete Data: The Analysis of Discrete Choice." In Samuel Leinhardt (Ed.), *Sociological Methodology.* San Francisco: Jossey-Bass.

Manski, Charles, and Steven Lerman. 1977. "The Estimation of Choice Probabilities from Choice Based Samples." *Econometrica* 45:1977–88.

Martinez, Celorrio. 1992. "Captive Marginality and Despicable Poverty: Careers of Deculturation among Homeless Youth." *Revista Internacional de Sociologia* 3:113–39.

Matsueda, Ross. 1982. "Testing Control Theory and Differential Association: A Causal Modeling Approach." *American Sociological Review* 47:489–504.

——— 1988. "The Current State of Differential Association Theory." *Crime and Delinquency* 34:277–306.

Matsueda, Ross, Rosemary Gartner, Irving Piliavin, and Michael Polakowski. 1992. "The Prestige of Criminal and Conventional Occupations: A Subcultural Model of Criminal Activity." *American Sociological Review* 57:752–70.

Matza, David. 1966. "The Disreputable Poor." In Reinhard Bendix and Seymour Lipset (Eds.), *Class, Status and Power.* New York: Free Press.

McAllister, Ronald, Steven Goe, and Edgar Butler. 1973. "Tracking Respondents in Longitudinal Surveys: Some Preliminary Considerations." *Public Opinion Quarterly* 37:413–16.

McBroom, William. 1988. "Sample Attrition in Panel Studies: A Research Note." *International Review of Modern Sociology* 18:231–45.

McCarthy, Bill. 1990. *Life on the Street: Serious Theft, Drug-Selling, and Prostitution among Helpless Youth.* Unpublished Ph.D. dissertation. Department of Sociology, University of Toronto.

——— 1996. "The Attitudes and Actions of Others: Tutelage and Sutherland's Theory of Differential Association." *British Journal of Criminology* 36:135–47.

McCarthy, Bill, and John Hagan. 1991. "Homelessness: A Criminogenic Situation?" *British Journal of Criminology* 31:393–410.

——— 1992. "Mean Streets: The Theoretical Significance of Situational Delinquency Among Homeless Youths." *American Journal of Sociology* 98:597–627.

——— 1995. "Getting into Street Crime: The Structure and Process of Criminal Embeddedness." *Social Science Research* 24:63–95.

McCord, Joan. 1983. "A Forty Year Perspective on Effects of Child Abuse and Neglect." *Child Abuse and Neglect* 7:265–70.

McLoyd, V. C. 1989. "Socialization and Development in a Changing Economy: The Effects of Paternal Job and Income Loss on Children." *American Psychologist.* 44:293–302.

Mead, George Herbert. 1918. "The Psychology of Punitive Justice." *American Journal of Sociology* 23:577–602.

———. 1934. *Mind, Self and Society.* Chicago: University of Chicago Press.

Mensch, Barbara, and Denise Kandel. 1988. "Underreporting of Substance Abuse in a National Longitudinal Youth Cohort: Individual and Interviewer Effects." *Public Opinion Quarterly* 52:100–24.

Merton, Robert. 1938. "Social Structure and Anomie." *American Sociological Review* 3:672–82.

———. 1995. "Opportunity Structure: The Emergence, Diffusion, and Differentiation of a Sociological Concept, 1930s–1950s." In Freda Adler and William S. Laufer (Eds.). *Advances in Criminological Theory, Volume 6: The Legacy of Anomie.* New Brunswick, NJ: Transaction Press.

Messner, Steven, and Marvin Krohn. 1990. "Class, Compliance Structures, and Delinquency: Assessing Integrated Structural-Marxist Theory." *American Journal of Sociology* 96:300–28.

Messner, Steven, Marvin Krohn, and Allen Liska (Eds.). 1989. *Theoretical Integration in the Study of Deviance and Crime: Problems and Prospects.* Albany: State University of New York at Albany Press.

Miller, Walter. 1958. "Lower Class Culture as a Generating Milieu of Gang Delinquency." *Journal of Social Issues* 14:5–19.

Minehan, Thomas. 1934. *Boy and Girl Tramps of America.* New York: Farrar & Rinehart.

Mingione, Enzo, and Francesca Zajczky. 1992. "The New Urban Poverty in Italy: Risk Models for the Metropolitan Area of Milan." *Inchiesta* 22:63–79.

Mohr, L. 1990. *Understanding Significance Tests.* Newbury Park: Sage.

Momeni, Jamshid (Ed.). 1989. *Homelessness in the United States.* New York: Greenwood.

Monti, Daniel. 1994. *Wannabe: Gangs in Suburbs and Schools.* Oxford: Blackwell.

Moore, Joan. 1991. *Going Down to the Barrio: Homeboys and Homegirls in Change.* Philadelphia: Temple University Press.

Mortimer, Jeylan. 1996. "The Transition to Adulthood: U.S. Research on Work Role Acquisition and Attainment." In Burt Galaway and Joe Huson (Eds.), *Youth in Transition: Perspectives on Research and Policy.* Toronto: Thompson Educational Publishing.

Moynihan, Daniel. 1965. "The Negro Family: The Case for National Action." Washington: Office of Policy Planning and Research, U.S. Department of Labor.

Mueller, John, Karl Schuessler, and Herbert Costner. 1977. *Statistical Reasoning in Sociology*, 3rd Edition. Boston: Houghton Mifflin.

Nagin, Daniel, and Raymond Paternoster. 1991. "On the Relationship of Past to Future Participation in Delinquency." *Criminology* 29:163–89.

National Research Council. 1993. *Losing Generations: Adolescents in High Risk Settings*. Washington: National Academy Press.

Needle, Richard, Sue-Ching Jou, and Susan Su. 1989. "The Impact of Changing Methods of Data Collection on the Reliability of Self-Reported Drug Use of Adolescents." *American Journal of Drug and Alcohol Abuse* 15:275–89.

Nye, F. Ivan. 1958. *Family Relationships and Delinquent Behavior*. New York: Wiley.
1980. "A Theoretical Perspective on Running Away." *Journal of Family Issues* 1:274–99.

Nye, F. Ivan, and James Short. 1957. "Scaling Delinquent Behavior." *American Sociological Review* 22:326–32.

Olson, Lucy, Elliot Liebow, Fortune Mannino, and Milton Shore. 1980. "Runaway Children Ten Years Later." *Journal of Family Issues* 1:165–88.

Padilla, Felix. 1992. *The Gang as an American Enterprise*. New Brunswick, NJ: Rutgers University Press.

Palenski, Joseph. 1984. *Kids Who Run Away*. Saratoga, CA: R. E. Publishers.

Paternoster, Raymond, and Ruth Triplett. 1988. "Disaggregating Self-Reported Delinquency and Its Implications for Theory." *Criminology* 26:591–625.

Patterson, Gerald. 1980. "Children Who Steal." In Travis Hirschi and Michael Gottfredson (Eds.), *Understanding Crime: Current Theory and Research*. Beverly Hills: Sage.
1982. *Coercive Family Process*. Eugene, OR: Castalia.

Piliavin, Irving, Michael Sosin, Alex Westerfelt, and Ross Matsueda. 1993. "The Duration of Homeless Careers: An Exploratory Study." *Social Science Review* 67:576–98.

Piliavin, Irving, Craig Thornton, Rosemary Gartner, and Ross Matsueda. 1986. "Crime, Deterrence, and Rational Choice." *American Sociological Review* 51:101–19.

Prentice, R. L., and R. Pyke. 1979. "Logistic Disease Incidence Models and Case-Control Studies." *Biometrika* 66:403–11.

Puffer, J. Adams. 1912. *The Boy and His Gang*. Boston: Houghton Mifflin.

Reckless, Walter. 1961. "A New Theory of Delinquency and Crime." *Federal Probation* 25:42–46.

Reisman, David. 1964. *Abundance for What?* Garden City, NY: Doubleday.

Reiss, Albert. 1961. "The Social Integration of Queers and Peers." *Social Problems* 9:102–20.

Revenga, Ana. 1992. "Exporting Jobs? The Impact of Import Competition on Employment and Wages in U.S. Manufacturing." *Quarterly Journal of Economics* 107:255–84.

Robey, Ames, Richard Rosenwald, John Snell, and Rita Lee. 1964. "The Runaway

Girl: A Reaction to Family Stress." *American Journal of Orthopsychiatry* 34:762–67.

Robins, Lee, and Patricia O'Neal. 1959. "The Adult Prognosis for Runaway Children." *American Journal of Orthopsychiatry* 29:752–61.

Robins, Lee, and Michael Rutter (Eds.). 1990. *Straight and Devious Pathways from Childhood to Adulthood.* Cambridge: Cambridge University Press.

Rosenbaum, James, Takehiko Kariya, Rick Settersten, and Tony Maier. 1990. "Market and Network Theories of the Transition from High School to Work: Their Application to Industrialized Societies." *Annual Review of Sociology* 16:263–99.

Rosenberg, Morris. 1975. "The Dissonant Context and the Adolescent Self-Concept." In Sigmund Dragastin and Glenn Elder, Jr. (Eds.), *Adolescence in the Life Cycle: Psychological Change and Social Context.* New York: Halstead Press.

Rosenwald, Richard, and Joseph Mayer. 1967. "Runaway Girls from Suburbia." *American Journal of Orthopsychiatry* 37:402–3.

Rossi, Peter. 1989. *Down and Out in America: The Origins of Homelessness.* Chicago: University of Chicago Press.

Rossi, Peter, Emily Waite, Christine Bose, and Richard Berk. 1974. "The Seriousness of Crimes: Normative Structure and Individual Differences." *American Sociological Review* 39:224–37.

Rumptz, Maureen, Chris Sullivan, William Davidson, and Joanna Basta. 1991. "An Ecological Approach to Tracking Battered Women over Time." *Violence and Victims* 6:237–44.

Russell, Whitworth. 1847. "Abstract of the Statistics of Crime in England and Wales from 1839–1843." *Journal of Statistical Society of London* 10:38–61.

Rutter, Michael. 1989. "Pathways from Childhood to Adult Life." *Journal of Child Psychology and Psychiatry and Allied Disciplines* 30:23–51.

Sah, Raaj. 1991. "Social Osmosis and Patterns of Crime." *Journal of Political Economy* 99:1272–95.

Sampson, Robert. 1986. "Effects of Socioeconomic Context on Official Reaction to Juvenile Delinquency." *American Sociological Review* 51:876–85.

———. 1992. "Family Management and Child Development: Insights from Social Disorganization Theory." In Joan McCord (Ed.), *Advances in Criminological Theory, Volume 3: Facts, Frameworks, and Forecasts.* New Brunswick, NJ: Transaction Publishers.

Sampson, Robert, and W. Byron Groves. 1989. "Community Structure and Crime: Testing Social Disorganization Theory." *American Journal of Sociology* 94:774–802.

Sampson, Robert, and John Laub. 1993. *Crime in the Making: Pathways and Turning Points Through Life.* Cambridge: Harvard University Press.

———. 1994. "Urban Poverty and the Family Context of Delinquency: A New Look at Structure and Process in a Classic Study." *Child Development* 65:523–40.

1996. "Socioeconomic Achievement in the Life Course of Disadvantaged Men: Military Service as a Turning Point, Circa 1940–1945." *American Sociological Review.*

Saunders, B. 1986. *Homeless Young People in Britain.* London: Bedford Square.

Schatzman, Leonard, and Anslem Straus. 1973. *Field Research: Strategies for a Natural Society.* Englewood Cliffs, NJ: Prentice-Hall.

Scheff, Thomas. 1988. "Shame and Conformity: The Deference-Emotion System." *American Sociological Review* 53:395–406.

Scheff, Thomas, and Suzanne Retzinger. 1991. *Emotions and Violence: Shame and Rage in Destructive Conflicts.* Lexington, MA: Lexington.

Scheper-Hughes, Nancy. 1992. *Death Without Weeping: The Violence of Everyday Life in Brazil.* Berkeley: University of California Press.

Schmidt, Peter, and Ann Witte. 1984. *An Economic Analysis of Crime and Justice.* Orlando, FL: Academic.

Schultz, Theodore. 1961. "Investment in Human Capital." *American Economic Review* 51:1–17.

Sellin, Thorsten. 1937. *Research Memorandum on Crime in the Depression.* New York: Social Science Research Council.

Sewell, William, and Robert Hauser. 1975. *Occupations and Earnings: Achievement in the Early Career.* New York: Academic Press.

Sewell, William, Archibald Haller, and Alejandro Portes. 1969. "The Educational and Early Occupational Attainment Process." *American Sociological Review* 34:82–93.

Sewell, William, Archibald Haller, and George Ohlendorf. 1970. "The Educational and Early Occupational Status Attainment Process: Replication and Revision." *American Sociological Review* 35:1014–27.

Shane, Paul. 1989. "Changing Patterns among Homeless and Runaway Youth." *American Journal of Orthopsychiatry* 59:208–14.

Shaw, Clifford. 1929. *Delinquency Areas.* Chicago: University of Chicago Press.

1930. *The Jack-Roller.* Chicago: University of Chicago Press.

1938. *Brothers in Crime.* Chicago: University of Chicago Press.

Shaw, Clifford, and Henry McKay. 1931. *Social Factors in Juvenile Delinquency.* Washington: USGPO.

1942. *Juvenile Delinquency and Urban Areas.* Chicago: University of Chicago Press.

Shellow, Robert, Juliana Schamp, Elliot Liebow, and Elizabeth Unger. 1972. "Suburban Runaways of the 1960s." Paper in the United States Senate Hearings on Runaway Youth before the Subcommittee to Investigate Juvenile Delinquency of the Committee on the Judiciary 92 Congress, 1st Session. Washington: Government Printing Office.

Sherman, Lawrence. 1993. "Defiance, Deterrence, and Irrelevance: A Theory of the Criminal Sanction." *Journal of Research in Crime and Delinquency* 30:445–73.

Shlay, Ann, and Peter Rossi. 1992. "Social Science Research and Contemporary Studies of Homelessness." *Annual Review of Sociology* 18:129–60.

Short, James, and Fred Strodtbeck. 1965. *Group Process and Gang Delinquency.* Chicago: University of Chicago Press.

Silbert, Mimi, and Ayala Pines. 1982. "Entrance into Prostitution." *Youth and Society* 13:471–500.

Simons, Ronald, and Les Whitbeck. 1991. "Sexual Abuse as a Precursor to Prostitution and Victimization among Adolescent and Adult Homeless Women." *Journal of Family Issues* 12:361–79.

Simons, Ronald, Les Whitbeck, Janet Melby, and Chyi–In Wu. 1994. "Economic Pressure and Harsh Parenting." In Rand Conger and Glen Elder, Jr. (Eds.), *Families in Troubled Times.* New York: Aldine de Gruyter.

Smith, Douglas. 1986. "The Neighborhood Context of Police Behavior." In Albert Reiss and Michael Tonry (Eds.), *Communities and Cities.* Chicago: University of Chicago Press.

Smith, D. Randall, William Smith, and Elliot Noma. 1984. "Delinquent Career-Lines: A Conceptual Link Between Theory and Juvenile Offenses." *The Sociological Quarterly* 25:155–72.

Snow, David and Leon Anderson. 1987. "Identity Work among the Homeless: The Verbal Construction and Avowal of Personal Identities." *American Journal of Sociology* 92:1336–71.

1993. *Down on Their Luck: A Study of Homeless Street People.* Berkeley: University of California Press.

Snow, David, Susan Baker, and Leon Anderson. 1989. "Criminality and Homeless Men: An Empirical Assessment." *Social Problems* 36:532–49.

Sosin, Michael, Irving Piliavin, and Alex Westerfelt. 1990. "Toward a Longitudinal Analysis of Homelessness." *Journal of Social Issues* 46:157–74.

Spergel, Irving. 1989. *Youth Gangs: Problems and Response.* Chicago: University of Chicago School of Social Service Administration.

Starr, Jerrold. 1986. "American Youth in the 1980s." *Youth and Society* 17:323–45.

Steel, Lauri. 1991. "Early Work Experience among White and Non-White Youths: Implications for Subsequent Enrollment and Employment." *Youth and Society* 22:419–47.

Steffensmeier, Darrell. 1980a. "Sex Differences in Patterns of Adult Crimes, 1965–77: A Review and Assessment." *Social Forces* 58:1080–108.

1980b. "Trends in Female Delinquency: An Examination of Arrest, Juvenile Court, Self-Report, and Field Data." *Criminology* 18:62–85.

1993. "National Trends in Female Arrests, 1960–1990: Assessment and Recommendations for Research." *Journal of Quantitative Criminology* 9:411–41.

Stern, David, and Yoshi-Fumi Nakata. 1989. "Characteristics of High School Students' Paid Jobs, and Employment Experience after Graduation." In David Stern and Dorothy Eichorn (Eds.), *Adolescence and Work: Influences of*

Social Structure, Labor Markets, and Culture. Hillsdale, NJ: Lawrence Erlbaum Associates.

Stierlin, H. 1973. "Family Perspective on Adolescent Runaways." *Archives of General Psychiatry* 29:56–62.

Stinchcombe, Arthur. 1963. "Institutions of Privacy in the Determination of Police Administrative Practice." *American Journal of Sociology* 69:150–60.

Stolzenberg, Ross, and Daniel Relles. 1990. "Theory Testing in a World of Constrained Research Design: The Significance of Heckman's Censored Sampling Bias Correction for Nonexperimental Research." *Sociological Methods and Research* 18:395–415.

Straus, Murray. 1979. "Measuring Intrafamily Conflict and Violence: The Conflict Tactics (CT) Scale." *Journal of Marriage and the Family* 41:75–88.

——— 1990. "The Conflict Tactics Scales and Its Critics: An Evaluation and New Data on Validity and Reliability." In Murray Straus and Richard Gelles (Eds.), *Physical Violence in American Families: Risk Factors and Adaptations to Violence in 8,145 Families.* New Brunswick, NJ: Transaction Publisher.

——— 1991. "Discipline and Deviance: Physical Punishment of Children and Violence and Other Crime in Adulthood." *Social Problems* 38:133–54.

Straus, Murray, Richard Gelles, and Suzanne Steinmetz. 1980. *Behind Closed Doors: Violence in the American Family.* Garden City, NY: Doubleday.

Sudman, Seymour, and Norman Bradburn. 1974. *Response Effects in Surveys: A Review and Synthesis.* Chicago: Aldine Publishing.

——— 1982. *Asking Questions.* San Francisco: Jossey-Bass.

Sullivan, Mercer. 1989. *Getting Paid: Youth Crime and Work in the Inner City.* Ithaca: Cornell University Press.

Sutherland, Edwin. 1937. *The Professional Thief: By a Professional Thief.* Annotated and Interpreted by Edwin Sutherland. Chicago: University of Chicago.

——— [1942] 1956. "Development of the Theory." In Albert Cohen, Alfred Lindesmith, and Karl Schuessler (Eds.), *The Sutherland Papers.* Bloomington: Indiana University Press.

——— [1944] 1956. "Critique of the Theory." In Albert Cohen, Alfred Lindesmith and Karl Schuessler (Eds.), *The Sutherland Papers.* Bloomington: Indiana University Press.

——— 1947. *Principles of Criminology,* 4th edition. Philadelphia: J. B. Lippincott.

——— [1949] 1983. *White Collar Crime: The Uncut Version.* New Haven: Yale University Press.

Sutherland, Edwin, and Harvey Locke. 1936. *Twenty Thousand Homeless Men: A Study of Unemployed Men in the Chicago Shelters.* Philadelphia: J. B. Lippincott.

Suttles, Gerald. 1968. *Social Order of the Slum.* Chicago: University of Chicago Press.

Tannenbaum, Franklin. 1938. *Crime and the Community.* Boston: Ginn.

Taylor, Carl. 1990. *Dangerous Society.* East Lansing: Michigan State University Press.

Tebes, Jacob, David Snow, and Michael Arthur. 1992. "Panel Attrition and External Validity in the Short-Term Follow-Up Study of Adolescent Substance Abuse." *Evaluation Review* 16:151–70.

Thoits, Peggy. 1983. "Dimensions of Life Events that Influence Psychological Distress: An Evaluation and Synthesis of the Literature." In Howard Kaplan (Ed.), *Psychosocial Stress: Trends in Theory and Research*. New York: Academic Press.

Thomas, W. I. 1923. *The Unadjusted Girl*. New York: Harper & Row Torchbooks.

Thornberry, Terence, and R. L. Christenson. 1984. "Unemployment and Criminal Involvement: An Investigation of Reciprocal Causal Structures." *American Sociological Review* 49:398–411.

Thornberry, Terence, Melanie Moore, and R. L. Christenson. 1985. "The Effect of Dropping Out of High School on Subsequent Criminal Behavior." *Criminology* 23:3–18.

Thornton, Arland, Deborah Freedman, and Donald Camburn. 1982. "Obtaining Respondent Co-operation in Family Panel Studies." *Sociological Methods and Research* 11:33–51.

Thrasher, Frederick. 1927. *The Gang: A Study of 1,313 Gangs in Chicago*. Chicago: University of Chicago Press.

Tittle, Charles, Elton Jackson, and Mary Burke. 1986. "Modeling Sutherland's Theory of Differential Association: Toward an Empirical Clarification." *Social Forces* 65:405–32.

Tittle, Charles, and Robert Meier. 1990. "Specifying the SES/Delinquency Relationship." *Criminology* 28:271–99.

Tittle, Charles, Wayne Villemez, and Douglas Smith. 1978. "The Myth of Social Class and Criminality: An Empirical Assessment of the Empirical Evidence." *American Sociological Review* 43:643–56.

UNICEF. 1989. *Annual Report*. New York: UNICEF.

Visano, Livy. 1987. *This Idle Trade: The Occupational Patterns of Male Prostitution*. Concord, ONT: VitaSana.

Walker, Deborah. 1975. *Runaway Youth: Annotated Bibliography and Literature Overview*. Washington: Department of Health, Education, and Welfare.

Warr, Mark, and Mark Stafford. 1983. "Fear of Victimization: A Look at the Proximate Causes." *Social Forces* 61:1033–43.

Weber, Marlene. 1991. *Street Kids: The Tragedy of Canada's Runaways*. Toronto: University of Toronto Press.

Weis, Joseph. 1987. "Social Class and Crime." In Michael Gottfredson and Travis Hirschi (Eds.), *Positive Criminology*. Newbury Park, CA: Sage.

Weisberg, D. Kelly. 1985. *Children of the Night: A Study of Adolescent Prostitution*. Lexington, MA: Lexington Books.

Whitbeck, Les, and Ronald Simons. 1990. "Life on the Street – The Victimization of Runaway and Homeless Adolescents." *Youth and Society* 22:108–25.

1993. "A Comparison of Adaptive Strategies and Patterns of Victimization among Homeless Adolescents and Adults." *Violence and Victims* 8:135–52.

White, Jennifer, Terrie Moffitt, Felton Earls, Lee Robins, and Phil Silva. 1990. "How Early Can We Tell? Predictors of Childhood Conduct Disorder and Adolescent Delinquency." *Criminology* 28:507–33.

Whyte, William. 1943. *Street Corner Society.* Chicago: University of Chicago Press.

Wiatrowski, Michael, David Griswold, and Mary Roberts. 1981. "Social Control and Delinquency." *American Sociological Review* 46:525–41.

Widom, Cathy Spatz. 1989. "Child Abuse, Neglect, and Violent Criminal Behavior." *Criminology* 27:251–71.

Wilson, James, and Richard Herrnstein. 1985. *Crime and Human Nature.* New York: Simon and Schuster.

Wilson, Margo, and Martin Daly. 1987. "Risk of Maltreatment of Children Living with Step Parents." In Richard Gelles and Jane Lancaster (Eds.), *Child Abuse and Neglect: Biosocial Dimensions.* New York: Aldine de Gruyter.

Wilson, Margo, Martin Daly, and Suzanne Weghorst. 1980. "Household Composition and the Risk of Child Abuse and Neglect." *Journal of Biosocial Science* 12:333–40.

Wilson, William. 1987. *The Truly Disadvantaged.* Chicago: University of Chicago Press.

Winship, Christopher, and Robert Mare. 1992. "Models for Sample Selection Bias." *Annual Review of Sociology* 18:327–50.

Witte, Ann. 1980. "Estimating the Economic Model of Crime with Individual Data." *Quarterly Journal of Economics.* 94:57–84.

Wolfgang, Marvin, Robert Figlio, Paul Tracy, and Simon Singer. 1985. *The National Survey of Crime Severity.* Washington: U.S. Department of Justice, Bureau of Justice Statistics.

Wolfgang, Marvin, Terence Thornberry, and Robert Figlio. 1987. *From Boy to Man, From Delinquency to Crime.* Chicago: University of Chicago Press.

Wolk, Steven, and Janet Brandon. 1977. "Runaway Adolescents' Perceptions of Parents and Self." *Adolescence* 12:175–87.

Wright, Erik Olin. 1978. *Class, Crises and the State.* London: New Left Books.
1985. *Classes.* London: Verso.

Wright, Erik Olin, and Luca Perrone. 1977. "Marxist Class Categories and Income Inequality." *American Sociological Review* 42:32–55.

Wright, James. 1989. *Address Unknown: Homelessness in Contemporary America.* Hawthorne, NY: Aldine de Gruyter.
1991. "Health and the Homeless Teenager: Evidence from the National Health Care for the Homeless Program." *Journal of Health and Social Policy* 2:15–35.

Wright, James, Martha Wittig, and Donald Kaminsky. 1993. "Street Children in North and Latin America: Preliminary Data from Projecto Alternativos in

Tegucigalpa and Some Comparisons with the U.S. Case." *Studies in Comparative International Development* 28:81–92.

Xie, Yu, and Charles Manski. 1989. "The Logit Model and Response-Based Samples." *Sociological Methods and Research* 17:283–302.

Zorbaugh, Harvey. 1929. *The Gold Coast and the Slum.* Chicago: University of Chicago Press.

Index

9   INDEX

Sullivan, Mercer: *Getting Paid*, 4
surplus population families, 66, 231; and taking to the street, 68, 70, 77, 78
survey research, 1, 7, 258–9
survival issues, 9, 162–3, 233; membership in street families and, 177–8
Sutherland, Edwin, 136–7, 138, 139, 140, 142, 155–6, 225; *Professional Thief, The*, 156; *Twenty Thousand Homeless Men* (with Harvey Locke), 4, 6, 155–6
Suttles, Gerald: *Social Order of the Slum*, 4

taking to the streets, 55–79, 96, 103, 110; and serious theft, 71–7
Tally's Corner (Liebows), 4
temporal sequence, 185, 186
territoriality, 174, 177
theft, 54, 106, 113, 115, 122, 127, 133, 232; to acquire necessities, 84–7; of clothing, 86; embeddedness and, 139, 140, 143; and employment, 214, 234; of food, 84–6, 89–90, 92–6, 93t, 101, 102t, 103–4; in hostels, 44–5; minor, 91; on the street, 46; street families and, 169–70; tutelage in, 147, 149, 155
theft, serious, 80; decomposition of difference in: street and school youth, 77t; embeddedness/capital in, 150–1; lack of food, shelter, and employment and, 89–96, 93t, 101, 102t, 103–4; logit based estimates of participation in, 75t; measure of, 67–8; modeling, 71; participation/ frequency, 71, 73–4; taking to the street and, 71–7; tobit estimates of probabilities of, 76t
theoretical orientations, 224, 225–7, 232, 235; *see also* criminological theory
Thomas, W. I.: *Unadjusted Girl, The*, 4
Trasher, Fredrick: *Gang, The*, 4, 140
tobit models, 71, 74, 76t
Toronto, 9–10, 12–14, 15f, 23–4, 104, 141, 204; access to social capital in, 232; cross-sectional study, 20; initial study, 22–3; panel study, 20, 23, 118–19, 186; school sample, 92, 96, 99–101; social environment of, 18–19; social policies in, 113; social services in, 18; street crime in, 119–30; street families in, 174–7; street population of 62–3; street youth and crime in, 1, 8, 107–10; streets of, 130–4
turning points, 201, 204–9; employment as, 210

tutelage, 138, 141, 142–6, 233; crime-specific nature of, 155–7; differential association and, 136–7
tutelage relationships, 147–9, 150–5, 156, 158, 170
Twenty Thousand Homeless Men (Sutherland and Locke), 4, 6, 155–6
two-stage estimator, 99–100

Unadjusted Girl, The (Thomas), 4
unemployment, 8, 83, 91, 202, 218; and crime, 92, 94, 96, 101, 104, 202–4, 221, 232–3; parental, 56, 59, 61, 66; in Toronto, 13
United States, 227–8
urban anthropologists, 4
urban neighborhoods, 3
urban underclass, 103, 227
urbanization, 3, 225

validity, 255–8; external/internal, 62, 78, 79, 80, 92, 96–101, 104
Vancouver, 12, 116–18, 17f, 104, 150, 233; access to social capital in, 232; panel study, 20, 23, 118–19, 186; social environment of, 18–19; social policies in, 113; street families in, 166–8, 174–7; street youth and crime in, 1, 107–10, 119–30; streets of, 130–4
victimization, 2, 8, 46, 48, 163
violence, 106, 122–3; situational destitution and, 266n1; on the street, 46–7, 116–18, 163; *see also* family physical abuse/ violence; parental abuse/violence
violent crime, 127, 133, 232; ontogenetic factors in, 115; origins of, 134; in Toronto and Vancouver, 130, 131f
War on Poverty, 225
welfare services: Toronto, 108; Vancouver, 108–9; *see also* social services
Whyte, William: *Street Corner Society*, 4
work: finding, 211–18; importance of, 221; lack of, and crime, 231; testing effects of, 209–11; and transition to adulthood, 200, 202–1; *see also* employment
work experiences, 49–51; and employment, 212

youth: abusing parents, 108, 111, 113, 122, 126, 127, 130; definition of, 10–11